SANCTIONING MATRIMONY

SAL ACOSTA

SANCTIONING MATRIMONY

*Western Expansion and Interethnic Marriage
in the Arizona Borderlands*

The University of
Arizona Press
TUCSON

The University of Arizona Press
www.uapress.arizona.edu

We respectfully acknowledge the University of Arizona is on the land and territories of Indigenous peoples. Today, Arizona is home to twenty-two federally recognized tribes, with Tucson being home to the O'odham and the Yaqui. Committed to diversity and inclusion, the University strives to build sustainable relationships with sovereign Native Nations and Indigenous communities through education offerings, partnerships, and community service.

© 2016 The Arizona Board of Regents
All rights reserved. Published 2016
First paperback edition published 2024

ISBN-13: 978-0-8165-3237-7 (cloth)
ISBN-13: 978-0-8165-5528-4 (paper)
ISBN-13: 978-0-8165-3376-3 (ebook)

Cover designed by Leigh McDonald
Cover photo courtesy of the Arizona Historical Society/Tucson

Publication of this book is made possible in part by funding from the Office of Research at Fordham University.

Library of Congress Cataloging-in-Publication Data
Names: Acosta, Sal, author.
Title: Sanctioning matrimony : western expansion and interethnic marriage in the Arizona
    borderlands / Sal Acosta.
Description: Tucson : The University of Arizona Press, 2016. | Includes bibliographical references
    and index.
Identifiers: LCCN 2015028629 | ISBN 9780816532377 (cloth : alk. paper)
Subjects: LCSH: Interracial marriage—Arizona—Tucson—History—19th century. | Interracial
    marriage—Arizona—Tucson—History—20th century. | Mexican Americans—Arizona—
    Tucson—Social conditions—19th century. | Mexican Americans—Arizona—Tucson—Social
    conditions—20th century. | Social classes—Arizona—Tucson—History—19th century. | Social
    classes—Arizona—Tucson—History—20th century. | Interracial marriage—Law and legislation—
    Arizona—Tucson—History—19th century. | Interracial marriage—Law and legislation—Arizona—
    Tucson—History—20th century. | Miscegenation—Arizona—Tucson—History—19th century. |
    Miscegenation—Arizona—Tucson—History—20th century.
Classification: LCC HQ1031 .A325 2016 | DDC 306.84/609791776—dc23 LC record available at
    http://lccn.loc.gov/2015028629

Printed in the United States of America
♾ This paper meets the requirements of ANSI/NISO Z39.48–1992 (Permanence of Paper).

*To Araceli,
the love of my life,
the life of my love*

CONTENTS

	List of Illustrations	*ix*
	Acknowledgments	*xi*
	Introduction	3
1	Arizona's Miscegenation Law and Racial Prescriptions	22
2	The Discourse of Manifest Destiny and the Mexican Question	44
3	Intermarriage in Tucson, 1860–1930	71
4	"The woman in question is not a white woman, but a Mexican": Relationships with Blacks and Chinese	101
5	Marital Expectations in the Borderlands	132
	Epilogue	159
	Notes	*165*
	Bibliography	*213*
	Index	*235*

ILLUSTRATIONS

FIGURES

1. Hiram Stevens, Petra Santa Cruz, Sam Hughes, and Atanacia Santa Cruz — 9
2. The Dalton-Vásquez family — 11
3. Alexander Levin and Zenona Molina — 69
4. Theatrical production at Tucson's Safford School — 72
5. Beatriz Ferrer, Jesús Barceló, and Sofía Hughes — 81
6. Tucson, 1910: white and white-Mexican households and single white women, by district — 87
7. Tucson, 1930: white and white-Mexican households and single white women, by district — 91
8. Tucson, 1930: black and Chinese residents and Mexican households, by district — 110
9. Hi Wo, Emeteria Moreno-Wo, and children — 119
10. Mónica, Francisca, Luisa, and Lidia Flin — 137

TABLES

1. Population, couples, and single residents, Tucson, 1860–1880 77
2. Mexican, white, and white-Mexican unions per census year, Tucson, 1860–1930 79
3. Marriage licenses involving interethnic partners, Pima County, 1872–1930 83
4. Intermarriage rates for whites based on certain scenarios, Tucson, 1860–1930 95
5. Unmarried black and Chinese residents sixteen years of age or older, Tucson, 1880–1930 106
6. Chinese men forty years of age and older, by marital status, Tucson, 1880–1930 107
7. Unions of Mexicans or mixed ancestry with blacks or Chinese, 1880–1930 123
8. Marriages and divorces among interethnic couples, Pima County, 1873–1930 147
9. Divorce petitions of intermarried couples, Pima County, 1873–1930 149

ACKNOWLEDGMENTS

I BECAME A HISTORIAN at the University of Arizona. Instrumental in that formation were professors Karen Anderson, Katherine G. Morrissey, Jack D. Marietta, Kevin Gosner, Jadwiga Pieper Mooney, and William Beezley. I offer my special gratitude to Professor Anderson for directing my dissertation and for her personable approach. I thoroughly enjoyed my graduate courses, and I must single out a few of my fellow students who contributed to those good times: Ryan Alexander, Tom Finger, Matt Furlong, Jane Haigh, Vilja Hulden, Katrina Jagodinsky, Amie Kiddle, Leesa Lane, and Emily Wakild. The History Department and the University of Arizona provided pivotal financial support to allow me to concentrate on my studies and research.

My eventual admission to the history program would not have occurred had I not arrived in Tucson to pursue a master's in Mexican American studies. I wish to thank professors Scott Carvajal, Raquel Rubio-Goldsmith, Greg Rodríguez, and Anna Ochoa O'Leary. The opportunity to enter the program I owe to the director, Dr. Antonio Estrada. I am but one of countless students who have benefited from his guidance and support and from his commitment to Tucson's Mexican American community.

I found great assistance during the past several years of research from Betty Wittenberg at the Catholic Diocese of Tucson Archives; Lisa Patton at the Pima County Superior Court; the Arizona Historical Society; the University of Arizona Special Collections Library; the Grant County Clerk's Office in

Silver City, New Mexico; the Hidalgo County Clerk's Office in Lordsburg, New Mexico; and Archives and Public Records at the Arizona State Library in Phoenix, Arizona.

Fordham University has consistently supported my research projects. The Office of Research under the leadership of Drs. Nancy Busch and Amy Tuininga facilitated my research trips and contributed financially toward the publication of this book. The university's early sabbatical program for junior faculty provided valuable release time during which I made great progress on my manuscript. The History Department welcomed me as a colleague in 2010. Their academic accomplishments are quite impressive—their friendliness much more.

I also thank the staff at the University of Arizona Press, in particular its encouraging and patient acquiring editor, Kristen Buckles. I greatly appreciate the dedication and insight of my copyeditor, Melanie Mallon. Earlier versions of chapter 4 benefited from comments by the editors and anonymous readers at the *Journal of the Southwest* and the *New Mexico Historical Review*, where two of my articles appeared.

My parents, Pedro Acosta and Eulalia Valtierra, made me. Although I have always known that they undoubtedly possess the intellect and dedication to become great scholars, they never had the opportunity to continue their education. But their hard work ensured that I did, and I am forever grateful. In the 1960s, they left their small village in central Mexico and took a train ride to Mexico City, the first of many migrations they undertook to build a better future for our family. My greatest debt to them, however, involves the moral direction and loving care they provided for my siblings and me. Your children—José, Juan, Pedro, Norma, Rocío, and I—love you and each other very much because we had the fortune to grow up Acosta Valtierra.

The untimely death of Professor Guillermo E. Hernández in 2006 left a great void in the lives of all his students. I will never forget his continuous support after I graduated from UCLA or the laughter we shared during our lunch sessions. Besides my family, he, most of all, would have been happy to see this book in his hands.

Charro García and Bolillo Jiménez offered friendship, companionship, wisdom, and, especially, perspective and balance. I will never forget you, my friends.

My wife, Araceli, is the sweetest and strongest person. Your love, support, and unconditional sacrifices have allowed me to pursue my academic goals. My life has meaning because of you. May we spend eternity together, and if life blossoms again, may we live as sunflowers.

SANCTIONING MATRIMONY

INTRODUCTION

I N 1872 EMMETT WOODLEY AND LEONICIA TERRAZAS decided to enter into marriage in Tucson. They met in town, but considerably different journeys had brought them to the new Arizona Territory. Like countless other Americans, Emmett had migrated west. A native of Virginia, he had served in the U.S. Army before settling in southern Arizona. Leonicia, meanwhile, had ventured north from the border state of Sonora, following a path that Mexicans had wrought for more than a hundred years. Their working-class backgrounds and recent migrant experiences probably generated a sense of compatibility and reassurance to help them overcome linguistic and other cultural differences, but the couple still had to negotiate two potential obstacles before being able to marry, one with the Catholic Church and the other with Arizona's miscegenation law (1865–1962). Emmett was an African American Protestant; Leonicia was Catholic and, as an ethnic Mexican, was legally white. The Church begrudgingly condoned this type of interfaith union, and Arizona had prohibited marriages between blacks and whites during its very first legislative session. Emmett and Leonicia's plans to marry nonetheless proceeded uneventfully: they encountered no difficulties in securing a license from the county clerk, and the priest at Saint Augustine granted an interfaith dispensation and married them on March 23, 1872.[1] The local church preferred conversion prior to marriage but did allow interfaith ceremonies—as long as the non-Catholic partner agreed to certain stipulations. The consent of clerks, on the other hand, did not come automatically when partners belonged to different races. In fact, marriages between blacks and Euro-American whites were all but nonexistent in Arizona during the life of the miscegenation law.

The existence of any such relationships in light of an ostensibly rigid miscegenation law and the ambiguous racial classification of some groups demonstrates that race could be both meaningful and meaningless in the American Southwest. During the second half of the nineteenth century, the region offered domestic and foreign migrants economic opportunities that they could not find in their places of origin, but race was meaningful because economic, political, and social entities often used it as a differentiating and discriminating factor in their decisions and policies. Thus, in addition to the obstacles all settlers encountered—such as difficulties in travel, the threat of Indian raids, and unbalanced sex ratios—racial discrimination added more barriers to the experiences of nonwhites. Efforts to maintain racial classifications rested in ascribing meaning to race and relying on human beings to identify it uniformly and record it accurately. But inconsistent racial attitudes, lack of awareness, or mere disinterest indicated that race was often meaningless.

For example, Emmett succumbed to heart disease in 1935, more than twenty-five years after Leonicia had passed away. As often occurred with other transplanted men who died as widowers or bachelors in the West, the hospital reported only scant information. He had suffered from senility, and the staff could only establish his age and birthplace. Notably, they initially listed him as Mexican, overlooking the incongruity of assigning that category to a black man they identified as born in Petersburg, Virginia. They eventually amended their original classification and added "colored," but left "Mexican" in place. He died in Phoenix, and after spending the previous seven decades so far from his native Virginia, perhaps Emmett's classification as Mexican had to do with the visitors he received, who necessarily were his black-Mexican descendants or his Mexican in-laws. The staff probably labeled him a "colored Mexican" based on the bilingual interaction of those relatives or on the likely Spanish fluency of Emmett himself.[2]

The inability of hospital staffs—and at times, their seeming lack of concern—to determine the racial background of some people resembled the vacillation of census takers and the forbearance of county clerks, who often sanctioned marriages of Mexicans with blacks and Chinese. Thus, disjunction between legal prescriptions and local practices could occur when officials intentionally disregarded race-based laws or could not ascertain or agree on the racial identity of some groups, especially people of mixed ancestry. On paper,

Arizona law strictly forbade interracial marriage, eventually even including multiracial ancestry in this prohibition. In practice, however, the law proved ineffective with marriages involving Mexicans, a group that occupied a racially ambiguous space. Technically, their legal whiteness permitted them to marry only other whites, but their social nonwhiteness meant that county officials frequently permitted their unions with nonwhites.

Although miscegenation laws in the United States always allowed Mexicans to marry Euro-Americans, one cannot necessarily view those relationships as logical or automatic in light of the occasional sanctioning of marriages between Mexicans and blacks or Chinese. For instance, it is unlikely that a county clerk would issue a license to a black-Mexican couple and, upon the death of the spouse, allow the same Mexican to marry a white partner. He would necessarily have to view one of the marriages as legally unacceptable, depending on whether he viewed Mexicans as white or nonwhite. The conscious endorsement of the two unions would in effect confer on Mexicans an intermediate, or transitional, racial status, a designation that has never existed in American law. Socially speaking, however, Mexicans occupied precisely such a position in the Southwest: they could be both white and nonwhite. They could always marry whites, but at times, the legal and the social spaces merged, and they could also marry nonwhites.

Several factors suggest that of the two types of relationships, marriages between Mexicans and whites should have occurred only sporadically in the nineteenth-century Southwest, if ever: (1) the frequency and tone of the anti-Mexican rhetoric of the mid-nineteenth century, especially its opposition to any kind of relationships with Mexicans, let alone marriages; (2) the antagonism that surrounded the political, economic, and social displacement of the Mexican population in the Southwest; and (3) cultural differences, especially in religion, language, and customs. In Arizona, after all, politicians, judges, and civil officials of the second half of the nineteenth century were primarily transplanted Americans from east of the Mississippi, many from the South, who had lived through the U.S.-Mexico War (1846–1848) and the Civil War. They hardly viewed Mexicans as racially or culturally compatible.

During the years surrounding the war with Mexico, Americans described Mexicans as sacrilegious half-breeds, indolent and dirty, and compared them to Indians and blacks.[3] Their admission as white under the Treaty of Guadalupe Hidalgo did not change widespread anti-Mexican attitudes among Euro-Americans. Mexicans joined the U.S. populace effectively as a racial underclass. After the war, courts and legislatures in the West frequently violated the legal stipulations of the treaty, exploiting the individual and collective multiracial background of Mexicans and granting rights only to certain cohorts. Thus, large groups—especially dark mestizos, Christianized Indians, and Mexicans of African ancestry—who had enjoyed the benefits of citizenship under Mexican law suddenly lost the right to vote, hold some political offices, practice law, testify in cases involving whites, and serve on juries. Statutes, such as the foreign miners' tax and vagrancy laws, focused on the ascribed foreignness and purported deviancy of Mexicans. Subsequently, the creation of barrios perpetuated exclusion and poverty, and anti-Mexican rhetoric had a direct effect on Mexican interactions with whites.[4]

The legal and social standing of Mexicans in Arizona resembled their experiences in the rest of the Southwest. Almost immediately upon achieving territorial status in 1863, Arizona's legislature limited the franchise to "[e]very white male citizen of the United States, and every *white* male citizen of Mexico," thus undermining the peace treaty by indicating that not all Mexicans qualified for the rights of citizenship.[5] That limited whiteness often led to legal and social intolerance during Arizona's territorial years (1863–1912). Mexicans encountered discrimination and violence in social spaces and on labor sites, problems the legal system frequently exacerbated with unequal treatment.[6]

But these attacks did not—could not—occur in all places all the time. The American settlement of the West suffered from an unstable domestic environment. As Americans moved to the Southwest in the nineteenth century— whether in the form of massive sudden migrations, like the gold and silver rushes in California and Colorado, or in slower movements, like the migrations produced by trade and agricultural ventures in Arizona and New Mexico—one situation consistently emerged in burgeoning towns: the ratio of white men to white women became extremely high. But the annexation of the Southwest between 1848 and 1854 had incorporated a balanced population of approximately one hundred thousand Mexican residents into the United States. Consequently, for the most part, the only non-Indian women white men found as potential spouses were Mexican—and a few places, like Arizona, barred white-Indian marriages. Mexican American historiography accurately points out that some white men found a welcoming situation among Mexicans. That narrative, however, tells only part of the story.

Until recently, historians have undertaken a narrow approach to race and class in examining the role of intermarriage among Mexicans in the Southwest in the late nineteenth and early twentieth centuries, resulting in two gaps in the historiography, the study of lower classes and intermarriage with nonwhites: (1) scholars have primarily focused on intermarriages between prominent white men and the daughters of Mexican landowners; and (2) even in studies of the lower classes, marriages with whites have tended to dominate the scholarship. The elite-centered narrative still permeates syntheses and overviews in particular, originating from a tendency in the most influential works to highlight the lives of dominant classes or figures, people who leave more historical records. These works frequently emphasize the alliances formed through intermarriage by social and political leaders. They posit that wealthy Mexican families tried to maintain power or to whiten their lineage, and that whites sought access to trade, land, inheritance, and political influence. As whites ascended in power, and white women arrived in large enough numbers, intermarriage declined.[7]

Studies that discuss intermarriage in Tucson offer similar conclusions. They focus on relationships between enterprising white men and local Mexican elites and maintain that white-Mexican marriage increased or declined in relation to the presence of single white women.[8] For instance, sociologist James Officer proposes that in the early territorial years, these unions helped whites gain connections to prominent Mexican power players. "In the years which followed," he adds, these interethnic families "and their descendants provided important links between the Anglo and Mexican communities and they have helped to maintain good relations between the two ethnic groups in Tucson down to the present day [1960]." Officer nonetheless credits the positive relations as much to other reasons, such as trade ventures, shared antagonism toward Apache Indians, and even the lack of lower-class Mexican immigration during the 1910s. He also points out the limits of the harmony, discussing examples of discrimination and alienation.[9]

Paralleling studies on other parts of the Southwest, Officer and Thomas Sheridan suggest that intermarriage began to decline as the white population started to increase upon the pacification of Indians and the arrival of the railroad in 1880. Those events, according to Officer, produced two transformations: "Anglo women entered the territory to provide wives for Anglo men," and the "pattern of intermarriage in Tucson would change dramatically." Although he does not explain what made the change dramatic, he follows his statements by underscoring, and thus connecting them to, the end of commercial partnerships between whites and Mexicans. After that, he adds, few Mexicans participated in social events with whites. Economic and political separation soon followed, and even elites experienced prejudice. One can only conclude, therefore, that Officer meant that the change in intermarriage was downward.[10] Sheridan also identifies the deterioration in white-Mexican relations, but he makes the connection between the arrival of white women and the decline in intermarriage explicit: "As more and more Anglo women followed the Southern Pacific into town," he explains, "Anglo men increasingly chose them rather than Mexican women as brides." He further posits that the "increasing gulf between Tucson's two major ethnic groups soon extended from the work place and the political arena into the marital bedroom as well."[11] The decline in interethnic unions accelerated, Sheridan concludes, and by the early twentieth century, whites and Mexicans "rarely chose one another as husbands or wives."[12] In sum, these interpretations render Mexican women as temporary substitutes for white women, and race emerges as the driving force that corrected marriage practices.

The predominance of elite marriages in the regional and local historiography distorts their frequency among the Mexican population of the Southwest. Demographic logic suggests that the potential intermarriages among the more than one hundred thousand lower-class Mexicans who lived in the area in the nineteenth century could easily surpass the number of unions among the few dozen elite Mexican families. Indeed, recent studies point to interethnic unions among the lower classes representing the norm. Along with emphases on white-Mexican marriage among the poor, some of these works also focus on different types of relationships. For instance, they analyze marriages of Mexican men and women with working-class blacks and Indians and, in the twentieth century, between working-class Mexican women and working-class Punjabi and Filipino immigrants.[13] The case study of the Tucson area corroborates the primacy of these different and far more common types of intermarriage. It reveals that interethnic relationships took place almost exclusively among working-class partners, primarily between Mexicans and whites, but also between Mexicans and blacks or Chinese. This study thus fits within the recent scholarship demonstrating that class similarities can sometimes counterweigh racial differences.[14]

Intermarriage among the city's few but historically famous elites did take place and does matter, but virtually all studies that deal with early Arizona history address its existence and significance. In a way, the decline in those renowned marriages has added to the perception that white-Mexican marriage became rare by the early twentieth century. Take, for instance, the case of Sam Hughes and Atanacia Santa Cruz, one of the most famous intermarriages in Arizona history. The thirty-two-year-old Sam married twelve-year-old Atanacia

FIGURE 1. From left to right: Hiram Stevens and Petra Santa Cruz (married c. 1858) and Sam Hughes and Atanacia, Petra's sister. Sam married Atanacia in 1863, when she was twelve years old and he was thirty-two. In the picture (c. 1866), Atanacia is pregnant for the third time. Arizona Historical Society/Tucson, AHS Photo Number 14244.

in 1863, and they had fifteen children, ten of whom lived beyond childhood. They were one of twenty-two interethnic couples who lived in Tucson in 1864, some of whom also gained prominence, like Hiram Stevens and Petra Santa Cruz—Atanacia's sister—and Frederick Contzen and Margarita Ferrer. Sam founded the first bank in Tucson and was elected as council member and sheriff thanks to his entrepreneurship and Atanacia's properties and local networks. The Hughes's long marriage enjoyed local celebrity that had few rivals in town and that survived well after he died in 1917 and she in 1934. Their economic and social achievements made them extraordinary, but their willingness to cross ethnic lines and to inhabit and expand Tucson's multicultural space made them fairly commonplace. By 1880, they were one of ninety-seven interethnic relationships, and by the 1910s, they were but one of around two hundred such couples in town. But the census only captures a glimpse of what was happening all around them. By the time of Atanacia's death, almost two thousand interethnic couples had married in the Tucson area, dozens of whom were Mexicans partnered with either African Americans or Chinese, and many more who were among the descendants of interethnic partners. Marriages of the stature of the Hugheses never accounted for a large percentage of all interethnic couples. The larger working-class populace did, and they never stopped intermarrying.

The availability of records for prominent marriages does offer access to important insight into the complexity of multiethnic ancestries. The genealogy of singer Linda Ronstadt provides an excellent example. As the daughter of Gilbert Ronstadt and Ruth Mary Copeman, she is Dutch, German, and English on her mother's side. The ancestry of Linda's father, meanwhile, embodied a diversity that was characteristic of the U.S.-Mexico border region's history. Gilbert was born in 1911 in Tucson. He was five-eighths Mexican, descended from Federico José María "Fred" Ronstadt (b. 1868, Sonora) and María Guadalupe Agustina "Lupe" Dalton (b. 1882). A marriage where both partners were of white-Mexican ancestry was not that unusual in turn-of-the-century Tucson. Fred, who arrived in town in 1882, descended from Friedrich August "Federico Augusto" Ronstadt (b. 1816), a German immigrant from Hanover who meandered around the U.S.-Mexico borderlands and settled in Sonora. He married Margarita Redondo in 1866. Fred Ronstadt was thus half Mexican. His wife, Lupe Dalton, on the other hand, was three-quarters Mexican. She was born in Tucson to Winnall Dalton (b. 1850) and Jesús Vásquez (b. 1855, Mexico). Winnall descended from Henry Dalton, an Englishman who found his way to California after living and forming a family in Peru. Winnall's mother, Gua-

FIGURE 2. The Dalton-Vásquez family (c. 1890). The parents are Winnall Agustín Dalton and Jesús Vásquez. He was the son of Englishman Henry Dalton and Guadalupe Zamorano, from a Californio family. Jesús was born in Sonora, Mexico. The children, thus three-quarters Mexican, are, from left to right, Hortense, Henry, Natalie, and Guadalupe. In 1901 Hortense married José M. Ronstadt, son of Friedrich August Ronstadt, from Germany, and Margarita Redondo. Henry married Anita Jácome in 1913. Guadalupe "Lupe" Dalton is singer Linda Ronstadt's grandmother. In 1904 Lupe married another Ronstadt brother, Federico José María "Fred" Ronstadt. Their son Gilbert married Ruth Mary Copeman, from Michigan. Linda was the third child of Gilbert and Ruth. MS 407, folder 18, box 10, Ronstadt Family Collection, courtesy of University of Arizona Libraries, Special Collections.

dalupe Zamorano, was born in Monterey in 1832 to an elite Californio family. Although classifying women like Guadalupe, Margarita, and Jesús as Mexican oversimplifies and obscures their European and indigenous ancestries, Gilbert Ronstadt's eclectic genealogy, combined with Ruth Mary Copeman's ancestry, makes their daughter Linda eleven-sixteenths white. In other words, the ancestry of the performer who rose to fame singing American ballads in the 1960s, and in the 1980s recorded traditional Mexican music in *Canciones de mi padre* (Songs of My Father), is five-sixteenths Mexican but full of southwestern history.

The Tucson area offers an excellent opportunity to study that diversity in interethnic relations. Like the rest of the West, Tucson attracted domestic and foreign migrants whose very transplantation points to a general lack of economic stability. But Tucson differed from other areas with sizeable Mexican populations. It could not match the fertile land, natural resources, or geographic advantages of California, New Mexico, and Texas, and it thus witnessed only a gradual increase in its white populace until the early twentieth century. Its largely working-class population allows for the study of the connection between class and race. Broadly speaking, if intermarriage rates decline among the lower classes as the white population increases, one can hypothesize that race outweighs class. If, on the other hand, these relationships continue, then class might better explain not only their persistence but also their initial occurrence. The latter scenario played out in Tucson: interethnic relationships definitely continued even as the white population significantly increased. As the chapters in this book demonstrate, areas that continued to resemble the demographic composition of 1870s and 1880s Tucson consistently witnessed the practice of intermarriage. The importance of Tucson as the locus of this study thus stems from the need to examine not simply whether class played a role in intermarriage in other areas, but also whether one can find comparable demographic conditions in other parts of the Southwest. Did similar spaces—poor Mexican communities that witnessed the arrival of immigrants from other ethnic groups—experience increases in the practice of intermarriage? Until now, the emphasis on the intermarriages of elites has precluded a concrete answer to that question.[15]

This study identifies and explains important facts and incongruities in the history of intermarriage in the Tucson area in the late nineteenth and early twentieth centuries. It focuses on the experiences of interethnic couples and their descendants to illustrate how social and cultural attitudes can undermine or contravene racialist definitions and directives. The book argues that an emphasis on class best illuminates the practice of intermarriage in southern Arizona. Class permeates and dominates the entire study because it greatly shaped the experiences of these partners before and after they intermarried. Class parallelism proved conducive to interethnic relationships, as marriages of Mexicans with whites occurred primarily among the lower classes, but logically it also circumscribed intermarriage among elites. Class allowed black and

Chinese men to marry Mexican women: the working-class background of these women, combined with the racial nebulousness of Mexicans, made those ostensibly illegal unions acceptable to the Mexican community and, frequently, to civil officials. Neither rhetorical prescriptions nor codified racism managed to keep interethnic couples apart.

The fact that no elite Mexicans anywhere in the West intermarried with blacks or Chinese further demonstrates that class indeed mattered. The whiteness of those elites was not ambiguous, and their lives and decisions paralleled the experiences of middle- to upper-class whites, more than those of poor Mexicans. Furthermore, the sheer number of marriages between Mexican women and white, black, or Chinese men suggests that these spouses viewed each other as social equals. Class stands out even in divorce cases. The use of racialist discourse is highly noticeable for its absence in litigation. Neither Mexicans nor whites cited ethnic, racial, or cultural differences in their complaints or defenses, and almost no one used racial epithets in their testimony. Economic concerns played the primary role.

Class illuminates why white-Mexican intermarriage occurred so frequently despite the racist rhetoric of the period. The enunciations that developed into the discourse of manifest destiny originated primarily from middle- and upper-class men from the East Coast. That group necessarily had unique political and economic interests, goals, and views that differed from those of westering white men. The latter men, largely young and single, ventured west with more pragmatism than ideology. They wanted to improve their economic situation, not to engage in polemics on race. Yet, national and regional histories frequently emphasize phrases and ideas to describe the overall mood and meaning of an era, such as the speeches and declarations of politicians and prominent writers. These voices often bequeath memorable statements that seemingly encapsulate the quintessence of the times. In this case, John O'Sullivan's phrase "manifest destiny" purportedly captured the mission of the United States during the entire era of western expansion—too long a period for such a precise phrase. The corresponding discourse of manifest destiny depicted Mexicans as an inferior race unworthy of assimilation into white society.

Although examples of such enunciations appear frequently in speeches, periodicals, and travel accounts, one should not assume that all whites—or, more specifically, those who eventually settled in the Southwest—embraced those views. Placing primacy on the racialist ideologies of middle- and upper-class expansionists (politicians, journalists, and writers) leaves the impression that whites uniformly detested Mexicans and opposed interethnic unions. But those men never lived among Mexicans for long periods, if they visited the Southwest at all, and they therefore never had to decide whether to enter into interethnic relationships. They tended to oppose intermarriage as an abstract threat to notions of providential missions, and they envisioned ideologically united white settlements that would coalesce around national Anglo-Saxon racial purity. Their rhetorical proclamations presumed that white settlers would prioritize whiteness and national cohesiveness and intuitively or obediently play their role in building the burgeoning nation. In sum, expansionists inserted all whites within the unifying narrative of Anglo-Saxonism and in opposition to Mexicans, the latest antagonist in the conquest of the frontier. Yet, these enunciators, emanating primarily from the East Coast, ignored or misunderstood the concerns of potential settlers. Some of these migrants might have been unaware of—or in fact opposed to—such racial visions. Their western migration indicated, after all, that they embraced difference—or, at least, that they did not fear it.

Thus, these calls for unity around whiteness notwithstanding, westering men—American and foreign born alike—openly exercised their own prerogatives when they met Mexican populations in the conquered territory. These men probably lacked a sense of collectivity because they might not have believed they shared a common identity. The initial encounters between whites and Mexicans occurred during a period when several European groups occupied ambiguous positions in the Euro-American ethnic hierarchy. Some westering white men, furthermore, might have found more in common with poor Mexicans—like class, religion, and migration experiences—than with the East Coast expansionists who promoted the notion of manifest destiny. These migrants' visions focused on their immediate goals and needs, not on the future of the nation.[16] The multitude of intermarriages in Tucson demonstrates that essays and speeches held little sway over their marriage choices. Unlike proponents of racialist prescriptions, incoming white men did not muse about the West; they lived it. They did not theorize about intermarriage; they embraced it.

The work of cultural anthropologist Ann L. Stoler on the connection between colonialism and sexual behavior helps explain why such anti-Mexican rhetoric did not significantly influence the marriage choices of westering men. She points out, for example, that despite numerous efforts by French colonial officials to regulate marriage and sexual relationships in Indonesia, a consistent incongruity between prescription and practice developed. The French always worried about the allegiance of colonizers. They feared that excessive interaction with the native population might lead to a shift in loyalty. They maintained that "a man remains a man as long as he stays under the gaze of a woman of his race," but they also posited that the presence of white women—whom they considered more likely to empathize with the natives—would undermine colonial power. Thus, they repeatedly adopted regulations on conduct, living arrangements, and lengths of stay. French men, nonetheless, engaged in formal and informal relationships with native women regardless of the policies of colonial authorities.[17]

Stoler maintains that the failure of European powers to control sexual behavior stemmed in part from four realities. First, policymakers resided in Europe and remained distant from the experiences of colonial life. They codified modes of conduct based on theory, cultural values, and pragmatism, not on the actual wishes and concerns of white colonists. Second, officials measured success on assessments of public rather than private life—that is, the semblance of bachelorhood or endogamy often sufficed even if informal sexual relationships with native women remained prevalent, as the increasing number of biracial children indicated. Third, officials modeled rules of conduct on middle-class standards of living, making it almost certain that lower-class colonists—who represented a majority—could not observe them. Fourth, adherence to these rules rested on the false premise that colonists viewed themselves as a unified racial, cultural, and political entity and wished to remain isolated from the natives.[18] In a way, Stoler suggests, imperial attempts at regulating behavior and denigrating those who strayed from prescribed norms were signs not of power, but of powerlessness.[19]

Thus, although French officials had only tenuous control over colonizers' domestic and sexual choices, American expansionists, lacking coercive power, had even less influence over westering men. The discourse of manifest destiny delineated ideas, projects, and theories that depicted Mexicans in a primarily negative light. Ordinary white men, on the other hand, were either unaware of such tenets or simply disregarded them. They never referred to racial hierarchies or used scientific racialist terminology to refer to Mexicans. They certainly never spoke—or perhaps even heard—of such an abstract notion as a national project. Proponents of manifest destiny argued that racial amalgamation constituted a threat to the republic, but the men who actually moved west were only concerned with their individual happiness, and a large number of them decided to marry Mexican women. Indeed, the value of these women lay not in their role as concubines, as some expansionists predicted. White men and Mexican women entered into legal marriages from the start. Informal relationships did take place, but even those unions frequently became long-lasting common-law marriages. Mexican women and white men tended to enter into interethnic relationships because they found more similarities than differences. Their working-class, Christian, and migrant backgrounds and their desire to form families proved more powerful than any purported racial incompatibility. Just as important, these couples found companionship and stability during a transitional period for whites and Mexicans in southern Arizona.

Class also helps explain the relationships of Mexicans with blacks and Chinese. The legal, labor, and social discrimination against Mexicans after annexation largely relegated them to lower-class enclaves throughout the Southwest. In Tucson, the agglomeration occurred in the downtown area and west and southwest of the growing city. As settlers continued to arrive, middle- and upper-class whites occupied the expanding areas in the east and north. Poor whites and nearly all African Americans and Chinese moved into the predominantly Mexican neighborhoods. Class unquestionably shaped the interaction among these groups. The largest percentage of Mexican marriages with whites and all their unions with blacks and Chinese occurred in those working-class areas. The stereotype of the Chinese grocer leaves the impression that the average Chinese resident was upwardly mobile and thus an appealing prospective spouse. Such was not the case. Some Chinese did prosper in Tucson, as did some blacks, but for both groups, a working-class background best describes the economic status of their local populations and of a majority of those who married Mexicans. Undoubtedly, Mexican women took economic status into consideration but not as a primary motivation when choosing a partner.

The title of the book employs the term *sanctioning* to signify both endorsement and castigation. Mexican intermarriage encountered approval and disapproval. In general, expansionists, politicians, and pseudoscientists warned against white-Mexican unions, but their contempt never translated into marriage restrictions. Their sanctions remained rhetorical. As legally white, however, Mexicans could not marry either of the two major groups targeted by miscegenation laws, African Americans and Asians. Yet, Mexicans married among the three groups because enough people approved of these unions. Despite the animosity of the discourse of manifest destiny, the actions of westering white men conveyed their approval of Mexicans as spouses. In the case of nonwhites, local clerks often overlooked Arizona's miscegenation law and granted licenses that allowed Mexicans to marry blacks and Chinese, and when necessary, New Mexico offered the endorsement that Arizona denied. All these people—and Mexican families, local community, and the Catholic Church—positively sanctioned intermarriage. But the key endorsement came from the men and women who chose to form interethnic families, often despite the disapproval they encountered.

The chapters that follow offer a discussion of the meaning and significance of race, culture, and class in the West by looking at intermarriage practices in southern Arizona. They provide the most extensive statistical analysis to date of intermarriage patterns in a southwestern area. The study contributes to re-examining the perception that intermarriage in the late-nineteenth-century Southwest occurred exclusively or primarily between enterprising white men and the daughters of the old Mexican elites. It also calls for a reassessment of the common historiographical assumption that the arrival of single white women caused a decline in the incidence of white-Mexican marriage. Further, this book explains the apparent contradiction between the prevalence of intermarriage among westering white men and the frequency of anti-Mexican rhetoric at both the national and regional levels.

The focus on the period 1860 to 1930 stems from an attempt to capture early interaction between Mexicans and whites as well as from archival limitations. Although the study delves into earlier events, its demographic component starts in 1860 because that year witnessed the first U.S. census, one that included the generation of Americans who had moved into southern Arizona after the Treaty of Guadalupe Hidalgo (1848) and the Gadsden Purchase (1854). Over the next seventy years, Tucson grew from a largely Mexican populace of under one thousand residents to a white majority of more than thirty thousand. Marriage practices would reflect the demographic changes of the city. The analysis ends in 1930 because vital and census records extended only to 1930 when the study began. The 1940 census became available while the project was ongoing, but unfortunately census schedules for that year no longer include the birthplace of parents. That exclusion, combined with higher American nativity rates for people of Mexican ancestry and American naming practices that erase a woman's maiden name, make it very difficult to ascertain intermarriage rates effectively. One can still use it to find previously identified interethnic couples and their descendants, and this study occasionally extends beyond 1930 to later census, vital, civil, and legal records.

Chapter 1 examines the history of Arizona's miscegenation law. It argues that the strict yet porous law efficiently curbed interracial marriages of whites and nonwhites but not those of Mexicans with either group because those relationships never threatened white purity. The law underwent several modifications from the initial territorial efforts to prohibit marriages of whites with blacks. It eventually included Asians, Native Americans, Filipinos, and Asian Indians, as well as a practically unenforceable ancestry stipulation. Under this amendment, multiracial people—like mestizos—technically could not marry anyone, not even a partner of their exact racial background. Even ignoring the fact that all mestizos who married in Arizona violated the law, the sanctioned marriages of the descendants of black-Mexican and Asian-Mexican couples further illustrate the permeability of the law in preventing interracial marriage. Several court cases demonstrate, however, that litigants could sometimes employ the law to bolster their legal positions, especially when they sought to claim or to protect property by questioning the legitimacy of certain marriages.

Miscegenation laws never focused on Mexicans in theory or in practice. Yet, fictional and nonfictional narratives of the mid-nineteenth century generally indicate that Americans viewed marriages with Mexicans as unacceptable. The immediate postannexation period nonetheless witnessed hundreds—most likely thousands—of such relationships. Chapter 2 proposes that clues to resolving that incongruity lie in the narratives themselves. It analyzes the racialist and antimiscegenation components of the manifest destiny discourse as it involved Mexicans. It argues that the rhetoric seemed universally racist, but two subtexts undermined it: first, it often allowed for the inclusion of Mexican women; and second, it did not represent the views of the typical westering man. The chapter discusses the saliency of racial depictions in various forms of accounts, such as travelogues, fiction, and essays from the early nineteenth century to the 1860s. In particular, the years surrounding the U.S.-Mexico War (1846–1848) generated the so-called Mexican Question among politicians, journalists, and pseudoscientists. As these self-proclaimed pundits addressed the topic, racial difference became a major concern, especially when they considered the national and personal admixture that a territorial expansion entailed. The chapter then explains how Arizona fit the larger national pattern of racialist discourse when it, too, developed a Mexican Question. Yet, the rhetoric and the objectives proved fragile at both national and local levels. Their weaknesses help explain the prevalence of intermarriage with the purportedly despised Mexicans.

Chapters 3 and 4 discuss the extent and significance of interethnic relationships in Tucson between 1860 and 1930. They rely on analyses of all census reports and schedules for Tucson and complementary legal and civil records. The databases that support the discussion take into account the race, marital status, occupation, family, and other relevant information for every Tucson resident during census surveys from 1860 to 1930, approximately one hundred thousand new and continuing residents altogether. Chapter 3 focuses primarily on white-Mexican unions, which occurred extensively and remarkably consistently during this period. It argues that class, more than race, consistently shaped the practice of intermarriage. White-Mexican intermarriage increased as the population grew, but the decline in the number of interethnic families as a share of all households has cemented the predominant and erroneous conclusions that (1) the arrival of white women led to a decline in intermarriage, and (2) that white-Mexican marriage therefore became rare. Quantitative evidence contradicts those claims regarding the practice of intermarriage in the West. The case study of Tucson reveals that white men did not quite redirect their attention toward the arriving white women.

Although white-Mexican unions accounted for the great majority of intermarriages in the Tucson area, the interethnic unions of Mexicans with African Americans and Chinese offer important insight into contemporaneous racial attitudes. Chapter 4 argues that these relationships occurred primarily because the two groups entered the racially ambiguous space Mexicans occupied in the Southwest. The presence of a large Mexican community and class similarities combined to create a relatively receptive environment for black and Chinese migrants, especially since the social nonwhiteness of Mexicans generally superseded their legal whiteness and facilitated officially sanctioned and informal relationships with both groups. The fact that civil and religious officials sometimes contravened the miscegenation law when agreeing to marry some of these couples does not necessarily mean that they approved of marriages between whites and nonwhites. Rather, they probably perceived both groups as nonwhite, or they acted with indifference or obliviousness regarding racial prescriptions. In their view, black-Mexican and Chinese-Mexican couples seemed to belong together, at the lower end of the socioethnic ladder. The number of these unions pales in comparison to the hundreds of marriages between Mexicans and whites, but intermarriage was perhaps more important to black and Chinese in-migrants. In an era when a large number of black and nearly all

Chinese men faced an almost certain prospect of a lifetime of bachelorhood, Mexican women were a significant part of their lives.

Chapter 5 examines the lives and expectations of people who entered into interethnic relationships. It relies extensively on newspaper accounts, personal papers, church documents, and legal records to reveal the experiences, proclivities, and examples of satisfaction and dissatisfaction that characterized members of interethnic families. The chapter argues that the sociocultural nature of southern Arizona—as a fluid Mexican borderlands region—significantly influenced how these couples interacted. In particular, the Mexican background of the wives shaped the family life and even the self-identity of the spouses and the children. One can safely suggest that the Tucson that developed after American annexation largely became the cultural space that Mexican women crafted. They influenced the lives of all their endogamous Mexican families and a significant percentage of non-Mexican partners and their multiracial children. For some spouses, the actions of their partners became unbearable, and they used divorce as a necessary recourse. At that point, they often relied on their understanding of the law and on the advice and emotional support of relatives and friends as they sought to protect their interests.

This book seeks to add to the reexamination of the meaning of racial and ethnic classifications. Its origin dates back to the first of many readings of Peggy Pascoe's articles and eventual book on miscegenation law. In the midst of legal barriers and cultural and social opprobrium emerged the openness and determination of interracial couples to form families. Legal and statistical categories homogenize and systematize race and leave their definitions on record. But how did those most affected by such classifications view their own place/ placing in the racial catalog? Did they know where they did and did not belong? What does it say about their self-identity if they knowingly disregarded the racial proscriptions they acquired from their cultures and societies—if they acquired them at all? What did it mean to them to be Mexican, black, Chinese, or white in their places of origin, and how did that meaning change when they moved to the Southwest and met each other in a new land?

Recent works employ a transnational perspective to offer insight into what it meant to be Mexican. Studies by Geraldo L. Cadava, Julia María Schiavone Camacho, Grace Delgado, and Nicole M. Guidotti-Hernández suggest that homogeneity can hardly characterize Mexicans in the Southwest. On the contrary, they frequently crossed both cultural and political boundaries. They sometimes formed relationships with other nonwhites, but at times they participated in their persecution. They went back and forth between northern Mexico and the American Southwest, but even those who never moved came under the influence of transnational commerce, politics, ideas, and culture.[20] The Southwest that African Americans, Chinese, and whites entered in the second half of the nineteenth and the early twentieth centuries was thus highly Mexicanized. Slow economic development made southern Arizona even more so, as other groups arrived gradually.

Emmett Woodley, therefore, did die as a "colored Mexican" in 1935, but culturally, not racially, speaking. His Mexican wife and the cultural milieu they occupied greatly Mexicanized him. The hospital staff that watched over him during his last few days saw his Mexican side, even if they did not witness its development. He must have sounded and looked Mexican, socially Mexican, the type that one can associate with dark complexions: he looked like a working-class Mexican who had lived most of his life in the lower echelons of turn-of-the-century southern Arizona. Those hospital workers, had they met Leonicia Terrazas, would probably have viewed the couple as racially compatible, as had the county clerk and the Catholic priest who had sanctioned their marriage more than six decades earlier. The twenty-two-year-old former army private born in the antebellum South—probably into slavery—migrated west, married Leonicia, and lived most of his life with and among Mexicans. There was much about him that was indeed Mexican, as was the case with so many other men and women who made intermarriage part of their Southwest experience.

1

ARIZONA'S MISCEGENATION LAW AND RACIAL PRESCRIPTIONS

FRANK PASS WENT TO TRIAL in 1940 for the murder of Sai Han Ong. The homicide occurred in the Phoenix area only two weeks after Frank had married Ruby Contreras, and she, without his consent, agreed to testify against him. The judge in the trial allowed the testimony because he determined that the Pass-Contreras marriage contravened the state's miscegenation statute, which thus exempted Ruby from the law that prevented witnesses from testifying against their spouses. The jury convicted Pass based primarily on Ruby's account of the incident. Frank's lawyers appealed the conviction, and the Arizona Supreme Court eventually weighed in. Despite the couple's surnames, it was Frank Pass's ancestry that made him ineligible to marry whites. Both Frank and Ruby had Mexican ancestry. His father was Mexican, and his mother was born in Utah to a Paiute Indian mother and an English father. Ruby, on the other hand, declared that her father was Spanish and her mother was half French and half Mexican, making her, according to the high court, 100 percent white. "In her veins nothing but Caucasian blood flowed," the judges explained.[1]

The court thus upheld the initial ruling and affirmed the law that disallowed the descendants of Indians from marrying whites. Although the state's lawyers and the court justified their position by maintaining that Mexicans were white, such a step was unnecessary. Even if the judges had found that Ruby was only partially white, the marriage would still violate Arizona law because Frank's Indian ancestry disqualified him from marrying anyone with any percentage of white ancestry. Frank's marriage options were in fact nonexistent. As the descendant of a white forebear to any degree, he could not marry anyone with any percentage of black, Chinese, Filipino, or Asian Indian descent either. Incredibly, in the ethnically diverse Arizona, Frank could in effect never legally marry, not even a partner of his exact racial composition.

This chapter explores the peculiar history of Arizona's miscegenation law (1865–1962). It traces the prohibition on interracial marriage, which began as a short-lived racist statute in the New Mexico Territory and persisted long after Arizona became a separate territory in 1863. It slowly evolved into the confounding law that essentially forbade multiracial people from marrying anyone. The law was effective in preventing whites from legally marrying blacks, Indians, and Chinese, serving its primary, if not its sole, objective, but it sometimes proved porous. Yet, as this chapter argues, even though some couples managed to marry despite their banned combinations, legal and social entities consistently affirmed the power of the miscegenation law when disputes arose. The legislature never targeted white-Mexican marriage, since Mexicans were legally white, but the prohibition affected Mexicans in a different way: it limited their marriage options with nonwhites, for instance, with blacks and Chinese.

Historically, the definition of Mexicans as legally white has repeatedly come under attack. The Treaty of Guadalupe Hidalgo, which ended the U.S.-Mexico War (1846–1848), guaranteed Mexicans the same citizenship enjoyed by Euro-Americans and the equal protection of their rights, but institutional and social discrimination during the second half of the nineteenth and early part of the twentieth centuries demonstrated that Mexicans did not actually enjoy all the privileges of whiteness. This ambiguity and the enactment of Arizona's miscegenation law effectively produced a contradiction: Mexicans could legally marry whites and, often, also nonwhites. The first type of marriage rested on their legal whiteness, and the second one illustrated their social nonwhiteness. At times, the directives of legislators and high courts differed from the decisions of local clerks and religious officials, who typically followed their own racial understandings when deciding which marriages to solemnize. The law, therefore, sometimes failed to prevent some banned marriages, but as the Pass case helps illustrate, the courts adhered to a strict interpretation of the miscegenation law and consistently annulled marriages. The judges who heard the appeal by Pass even cited a law dictionary to emphasize that *descendants* signified every ancestor "to the remotest degree," and any Indian ancestor in the Pass lineage signified that his marriage to Contreras could not take place in Arizona.[2] Legally speaking, he was too Indian to marry a Mexican partner.

Ironically, one month after the Pass decision, an Indiana appellate court ruled that Mexicans were not necessarily white. In 1940 Estanislao Barcena suffered a job-related accident and died while employed by the Inland Steel Company. The local industrial board awarded death benefits to his common-law wife, Ruby, but the company appealed the decision on the grounds that their union violated the state prohibition on marriages between whites and partners with at least one-eighth black ancestry. The court disagreed. It explained that although Ruby was black, and Estanislao was certainly "whiter than [she]," the company could not prove that Estanislao, as a Mexican, was white. The judges grounded their decision in an entry from the *Encyclopedia Britannica*, which stated that the Mexican population contained blacks, Chinese, Indians, Japanese, whites, and mixed bloods, essentially like the United States. They thus concluded that logically one could not automatically establish that Mexicans—or Americans, for that matter—were white based on country of origin. Notably, the court underscored that the Mexican constitution had since 1824 eliminated "race distinctions" and recognized all groups as "free and equal." *Mexican*, the judges concluded, should not "necessarily be construed to be a white person." Ruby Barcena won her case, but the decision once again left Mexicans in racial limbo.[3]

ENCODING RACIAL PURITY

American courts and legislatures had targeted interracial marriages since colonial times. Legal decisions and legislative resolutions had restricted the ability of white-black couples to engage in sexual and reproductive practices since the early seventeenth century. But in 1664, Maryland enacted the first American miscegenation law. It punished white-black marriage but did not ban it. In the same act establishing that slaves would serve for life, the assembly determined that (1) a white woman who, "to the disgrace of our Nation," intermarried with a slave would serve the slaveholder during the lifetime of her husband; and

(2) the children of the marriage would become slaves for life.[4] The statute clearly benefited slaveholders but focused only on marriages between whites and slaves, and not on their informal relationships. Other colonies enacted similar laws, but in 1750, Georgia became the first colony to augment the punishment by actually nullifying intermarriages, a clause nearly all future laws would apply. By the early nineteenth century, every southern state as well as Maine and Rhode Island prohibited black-white marriage. Like other aspects of legal segregation, miscegenation laws expanded both their scope and severity of punishment after the Civil War.[5]

In the mid-nineteenth century, most western legislatures swiftly enacted miscegenation laws that both resembled and differed from the statutes of southern states. Every state and territory west of Missouri forbade white-black marriage at one point, but legislatures in the former Mexican land acted particularly quickly. By 1865, less than twenty years after the land cession, all of them had adopted a prohibition on interracial marriage. Of note, California instituted a ban in 1850, New Mexico in 1857, and Nevada became the first American legislature to target Chinese in a miscegenation law (1861). Soon after, Arizona, Idaho, and Oregon also included Chinese in the list of groups that could not marry whites. California and Montana eventually banned Chinese-white marriage as well.[6]

Interracial marriage first became illegal in Arizona while it still formed part of the New Mexico Territory, whose legislature prohibited the marriages and cohabitation of white women with black and mulatto men in 1857. The law punished both partners with two to three years of prison and hard labor. The ban originally encoded a gender bias. It did not apply to the unions of white *men* with black and mulatto women, but two years later, the legislature also prohibited those relationships.[7] The proscription of interracial unions by New Mexico fit within a broader slave code—as indicated by the punishment of hard labor and the original focus on the relationships of white women only. The territorial legislature actually passed elaborate and unnecessary laws that, among other things, prohibited emancipation in the territory and restricted the movement of free blacks. But pragmatism, not just racism, also explains these laws. New Mexico politicians enacted the legislation to seek congressional support from southern politicians in Washington. Never popular or enforced, as very few blacks resided in the territory, the law succumbed to the political landscape of the Civil War. By 1866, New Mexico had dropped every part of the slave code, including the ban on miscegenation.[8] But by the time of the repeal, New Mexico laws no longer applied to Arizona, as the two had become separate territories in 1863.

Upon gaining territorial status, Arizona quickly adopted its own miscegenation law, one that would be more rigid and enduring than its New Mexico counterpart.[9] The territory's first legislative action authorized Governor John N. Goodwin to hire Judge William T. Howell to write a legal code. Howell relied on the laws of New York and California, and the First Arizona Territorial Legislature (1864) promptly approved the statutes, which went into effect the next year.[10] New York, however, never forbade interracial marriage.[11] Thus, Howell copied California's miscegenation law verbatim. It made the following stipulation: "Marriages of white persons with negroes or mulattoes are declared to be illegal and void." Violations resulted in a misdemeanor, and fines ranged from one hundred to ten thousand dollars and prison terms from three months to ten years.[12] The punishment contradicted the designation as a misdemeanor, since the upper range of these prison terms corresponded only to felonies.[13] Unlike the New Mexico version, Arizona's law did not prohibit interracial cohabitation, but both laws targeted an all but nonexistent population: at the time of its adoption, fewer than thirty African Americans resided in Arizona.[14] The law recognized marriages that had occurred legally in other states—including interracial marriages—regardless of their legality in Arizona. Until the legislature closed that loophole in 1901, an Arizona couple could travel to another state or country, marry, return to Arizona, and enjoy the legal protections of legitimate marriage. But even after 1901, the marriages of couples using this tactic remained legal in Arizona as long as no one could prove that they had intentionally circumvented the law.[15]

Arizona legislators modified the statute several times between 1865 and 1942. The Second Arizona Territorial Legislature (1865) demonstrated its prejudice against the large Indian and minute Chinese populations by adding both groups to the list of people who could not marry whites. These additions separated Arizona from the less restrictive contemporary laws of California and New Mexico. Arizona's two legislative chambers subscribed to slightly different racial biases. The house version had included only "Mongolians"—and indeed, Arizona became the first American legislature to use such a racial classification in a miscegenation law—but the council added Indians, a move that endangered but did not prevent the bill's passage. The ban on these marriages represented yet another expression of the anti-Indian and anti-Chinese prejudices Arizonans exhibited at the time. The 1865 legislature openly called for the removal of friendly Indians and the pacification and even extermination of hostile tribes. Likewise, contemporary Arizona politicians and newspapers frequently spoke against Chinese residents, accusing them of polygamy, practicing coolie labor, living in unsanitary conditions, prostituting their women, and demonstrating an unwillingness to embrace American culture. Rhetoric and fear, more than actual complaints or interaction, prompted these attacks, since the 1860 census recorded no Chinese residents in Arizona.[16]

The early trajectory of Arizona's miscegenation law fit within overall political efforts to bring order and economic development, all within the framework of national debates over the meaning of race, society, and citizenship. During the early territorial period, Arizona governors and lawmakers supported statutes that paralleled federal laws and contributed to their efforts to appear civilized.[17] Acquiring territorial status during the Civil War and, more important, under the sponsorship of Abraham Lincoln, Arizona could not have instituted the slave code that had prevailed when it was part of the New Mexico Territory. Union forces, moreover, had quelled the efforts of Arizona southern sympathizers to join the Confederacy.[18] Arizona lawmakers, nonetheless, did adhere to racist sentiments, as the ban on interracial marriage and other laws demonstrate.

Legislators were fully aware of the perils of resembling anything but a white territory, as underscored by the comments of the U.S. congressmen who, in the early 1860s, argued that Arizona did not deserve territorial status because only 10 percent of its white residents were non-Mexicans.[19] Thus, Arizona politicians promptly insisted that Mexicans were white, because excluding them would have left only six hundred white residents in 1863. Furthermore, governors and legislators during the territorial period consistently sought ways to attract non-Hispanic white immigration. They pursued improvements in transportation (namely the railroad, whose absence easterners perceived as a sign of backwardness and disorder), communication (postal service), education (public schools), and safety (statutes, courts, jails, and law enforcement).[20] Granting equality and visibility to nonwhites, especially in the formal institution of marriage, seemed counterproductive. Attacks on Indians and on interracial marriage allowed Arizona politicians to claim a semblance of social order and reassured whites that they could migrate to the territory and enjoy the protection of both property and racial expectations.[21]

Although Arizona initially copied California's miscegenation law, the 1865 amendment illustrated the prerogatives of the new territory. Pro-southern

Democrats had dominated the California legislature that adopted the 1850 law, and they had focused their ban on white-black marriage.[22] In Arizona, on the other hand, the existing law had already addressed the racialist concerns of politicians with pro-southern attitudes. Although they represented a plurality in the legislature, they were politically weakened and did not vote as a bloc.[23] Their opposition to white-black relationships furthermore did not extend uniformly to other interracial marriages. In the 1865 legislature that added a ban on white-Chinese and white-Indian marriages, two of five southerners in the house actually opposed the ban on Chinese-white marriage, and one more joined them to vote against the bill when the council added a ban on white-Indian marriage. Prohibitions against white-Indian unions, after all, did not pervade the South. Antagonism toward Indians more likely emanated from associations Arizona legislators made between Indians and disorder, viewing them as impediments to investment and economic development. They maintained, for instance, that Indians were a threat "whose hostile presence is, and has been the chief obstacle to the growth and development of the Territory."[24] Mining interests, in particular, exerted great influence in Arizona politics throughout the nineteenth and early twentieth centuries, and they viewed Indians with fear and resentment. John N. Goodwin, the first territorial governor, shared their hatred and referred to Indians as "murdering savages" who impeded the expansion of the mining industry. At the second legislative session, miners outnumbered those in other professions ten to six, and they overwhelmingly supported the addition of Chinese and Indians to the list of targeted groups. In all likelihood, their antagonism toward Chinese workers and their concerns over Indian attacks prompted miners to vote for the ban on those marriages.[25] Their own racial prejudice and the depiction of these groups as threats to economic growth combined to produce the ostracism of Chinese and Indians. These legislators, therefore, could hardly welcome these ostracized groups into the institution of marriage.

Arizona eventually became one of the first western legislatures to adopt a strict definition of whiteness in a miscegenation statute. In 1887 it amended the law to prohibit marriages between "persons of Caucasian blood *or their descendants* with Africans, Mongolians *and their descendants.*"[26] The revision sought tighter control of intermarriage by forbidding whites from marrying people with any trace of African, Asian, or Indian ancestry—anticipating, if more vaguely, the rigid racial definitions that would appear in the early twentieth century.[27] The Arizona ancestry clause aimed for complete protection of white purity by conveying that descendants of white-nonwhite couples could never achieve legal whiteness. Other governments, however, were more specific. In 1907 Oklahoma enacted a miscegenation law that defined people of color as those who had any African ancestry, and southern states, including Alabama, Georgia, and Virginia, increasingly tightened their racial definitions until, in the 1920s, they settled on the so-called one-drop rule, whereby any traceable African ancestry defined a person as legally black. In 1912 as nativists endeavored to separate ethnic groups along stricter racial classifications, a U.S. congressman from Georgia introduced a bill to enact a national ban on marriages between whites and people of color, whom he defined as "all persons of African descent or having any trace of African blood."[28] Although unsuccessful, the bill demonstrated that anxieties over racial purity existed in Washington and in the nation. In theory, the language of the 1887 Arizona statute applied equally strict definitions of nonwhiteness but went further by applying the ancestry litmus test to Asians and Indians, not only to blacks. All challenges to the meaning and constitutionality of the law repeatedly yielded the same result: the courts upheld the intent of the law to keep whites apart from people with any percentage of nonwhite ancestry.

One effect, probably unintended, was that this version of the law forbade practically all people of mixed ancestry—and who had at least one white ancestor—from marrying anyone. American legislators have historically adopted miscegenation laws to protect only white racial purity—no American law had ever barred interracial marriage between two nonwhite groups. But the 1887 Arizona legislature essentially enacted such a ban. Since the law stipulated that whites (or the descendants of whites) could not marry Asians, blacks, or Indians (or the descendants of these groups), a person of mixed ancestry could enter a marriage only if neither partner had any white ancestry whatsoever—a virtual impossibility in Arizona. For example, a person who was fifteen-sixteenths white and one-sixteenth black could not legally marry anyone who had *any* trace of white, black, Indian, or Asian ancestry. His white ancestry prevented him from marrying nonwhites, and his black ancestry—minute as it was—disallowed marriages with whites. Ironically, the amendment occurred during the term of Governor Nathan O. Murphy, who had hired lawyers to revise and eliminate "improper and contradictory matter" from the statutes.[29] Nonetheless, strict enforcement of the ancestry clause would have been nearly impossible. Mexicans, for instance, a primarily mestizo population, could technically not marry each other unless both were 100 percent white or 100 percent Indian. Similarly, any person of African ancestry with even a trace of white ancestry could not marry anyone who was white, black, or any combination of the two.

Therefore, given Arizona's racial composition, all mestizos and multiracial residents who married anyone between 1887 and 1942 effectively broke the law.

The last addition to the list of groups that could not marry whites came in 1931, when the legislature targeted "Hindus" and "members of the Malay race." Prejudice against Asian Indians and Filipinos surged in the West at this time, especially in California, and this amendment to the law reflected the antagonism experienced in other states more than in Arizona itself. Asian Indians and Filipinos had migrated in significant numbers since the early 1900s and had become especially visible by 1930. The anti-immigration campaigns of the early 1920s led to the inclusion of Asians in miscegenation laws throughout the country. As with previous versions of the law in Arizona, the amendments seemed particularly unnecessary considering the insignificant size of its Asian Indian and Filipino populations. California had a much larger population of both Asian Indians (1,873) and Filipinos (30,470) in 1930, while Arizona counted only 50 and 472, respectively.[30] In California, men greatly outnumbered women in both groups and primarily married Mexican women in large numbers. Although Asian Indians and Filipinos both suffered discrimination, Filipinos faced even more antagonism, since they actively dated white women, and local newspapers frequently emphasized their sexuality.[31] In 1933 California also passed a law prohibiting Filipinos from marrying whites.[32] Both legislatures had followed national trends in banning Asian-white marriages, as the number of states that had such laws increased from seven in 1910 to fifteen in 1950, even as the size of their Asian populations declined or remained stable. Most of the bans occurred in the West, but they also emerged in states that had miniscule Asian populations but long histories of prohibiting intermarriage, including Georgia, Maryland, and Virginia.[33]

Soon after Arizona tightened its law, however, its grip on interracial marriage came under legal attack and began to weaken. When the Frank Pass case came before the Arizona Supreme Court in 1942, the judges affirmed the constitutionality of the state's miscegenation law but highlighted the irrationality of the ancestry clause, albeit more than five decades after its adoption. They based the annulment of the Pass-Contreras marriage on one important premise. They emphasized that when asked if she had Indian ancestry, Ruby had responded that she knew of none. Accepting her claim that her father was Spanish and her mother of French and Mexican ancestries, the judges surmised that in sum she was of French and Spanish descent. That is, they considered Mexicans to be Spanish unless proven otherwise. But although the judges fully supported the legislature's prerogative in protecting white purity, the vagueness of the ancestry clause disturbed them. They declared, "In trying to prevent the white race from interbreeding with Indians, Negros, Mongolians, etc., [the statute] has made it unlawful for a person with 99 per cent Indian blood and 1 per cent Caucasian blood to marry an Indian, or a person with 99 per cent Caucasian blood and 1 per cent Indian blood to marry a Caucasian."[34] The judges could have further underscored the severity of disallowing marriages where both partners had precisely 1 percent white and 99 percent Indian ancestries. They emphasized and agreed with the intent of encoding white supremacy. They simply wanted exact parameters.

The court thus called on the legislature to establish a specific percentage of "Indian or other tabooed blood that will invalidate a marriage." Of course, from its inception, the ancestry clause sought to prevent people with any amount of nonwhite ancestry from marrying whites. The legislature, nonetheless, acted swiftly and went beyond the court's mandate. After a few unsuccessful attempts to agree on a specific percentage of disqualifying Indian ancestry, the senate simply voted 16–1 to remove the ancestry clause altogether and to legalize marriages between Indians and whites. A special provision retroactively validated all marriages that the revised law now authorized—including, ironically, unions like the Pass-Contreras marriage but not that one itself. The house overwhelmingly assented on a 43–2 vote.[35] Seventy-seven years after the initial ban, a strong consensus settled the issue, and Indians could once again legally marry whites in the state, and ancestry calculations no longer mattered.

Changes in Arizona's miscegenation law in 1942 coincided with events at the state and national levels. Clearly, the hostility toward American Indians that had prompted politicians to prohibit Indian-white marriages no longer existed in the legislature. American Indians received better treatment under the Franklin D. Roosevelt administration and recognition for their participation in World War II, where approximately twenty-five thousand served. John Collier's tenure as commissioner of Indian affairs (1933–1945) was particularly constructive. He coordinated programs and legislation that provided more economic aid and promoted self-sufficiency for tribes. The so-called Indian New Deal placed emphasis on cultural preservation, civil rights, and local autonomy.[36] Arizona, too, moved toward granting Native Americans more rights, and the state supreme court finally gave them the right to vote in 1948, concluding that denying them the franchise constituted a form of "violence to the principles of freedom and equality."[37]

Arizona finally repealed the state's miscegenation law in 1962, which by then only prohibited marriages of whites with Asians, Asian Indians, blacks, and Filipinos. Successful assaults on miscegenation laws had begun in California in 1948, when its supreme court struck down that state's statute in *Perez v. Lippold*. In 1959 a Pima County Superior Court in Tucson declared Arizona's miscegenation law unconstitutional in *Oyama v. O'Neill*. But before the state's supreme court heard an appeal, the Arizona legislature repealed the law with large margins of 71–6 in the house and 20–6 in the senate.[38] The state had ended its nearly one-hundred-year prohibition on interracial marriage. In 1967 the U.S. Supreme Court dealt the final blow to all remaining miscegenation laws in the country. Its *Loving v. Virginia* decision maintained that such statutes violated the Fourteenth Amendment.[39]

No miscegenation law ever targeted Mexicans, but they clearly did not enjoy equal status with Euro-Americans. The legal endorsement of their marriages with whites therefore should not obscure the history of racial antagonism against Mexicans and their tenuous legal and social standing. The admission of Mexicans as white under the Treaty of Guadalupe Hidalgo (1848) did not change widespread anti-Mexican attitudes among whites.[40] True, the treaty purported to guarantee Mexicans "the enjoyment of all the rights of citizens," but southwestern lawmakers and judges frequently violated such stipulations, primarily because the treaty did not define *Mexican* elaborately enough to daunt those who would later slight Mexicans of the rights that the treaty putatively protected.[41] During the years surrounding the U.S.-Mexico War, whites described Mexicans as indolent, dirty, and sacrilegious half-breeds and compared them to Indians and blacks.[42] No treaty could suddenly eliminate those racist attitudes, and the conflation of the social and legal realms often mitigated Mexicans' rights. These violations occurred because lawmakers could identify Mexicans as members of different races, including white, mestizo, mulatto, and Indian. As early as 1856, the California Assembly passed an antivagrancy ordinance informally known as the Greaser Act, which focused on people "commonly known as 'Greasers' or the issue of Spanish or Indian blood."[43] The law vilified Mexicans beyond its denigrating language.[44] Idleness of any kind qualified them as vagrants. One year later, a California court forbade a Mexican landowner who had signed the state constitution from testifying in court because of his Indian ancestry. The creation of barrios perpetuated exclusion, and poverty and anti-Mexican rhetoric had a direct effect on daily interactions between whites and Mexicans.[45] Not surprisingly, various southwestern legislatures of the ceded territory immediately curtailed the rights of a significant portion of the Mexican population by conferring constitutional rights only on Mexicans of light complexion, a stipulation the treaty never made. Thus, many mestizos and all the civilized Indians and Afro-mestizos who had enjoyed the rights of Mexican citizenship saw their status reduced to the levels of American Indians and blacks.[46]

Arizona once again followed the lead of California lawmakers by limiting the franchise to "[e]very white male citizen of the United States, and every *white* male citizen of Mexico."[47] The legislature, of course, could have simply stated that only white men qualified, but the fact that they mentioned Mexicans separately indicates that, in their view, not all Mexicans were white. (Ironically, their effort to protect white supremacy by differentiating between Mexican Americans and Euro-Americans technically granted white men in Mexico the right to vote in Arizona.) The specification on white Mexicans appeared nowhere in Arizona's miscegenation law, meaning that mestizo and mulatto Mexicans could technically marry whites but could not vote for them. Nonwhite Mexicans, furthermore, suffered other legal restrictions in Arizona, since only whites could practice law, testify in cases involving other whites, and serve on juries.[48] Unlike legislatures in California and New Mexico, where Mexicans were well represented in early legislative sessions, in Arizona only three Mexicans took part in the first territorial legislature in 1864—which enacted the Howell Code—and none returned until 1868.[49] It is unlikely, however, that they would have advocated for the rights of nonwhite Mexicans, since Mexican delegates in the other states and territories primarily acted to protect their own rights as elites.[50] Nonetheless, Arizona politicians could not simply redefine all Mexicans as nonwhite, especially when including them suited their pleas in Washington, DC, for territorial status, and later, for statehood.

Mexicans in the West suffered social and legal discrimination, but state and federal courts generally validated the white citizenship of those who challenged discriminatory laws. The results, however, were equivocal. The courts affirmed the legal rights of Mexicans but often acted too late to prevent social, political, and economic consequences, or their rulings had no effect on local practices. For example, the California Supreme Court declared that American citizens of Mexican descent did not have to pay the foreign miners' tax, but white miners regularly forced them out anyway.[51] Similarly, in 1869, white businessmen in Santa Barbara contested the election of Pablo de la Guerra as district judge, arguing that he retained "the character of a Mexican citizen." The California Supreme Court validated de la Guerra's white citizenship and allowed him to keep his office, but it also recognized the prerogative of the government to deny rights to nonwhite Mexicans.[52] A similar case occurred in Tucson in 1893, when white political opponents argued that Lucas Estrella, a city marshal, was not an American citizen. Estrella successfully deflected the attacks, but his political career soon ended.[53] In effect, whites managed to manipulate the law to curtail the rights and opportunities of Mexicans.

Although a federal district court established in 1897 the legitimate right of Mexicans to American citizenship, their whiteness remained unclear. From 1878 to 1952, U.S. courts heard petitions from foreign nationals to decide whether they met the restrictions that limited naturalization to whites. The 1897 ruling *In re Rodriguez* determined that Mexicans indeed qualified, but the victory came with a distressing explanation. The judges based their decision on international treaties between the United States and Mexico, and added that the claimant was probably not white in the *anthropological* sense, which in this case meant that he did not descend solely from whites.[54] In other words, the court reiterated that Mexicans were legally white even if they did not match the description, even if they did not look the part.

The social experiences of Mexicans in Arizona proved that legal whiteness differed from how they were perceived in society. They were victims of mob violence and even lynchings; a sheriff could manipulate tax laws to strip them of their property; they participated on juries at lower rates than whites; they were subject to more prosecutions, longer sentences, and a disproportionate number of death penalties; hospitals often denied them services; some employers—mines in particular—used dual-wage systems, in which Mexicans received lower salaries for equal work and had no access to higher-paying positions; company mining towns consigned them to segregated, deplorable housing, and placer miners called their own towns "white men's camps" and passed resolutions to deny access to "Asiatics and Sonoranians." On the eve of statehood, nativist organizations and labor unions—many of which excluded Mexicans—endorsed propositions to ban aliens from public projects and from purportedly hazardous occupations (namely mines), to require all employers to maintain their foreign workforce at a maximum of 20 percent, and to administer literacy tests to potential voters.[55] These political maneuvers primarily targeted Mexicans, since both the Chinese and black populations remained fairly small.

The prospect of interracial relationships with Mexicans worried mid-nineteenth-century Americans, as chapter 2 explains. The issue had not disappeared by the early twentieth century. Concerns over miscegenation arose as opponents of Mexican immigration used the discourse of Madison Grant's *The Passing of the Great Race* (1917), in which he called Mexicans a mongrel race, incapable of self-government—arguments he had inherited from pseudoscientific treatises of the 1840s and 1850s.[56] Grant, an elitist conservationist from New York, maintained that new immigrants from non-Nordic regions would degrade American society.[57] U.S. congressmen used similar language and warned of the degeneration and danger of racial mixing and referred to Mexican intermarriage as "a mistake, a crime, . . . an absolute tragedy" since "the product is a Mexican."[58] Congressional debates illustrated that both opponents and defenders of Mexican immigration grounded their arguments in biological determinism and depicted Mexicans as racially inferior. Opponents argued that the inferiority of Mexicans posed a threat to the social and racial health of the United States, while supporters countered that such inferiority made them suitable for the stoop labor and that they could never improve enough to challenge the supremacy of whites.[59]

The 1924 U.S. Immigration Act sought to curtail the immigration of eastern and southern Europeans and nonwhites from other continents, but the exemption of the western hemisphere from these restrictions did not leave Mexicans unscathed. Western economic interests, which benefited from an abundance of Mexican labor, ensured that Mexican immigration remained unrestrained, but the anti-immigrant movements did result in the militarization of the U.S.-Mexico border, harsher penalties, the creation of the U.S. Border Patrol (1925), and the criminalization of illegal entry (1929). Early border agents frequently maintained ties to the Ku Klux Klan and used the vicious tactics of the Texas Rangers.[60] The exclusion of Mexicans from the immigration act also failed to prevent their racialization in the 1930 census, when the bureau adopted *Mexican* as a racial category. That census reaffirmed what social and political entities had expressed since the mid-1800s, that Mexicans were not white.[61]

Thus, their constitutional whiteness notwithstanding, the treatment Mexicans experienced in public, labor, and legal spaces placed them in a racially ambiguous position: marriages to whites, although legal, seemed like social transgressions, and marriages to nonwhites, although prohibited, might have seemed more logical and socially acceptable. Accordingly, in their relationships with blacks and Chinese, Mexicans sometimes obtained marriage licenses because all three groups occupied parallel racial spaces. Once married, however, only unions that factually adhered to the letter of the law were truly safe from potential legal and social challenges.

VALIDATING RACIAL PRESCRIPTIONS: ARIZONA'S MISCEGENATION LAW IN THE COURTROOM

During the nineteenth century, state and territorial legislatures adopted measures to promote order and facilitate the transmission of property. They expanded the recognition of Indian, interstate, and common-law marriages and vested more civil and religious officials with the ability to officiate ceremonies. The liberalization of marriage laws, however, posed a threat to the preservation of white privilege unless politicians could ensure that nonwhites—including the children of interracial couples—would not have access to the same rights. Thus, the reach and scope of miscegenation laws increased between 1820 and 1865. The power of these laws lay not only in preventing certain couples from marrying, but also in their potential for retroactive enforcement during legal disputes, particularly if those cases involved assets.[62] For prohibited unions, success in obtaining a marriage license therefore left the couples in a legally tenuous position and, in some cases, even more susceptible to challenges and litigation. For instance, an intermarried couple might have neglected to draft a will because they viewed it as unnecessary. Such a document, however, would have prevailed in court even if the court nullified the marriage. Several cases demonstrate that these unions lacked the legal protections of permitted marriages. If litigation, such as divorces and contested estates, ever involved the validity of the marriage, couples could suddenly discover that, as far as the law was concerned, they had never married.

A legal marriage ensures moral and social propriety as well as the right to property and financial protection in case of divorce or the death of a spouse. Thus, miscegenation laws focused on marriage more than on sexual relations, because it brought the economic benefits that the dominant group wanted to control. These laws came into play primarily in legal disputes over assets, as whites—almost always men—sought annulments and questioned people's whiteness in order to deny economic benefits to nonwhites.[63] For instance, white relatives could claim the estates of men who had managed to marry nonwhite women in states and territories that prohibited those unions by calling for the nullification of marriages.[64] Courts that decided cases involving Arizona's miscegenation law always adhered to a strict interpretation of the law and disallowed marriages that contravened the statute.

The Arizona Supreme Court established this precedent relatively early. In 1896 it ratified the legality of the miscegenation law and the primacy of territorial law over Indian customs. The case involved the inheritance of Juana Walker, daughter of John D. Walker, a white man, and Chur-ga Walker, a Pima Indian. Walker's relatives had claimed his estate by arguing that Juana was not a legitimate heir. A former captain in the Union Army, Walker had settled among the Pima after the Civil War and soon after had married Chur-ga in an Indian ceremony in 1871. Both had died by 1891. Before 1901 Arizona law recognized (1) endogamous marriages that took place on Indian lands and (2) any marriages that occurred legally in other states and countries, even if such marriages involved partners of races that could not intermarry in Arizona. The first provision did not apply because the case involved an exogamous marriage banned by the law. The supreme court thus had to decide whether Arizona should treat an Indian tribe as a sovereign nation or rule that territorial statutes superseded tribal laws and customs. The case came before the court during a period when states and territories were demanding and receiving from the federal government more authority over Indian nations.[65] Accordingly, the Arizona judges affirmed the constitutionality of the miscegenation law and ruled that it applied to all citizens within the territorial borders, regardless of the existence of Indian tribes. It determined that John had never legally married Chur-ga because no legal ceremony of any kind could have taken place in Arizona since its laws forbade white-Indian marriage. It absurdly added that if Walker had adopted Juana—his own daughter—her claim to his estate *might* hold some validity.[66] The qualification itself was problematic, because the judges implied that the right of a white man to control property did not automatically transfer even to an adopted biracial daughter. The estate thus remained with his siblings.

Invoking laws against certain marriages, however, could also become a valuable recourse for disgruntled spouses. Joe Kirby, the son of a white man and a Mexican woman, married Mayellen Conner, a black woman from Kansas, in Tucson in 1914, when both were in their early thirties.[67] By 1920 the Kirbys were probably experiencing marital problems. They still resided in Tucson, but Joe had moved in with his mother and siblings, and Mayellen and their daughter lived with a black female friend. In 1921 Joe decided to end the marriage and went to court to seek not a divorce, but an annulment. Although Arizona statutes offered various grounds for divorce—such as abandonment, failure to provide, abuse, and infidelity—all spouses in prohibited unions could, at any time, employ the miscegenation law to invalidate their marriage retroactively.

Pursuing an annulment was not necessarily easier—divorce cases typically proceeded smoothly—but it did offer a substantial incentive to men: by invalidating the marriage, a husband did not have to divide his property or pay spousal or child support. Such was precisely the outcome of the Kirby trial.[68]

Joe and his lawyer argued that Mayellen, a black woman, could not have legally married Joe. Everyone involved, including the judge, presumed that Mayellen was black solely based on visual scrutiny. She did not indicate otherwise. The question then rested on Joe's race. His mother testified that she was half Spanish and half Mexican, and Joe added that his father was Irish—a first-generation American from Kentucky, according to the census—which made Joe, in his own view, "of the white race."[69] Mayellen's lawyer argued that Joe's mother was at most one-fourth white and three-fourths "native," but the judge retorted that Mexicans technically belonged to the Caucasian race and could not legally marry blacks. The court thus annulled the marriage.[70]

In establishing their positions, the participants in the trial employed differing racial interpretations. Joe's mother and his lawyer relied on family lore to claim a Spanish lineage. Joe expressed his own sense of identity in surmising that he was indeed white. Mayellen's lawyer presumed that Mexicans were not necessarily white and argued that, unless they had Spanish ancestry, they were indigenous. The judge simply relied on legal precedent to conclude that Mexicans were white. In effect, however, lawyers and judge wasted their time in arguing over the whiteness of Mexicans. The trial could have summarily ended when the court accepted that Joe's father was white, since having even one white ancestor disqualified him from marrying a person with any amount of black ancestry. Thus, Joe would have won the case even if his mother had been 100 percent Indian—or any other race—because any percentage of white ancestry fully disallowed his marriage to Mayellen.

The ancestry clause of Arizona's miscegenation law also came into play in a dispute over the inheritance of a white man in California, when a federal court in San Diego rejected the claim filed by Antoinette Giraudo-Monks for the estate of her late husband, Allan Monks. In December 1930, Allan and Antoinette had traveled from their home in the San Diego area to Yuma, Arizona, to get married. By 1932, Allan, whose mental condition had been deteriorating since a motorcycle accident in 1928, required confinement in a state hospital. He never recovered and died there in 1937. The distribution of his estate soon evolved into a five-year legal dispute when three claimants stepped forward: Antoinette, who presented a will dated in 1928—two years before their marriage and six months after Allan's accident; Ida Lee, the wife of one of Allan's childhood friends, who brought a will dated in 1913; and Louisa D. Hemple, Allan's aunt, whose claim to his estate on the basis of kinship ended when she died soon after.

The court promptly admitted the 1913 will of Ida Lee, and the proceedings then focused on Antoinette's claim. First, Lee's lawyer argued that Allan had drafted the 1928 will under the undue influence of Antoinette. The most serious accusations against Antoinette included attempts to distance Allan from all his friends, moving Allan to her friend's home after the accident, using two of her friends as the sole witnesses of the 1928 will, selling Allan's business interest in a motorcycle store, securing a lien against Allan's trust fund, and controlling his every decision. This argument proved overwhelming, supported by several witnesses, and would have sufficed, according to the appellate judges, to invalidate Antoinette's will. Yet, Antoinette's race became the focus of the trial when Ida Lee's lawyers sought to buttress their position even further by arguing that Antoinette could not have legally married a white man in Arizona. They even claimed that Antoinette had willfully deceived Allan when she purportedly told him that she was of pure French descent, when in fact, the lawyers asserted, she was partially black.[71]

Although both Allan and Antoinette stated in their marriage license that they were white, the burden of visual proof rested exclusively on her. Lawyers from both sides and the judges accepted that Allan was white. Lee's lawyers called on three expert witnesses to establish that Antoinette was of mixed ancestry. First, a hairdresser testified that based on the appearance of Antoinette's fingernails, the palms of her hands, and her hair, she was certainly of mixed descent. She added that Antoinette had once lamented that her hands revealed her true ancestry, since she might otherwise pass as white and thus enter the beauty salon during regular hours—whereas she always had to wait until the salon closed to white clients. Second, a physical anthropologist maintained that Antoinette's face, hands, and heels proved that she was "at least one-eighth Negroid." Finally, a surgeon concluded that she was one-eighth black based on the shape of her calves, heels, neck, and face. All testimony thus pointed to admixture, and Mayellen faced a difficult task to prove her whiteness.[72]

Although the use of physical characteristics to establish a person's race had proved effective since the nineteenth century, Antoinette's lawyers decided to use science to stake their position. They called an anthropologist and added a biologist to argue that no one could accurately surmise a person's race based solely on appearance. People of mixed ancestry, the experts stated, presented even more difficulties. In the end, the judges lent most credence to the testimony of the surgeon, concluding that he personified both scientific expertise and common sense. They ruled that as a woman with one-eighth black ancestry, Antoinette had never legally married Allan in Arizona.[73] No one, except Antoinette, even suggested that she had no African ancestors. She thus came under the scope of the ancestry clause of Arizona's miscegenation law: any trace of black, Asian, or Indian ancestry automatically disqualified a person from marrying someone with any trace of white ancestry. The court added that when agreeing to marry Antoinette and when writing his will, Allan must have acted under the false premise that Antoinette was a white woman, although they did not explain how they surmised that Antoinette deceived him. The court nullified the Monks's marriage and awarded the entire estate to Ida Lee.[74] The thirty-year-old will to the wife of a childhood friend held more legal sway.

Apparently, the judges could so easily determine not only that Allan was white, but also, for the purpose of Arizona law, that he had no racial admixture at all. The cursory nature of their analysis notwithstanding, the decision held much importance. Antoinette argued that the law greatly limited her ability to marry, and the court's ruling underscored that if both Antoinette and Allan had been of mixed ancestry—any combination would suffice—it would have allowed Antoinette to challenge the constitutionality of Arizona's miscegenation law under the Fourteenth Amendment. The judges relied on an old photograph to conclude that Allan was clearly and completely white—evidently, they needed no scientific proof in his case. In rejecting Antoinette's argument, the appellate court cited and distorted the precedent of the Arizona Supreme Court decision in *Kirby v. Kirby*. The California judges correctly indicated that the Arizona ruling had denied Mayellen Kirby the opportunity to challenge the constitutionality of Arizona's miscegenation law. The Arizona judges had determined that she could not ground her case in the inability of people of mixed ancestry to marry because *she* was black, and not of mixed ancestry. In other words, Mayellen was not someone like Antoinette. Yet, the California judges claimed that the Arizona court had indicated that both bride *and* groom would have to be of mixed ancestry for a challenge to proceed. Thus, it rejected Antoinette's argument, whereas the Arizona court would have allowed it. The California court in fact reached an illogical decision. Under Arizona law, it was not necessary for both partners to be of mixed ancestry for Antoinette's argument to apply. Whatever the race of the other partner, in 1930, a person of her mixed descent could not marry any other person in Arizona unless the marriage involved a hypothetical partner who had no trace whatsoever of the following ancestries: Asian, black, Indian, or white. Such a person would have been difficult to find anywhere in America, signifying that Antoinette effectively lacked the ability to marry legally in Arizona.

These court cases demonstrate that even when partners deliberately or innocently thwarted the miscegenation law, their marriages never entirely escaped its scope. The most effective preventive measure undoubtedly lay in the hands of court officials. In 1909, for instance, authorities in Prescott denied repeated requests for a marriage license to a Japanese man who wanted to marry a white woman. Annie Brown responded to the initial rejection by making a personal appeal, declaring that she was born in Germany and willfully wished to marry C. Togo, a man she understood was Japanese. By the time of the rejection, the couple was expecting their first child and stated that they would marry outside Arizona if necessary. Their insistence did not convince the judge and the district attorney. Togo and Brown remained in Prescott and had at least one more illegitimate child three years later.[75]

But local residents could also use the law to impose their racial attitudes. Two incidents in Arizona towns illustrate how whites specifically targeted interracial relationships. In 1904 residents in Bowie, a former army outpost near southern New Mexico, forcibly separated a white man from his African American wife. J. J. Rowell and "Sis" Hitchins at first only cohabitated without marrying. Highly visible for running a lodge and restaurant, the couple heard rumors of impending legal trouble for their informal relationship. Undoubtedly aware of the Arizona ban on white-black marriages, they decided to marry in nearby Lordsburg, New Mexico. Soon after, however, an Arizona judge disallowed their marriage, stating that the couple had "entered into collusion by going to New Mexico and by being married to evade the law." The illegitimacy of the marriage in Arizona fell within the prevailing statutes, but the judge went beyond his authority when he sentenced Rowell to six months in jail and fined his now ex-wife twenty-five dollars. The legislature never enacted penalties for traveling outside Arizona to evade its miscegenation law, and in 1887, lawmakers had repealed the punishment for marrying illegally within its borders.[76] The judge's decision nonetheless pleased local whites and went unchallenged.

A similarly questionable interpretation of the law forced the separation of a Chinese man from his white wife in the mining town of Jerome. Ah Fee married Lucille Ellwood in New Mexico in 1918. They soon arrived in Jerome to honeymoon and decided to stay permanently. "The rare racial combination," the *Prescott Journal Miner* reported, soon attracted attention and problems with Arizona law. The *Journal* even claimed that an opium addiction explained the bride's irrational marriage choice—only in such circumstances would a white woman agree to marry a Chinese man, the paper implied. Local authorities incarcerated Lucille—and most likely also Fee—and did not release her until she agreed to leave her husband and relocate to her parents' home in California. Local officials ensured compliance by accompanying her until she boarded the train. Not only did the judge exceed his power by administering punishment for marrying outside Arizona, but, in this case, he also incorrectly prosecuted the case. The law only voided the marriages of couples that married in another place while living or intending to live in Arizona. Fee and Lucille apparently decided to settle in Arizona only after they had already married in New Mexico.[77] Technicalities notwithstanding, the newlyweds probably never saw each other again. These examples demonstrate that local coercion and intimidation, more than proper application of the law, sometimes determined who had the right to form families in Arizona. White residents separated these couples simply because they found them racially incompatible. Whatever the accuracy of these legal interpretations, local racial expectations dictated that whites should not marry blacks or Chinese.

CONCLUSION

Interracial relations threatened the purity of the white race, but importantly, actual marriages were a greater concern to whites because the institution carried legitimacy, respectability, and economic benefits—such as inheritance, alimony, and child support.[78] Centuries of racial inequality had led to a disproportionate accumulation of wealth among whites. Statutes that restricted the dissemination of property—as miscegenation laws ultimately did—in essence sought to maintain property in the hands of white men and their white relatives. In that sense, the recognition of Mexicans as white sometimes provided them benefits over nonwhites and people of mixed ancestry. Joe Kirby, for example, escaped all spousal responsibility when he used the miscegenation law to nullify a marriage he knowingly and willfully contracted with an African American woman. Of course, women involved in marriages that contravened the law had equal access to these dissolutions. For instance, a Mexican woman from Solomonville, Arizona, one hundred miles northeast of Tucson, pursued annulment rather than divorce when seeking to end her marriage to a Chinese man.[79] But the law clearly favored men, because voiding a marriage actually released the husband from financial responsibility. Legal disputes that involved miscegenation laws therefore primarily revolved around property. Clearly, the family of John D. Walker did not seem to object to his decision to live among Pima Indians or to marry Chur-ga. He, as a white man, exercised control over his decisions and over his property. After his death, however, his neglect in securing the financial future of his daughter left her vulnerable. Unbeknownst to him, officially naming her as his heir would have ensured that she received his estate—or adopting her, as the judges suggested. These procedures would have granted the legitimacy that she, as the daughter of an interracial couple, did not automatically receive.[80] All cases concerning the legality of interethnic unions in Arizona resulted in the loss of property or rights by nonwhites, particularly by nonwhite women and their mixed-race children.

But arguably the most important aspect of the story of John and Chur-ga Walker involves their very decision to form a family. True, Arizona and other jurisdictions prohibited this and other types of marriages between whites and nonwhites, and the long history of legal measures against interracial unions in the United States reveals much about the racial attitudes of lawmakers. Yet, these laws never reached all states and territories. Most notably, the ideology of the pertinent legislators did not necessarily represent the racial views of all their constituents. Men like Joe Kirby and John Walker consciously entered into relationships with nonwhite women and, importantly, decided to marry them. Their actions, in other words, contravened codified racial ideology. They, not politicians, decided who qualified as a worthy spouse. The law adhered to and promoted racist tenets that these men did not share. Chapter 2 explores a similar situation. The period of American expansion that brought Mexicans within the realm of the United States—and thus within the purview of its racial attitudes—witnessed the rise of the rhetoric of manifest destiny. The language of expansionists denigrated Mexicans and disdained the prospect of interethnic marriage. One must not, however, assume that those propagandists spoke for all Americans, especially for the Americans who ventured west in the second half of the nineteenth century.

2

THE DISCOURSE OF MANIFEST DESTINY AND THE MEXICAN QUESTION

I N FEBRUARY 1848, as news of the conclusion of the U.S.-Mexico War was about to reach the United States, Sam Houston presented his case for the annexation of Mexico at a meeting of the Democratic Party in New York. The famous leader of the independence of Texas and current U.S. senator recounted a narrative that he had developed since 1836: the despotic Mexican government, he explained, had oppressed freedom-loving Texans until they had justifiably declared their independence; the Texas legislature then announced to the world that the southern boundary of the new republic extended to the Rio Grande, a demarcation Mexico had recklessly and repeatedly ignored; by 1846 the United States had finally responded with military action, and, he concluded, Americans had thus acted honorably to defend their new state. The speech contained historical errors, but by 1848, the discourse of manifest destiny pervaded the arguments of American expansionists, and Houston proceeded to affirm the oft-made declaration that the Anglo-Saxon race ought to expand throughout North America, redeem backward peoples, and develop the resources of the West. Providence, he declared, was undoubtedly guiding American troops to victory over Mexico.[1] Houston sanctioned the expansionist vision of manifest destiny and its depreciation of Mexicans because he, and most other expansionists, generally considered them members of an inferior race. They expressed their goals and justification with unwavering boldness.

When Houston spoke of Mexican women, however, his views revealed one of the ambivalences of the rhetoric: its unstable conflation of racial and gender attitudes. Expansionists tended to promote the tenet that God had entrusted the United States to civilize the American West, since Indians and Mexicans purportedly lacked the capacity to achieve such a mission. Yet, although many disdained all Mexicans, Houston, like some others, condoned the partial assimilation of the Mexican population. Echoing previous and future arguments of support for annexing the Mexican territory, Houston asserted that Mexicans were as inferior as Indians and that Americans should take possession of their lands. But he also maintained that although Mexicans had proven incapable of self-government, Americans could then teach them republican principles and thus "elevate them far above what their tyrants have done." Houston went further, however, concluding his remarks on racial uplift by inviting his audience to visit the territorial acquisitions and "look out for the beautiful *señoritas*, or pretty girls, and if you should choose to annex them, no doubt the result of this annexation will be a most powerful and delightful evidence of civilization." Houston claimed to despise those who took pleasure in reaping the material spoils of victory, but he evidently viewed human spoils differently, since he posited that a national conquest afforded the victors sexual rights over conquered women.[2] He patently suggested that American men enter into relationships with the women of a group he had just described as racially inferior. His arrogant sense of entitlement, even within the context of conquest, thus drew attention to the sensitive issue of racial amalgamation.

This chapter explores how Americans depicted Mexicans in the nineteenth century, especially in the period surrounding the Mexican war. It argues that although the language of manifest destiny appeared exclusionist and racist regarding Mexicans, a gendered subtext and the words and actions of the average American who interacted with Mexicans often ignored it or undermined it. First, the chapter discusses the salience of racial depictions in the accounts of American travelers and fiction writers who introduced Mexico as a literary motif in the early nineteenth century. Mexico received ambivalent depictions until 1836, but the spectacle of the independence of Texas initiated a period of scathing, stereotypical, and racist narratives that would only multiply and intensify over the next ten years. Second, it examines how the attention garnered by the annexation of Texas (1845) and the U.S.-Mexico War (1846–1848) produced an increasing interest in Mexico, its culture, and its people. Thus, the so-called Mexican Question started to receive much coverage from travelers, writers, pseudoscientists, editors, and expansionist politicians, as the speech of Sam Houston demonstrates. As these self-proclaimed pundits offered answers to the question of annexation, the racial characteristics of Mexicans became focal points. The discourse of manifest destiny focused on, among other subjects, whether the United States should condone the national and social amalgamation that a territorial expansion entailed. Finally, the chapter explains how Arizona's version of the Mexican Question compared to the larger national pattern. An exploration of how these reflections and remarks addressed relationships of Americans and Mexicans reveals much about the extent and limitations of anti-Mexican rhetoric.

"THE MONGREL RACES KNOWN AS MEXICANS": ENTERING THE AMERICAN RACIAL IMAGINATION

From 1845 to 1860, in the midst of the success of the United States in the war with Mexico and the consolidation of American presence in the Southwest, the *Democratic Review* and other publications promoted what one might qualify as the discourse of manifest destiny. Its highly politicized rhetoric combined calls for expansion with theories on racial hierarchies. Its claims rested on the premise that providence intended Anglo-Saxons to dominate darker races, and since Mexicans belonged to a dark race, Americans had to rule over them. Any privileges granted to Mexicans would simply prove the benevolence and enlightenment of the superior Americans. Throughout the 1840s, the *Democratic Review* consistently defended the American intervention against Mexico, even developing a fourteen-point argument by 1848. The discourse of manifest destiny maintained that racial inferiority, especially mixed ancestry, made Mexicans unfit to possess their lands or to live in the United States. The *Review* frequently referred to the valuable lessons Mexicans could learn under American tutelage. They already held great admiration for Americans, the editor claimed, and they "desire a closer intimacy."[3] Ironically, their impending incorporation raised the danger of social and interpersonal admixture. Mexicans, in other words, complicated the very expansion that could bring them into the nation that did not want them.

But the racialist components of the discourse of manifest destiny had developed long before the expansionist rhetoric of the 1840s. The few American travelers and fiction writers who portrayed Mexicans in the early 1800s employed a condescending tone that underscored racial and cultural differences. The Philadelphia magazine the *American Register* published one of the earliest depictions of Mexicans in 1808, when it printed the chronicles of sailor William Shaler. These accounts described Mexican Indians in California as dull and stupid, and the Hispanic population as "a mixed breed . . . of an indolent and harmless disposition and fond of spirituous liquors." Only a few Spanish officers of light complexion escaped Shaler's disdain.[4] References to mixed ancestry and indolence became a leitmotif that persisted throughout the century. The narrative of Joel Roberts Poinsett, American congressman and emissary to Mexico, repeated those themes and left a more lasting and negative impression.[5] Cultural biases permeated his commentary in *Notes on Mexico* (1825), referring to Mexicans, especially the poor, as a lazy, immoral, and "swarthy race."[6] His influential account helped Americans form an opinion of the nascent republic of Mexico that would only become more negative in the next few years.

Fictional tales by American writers also introduced Americans to Mexican themes, including the topic of intermarriage. The literary integration of Mexico into American fiction coincided with the publication of Poinsett's observations in the mid-1820s and acquired most of its principal characteristics a few years after the U.S.-Mexico War. Mexico first appeared as a locale for American fiction in 1826 with the publication of Timothy Flint's *Francis Berrian*, which contains the first fictional American-Mexican intermarriage. The relationship occurs along elite class lines, and the Mexican bride must undergo an Americanization process in order to gain entry into her husband's New England society. Eventually she humbly acknowledges the superiority of Americans: "What a great country! What a noble people! Compare their faces and persons with those of the people [of Mexico], and what a difference!"[7] Although largely avoiding the racial stereotypes that dominated much of the later literature, Flint, who never visited Mexico, nonetheless provided a condescending, if romanticized, depiction of Mexicans.[8]

Other accounts were even less enlightening. Unlike Flint, Albert Pike did base his fictional accounts on personal experiences in Mexican territory—the first writer to do so—and he was also responsible for popularizing stereotypical generalizations about Mexicans. First published in 1834, Pike's short tales depict Mexicans as an ignorant, mendacious, lazy, and dirty people who waste their lives at fandangos. Like Flint, he positioned his Mexican characters to declare their admiration for Americans. He described women as immodestly dressed and lacking in virtue, qualifying most of them as ugly.[9] Portrayals became more derogatory during the four years surrounding the annexation of Texas and the end of the war with Mexico (1845–1848), a period that witnessed the proliferation of fictional narratives, mostly dime novels, that depicted Mexicans in primarily pejorative terms, as members of a degraded society.[10] These novels presented five recurring characters who seemed to be merely awaiting displacement or redemption at the hands of capable Americans: the decadent hidalgo, the corrupted Catholic priest, the bandit, and the lazy peon. The fifth character, the daughter of the elite hidalgo, was the lone female figure of importance and the only one who might, under the right circumstances, enter American society. As a precondition, however, she had to marry an American who could then vouch for her moral rectitude.[11]

The increase in popularity of Mexican themes in American literature and chronicles coincided with the larger discussion of American expansionism in the nineteenth century. American politicians had coveted Mexican territories since early in the century, as the attempts to purchase Mexican land by several administrations demonstrate, but Mexico attracted the public imagination with the independence of Texas in 1836 and more so in the mid-1840s due in part to the rhetoric of John O'Sullivan's *Democratic Review*.[12] O'Sullivan had a talent for answering all sorts of questions he cleverly posed. He frequently wrote editorials with titles like "The Texas Question," "The Indian Question," "The Canada Question," and "The Oregon Question," always promoting the unrelenting territorial advance of the United States. The debates over the annexation of Texas in 1845 prompted him to take a position. He phrased and answered "The Mexican Question" of whether Texas fell under the jurisdiction of Mexico with a resounding refutation. He suggested that Mexico might yet benefit from friendly relations between the two nations if it desisted from acting with ignorant aggression, conceit, and imbecility, but he doubted Mexicans could change their behavior.[13]

Accordingly, the *Democratic Review* maintained that the future of the United States should remain solely an Anglo-Saxon prerogative. O'Sullivan even suggested that because Mexico and the other Latin American nations contained populations of "mixed and confused blood," expansion could actually solve the slavery problem. The United States, he posited, could relocate emancipated blacks because these countries openly embraced amalgamation.[14] The *Review* would never abandon its initial position on the righteousness of American expansion, and its attacks on the character and racial background of Mexicans only increased over the next fifteen years. "Annexation," the editorial where O'Sullivan coined his most famous phrase, was simply a follow-up to "The Mexican Question," but it articulated the fundamental component of the expansionist bombast of the period: Anglo-Saxons, the editor proclaimed, were fulfilling their "manifest destiny to overspread the continent allotted by Providence." This tenet remained the foundation of the discourse of manifest destiny. Mexico and Mexicans allegedly did not fit within that divine plan, and admixture was to blame. The editor maintained that the Spanish conquistadores had degenerated after three centuries of intermixing with indolent Indians, reproducing only the vices of both races, and that Mexicans now needed a master to govern them. The small white population in Mexico, he argued, could not sustain self-government with such large numbers of nonwhites, and they desperately needed American intervention.[15]

The increasing interest in the racial background and attitudes of Mexicans soon led to theoretical treatises, and the rising wave of quasi-ethnological reports were primarily negative. These hypotheses frequently pointed out that the mixed composition of the population had initiated an imminent decay. The authors highlighted the variations and classifications of the multiracial population of Mexico, typically focusing only on whites, Indians, mestizos, and mulattoes, but at times creating lists with more than twenty other mixed categories. These publications claimed that the degraded condition of Mexicans resulted from their mixed racial background, allegedly demonstrated by their penchant for aggression and their inferiority on the battlefield. Their mongrel population, periodicals repeatedly maintained, possessed the ignorance of slaves and the misguided passion of savages, and even the white population proved inferior to its American counterpart not only because it failed to exploit the land, but also because it intermixed with nonwhites. In their opinion, a willingness to view Indians as equals signified that Spaniards were themselves inferior.[16]

The racial denigration of Mexicans eventually acquired a semblance of empiricism. Pseudoscientists first approached the Mexican Question by asserting that an analysis of Mexican skulls revealed high levels of combativeness, destructiveness, and secretiveness. The organization of their brains, a phrenology pundit concluded, appeared "rather animal than intellectual."[17] Similarly, a doctor asserted that the small statures of Mexicans—and Mexican animals, for that matter—evinced a continuous degeneration.[18] Others cited the theory of the Swiss naturalist J. J. von Tschudi, whose widely circulated book *Travels in Peru* (1847)—which attributed purported deficiencies to the descendants of interracial parents—influenced much of the thought on the inferiority of non-whites. American periodicals promptly applied Tschudi's ideas to Mexicans, claiming, for instance, that the inconsistent and deficient behavior of Mexican soldiers derived from their mixed ancestry.[19] The hypothesis combined premises from theories on polygenesis and zoology. Proponents argued that animals from different species could not produce healthy and fertile offspring, and since humans descended from many different and incompatible origins, mixed children inherited feebleness and infertility. Not surprisingly, pseudoscientists inserted Mexicans within their theories on blacks. They concluded that Mexican mestizos—and their mulatto counterparts in the United States—would fade into extinction, even incorrectly stating that Spain had therefore banned white-Indian marriage.[20]

Racial difference and admixture attracted much attention, and Americans found the mixed ancestry of Mexicans to be the most salient and difficult trait to conceptualize. Their descriptions of the complexions of Mexicans revealed as much racism as sheer perplexity. They used terms such as yellow, Indian, black, slightly white, brown, swarthy, olive, and combinations and variations of these and other labels, like "yaller-nigger."[21] Some surmised that Mexicans embodied the incompatibility of Spanish and Indian bloods, and the resulting ugliness stemmed from their mixed heritage.[22] Before the end of the decades-long scientific debate (1840s–1870s) between monogenists and polygenists, the latter affirmed that Mexicans belonged to a different species altogether, descending from Spaniards (inferior Europeans) and Toltecs (inferior among nonwhites), a combination that automatically produced retrograde descendants.[23] As Americans realized that Mexicans would indeed live among them, some questioned the government's decision to grant them citizenship. They could not fathom that multiracial voters could decide political outcomes or that a person of Mexican ancestry could, in theory, become president of the United States.[24] Their backwardness, a veteran of the U.S.-Mexico War declared, stemmed from "the physical and moral differences between the Anglo Saxon and the mongrel races known as Mexicans."[25]

The potential integration of Mexicans into the country formed part of the larger debate over what portion of territory the United States would acquire after the war. Typically, both supporters and opponents of expansionism coincided in their opposition to the incorporation of too many Mexicans and expressed abhorrence at the prospect of absorbing mixed races and facilitating interracial relationships.[26] The difference in opinion lay in the fact that opponents of annexation viewed Mexicans as irredeemable, while supporters often argued that the United States could uplift or displace them.[27] For some, the prospect of relationships with Mexican women still produced concerns over racial admixture. Others partially acquiesced but affirmed that Mexicans were currently unprepared for American citizenship until American men should venture into the area and "attracted by the black eyes of Mexican beauty shall have found homes and wives."[28] Mexican women did not always represent a threat.

"GO TO WORK AND ANNEX HER DAUGHTERS": MEXICAN WOMEN IN THE DISCOURSE OF MANIFEST DESTINY

The racialist exclusionism of the discourse of manifest destiny was therefore somewhat porous. It sometimes allowed for a more accommodating perspective when it came to Mexican women by proclaiming both the superiority of whites and the possibility of interracial relations. From the beginning, anti-Mexican accounts had frequently delineated a clear distinction between men and women. Mid-nineteenth-century narratives often followed that pattern. They vilified Mexican men as ignorant, indolent, treacherous, cowardly, and mendacious but consistently included positive descriptions of women, typically by underscoring that the women were superior to the men.[29] For example, a self-proclaimed expert on Mexico stated that he had observed no redeeming quality in Mexicans, "excepting from this sweeping clause the women of the country, who, for kindness of heart and many sterling qualities, are an ornament to their sex, and to any nation."[30] On one occasion, a colonel wrote that Americans already knew of the character flaws of Mexican men, but that women were "a higher order of beings" who possessed "all the good qualities so wanting in the opposite sex."[31]

Negative depictions of Mexican women did exist, and they typically involved an infusion of racism. When depicting women unfavorably, chroniclers frequently attributed their purported deficiencies—such as immorality—primarily to racial traits. At times the writers injected references to the mongrel and mixed ancestries of Mexican women alongside accolades, not only to their superior morality, but also to their lovely feet and hair, beautiful dark eyes, and symmetrical shapely bodies.[32] In some cases, however, travelers might repeatedly pay Mexican women compliments for their beauty and manners—citing, for example, their "finely turned ankles, well developed busts . . . , dark and lustrous eyes"—yet generalize that they had "a sallow clayish hue to their skin" or "ugly dark countenances," or that they belonged to "a swarthy, copper-colored, half-Indian race."[33] Similarly, other visitors to Mexican territory lamented that Mexican women inherited the resemblance of their Indian ancestors or Cherokee Indians, with skin that looked "muslim [*sic*] having *once* been white, with such decay" that even the infusion of American blood might fail to improve it. In all cases, Americans associated Indian features with ugliness and admixture with regression.[34]

Race mattered, but so did class, and chroniclers who warned against interracial relationships with Mexican women frequently combined both in their descriptions. For example, a visitor to Santa Fe stated that some Mexican women were indeed beautiful but lamented that they married young and would "fade and become old & haggard in proportion. Indian blood is almost universally mixed througout [*sic*] the population."[35] Similarly, Lewis H. Garrard, who visited New Mexico in the mid-1840s, warned Americans of the consequences of having relationships with Mexicans. The author found a certain charm in the penchant for smoking of Mexican women, who "with neatly rolled-up shucks between coral lips, perpetrate winning smiles." Such practices and signals, however, seemed appealing only in the proper context: these women, he warned, were vixens trying to lure unsuspecting victims. The idea of marrying a Mexican woman, he added, might initially seem romantic to naive Americans, but one might eventually become aware of the lack of morals, intellect, modesty, virtue, and other traits that American women possessed.[36] The conflation of race with immorality and ugliness certainly explains why these men felt such contempt toward Mexican women. Perhaps they were predisposed to finding beauty only in white women, or perhaps their xenophobic bellicose attitudes shaped how they perceived all Mexicans. More important, however, is that these men based their descriptions solely on the type of women they met. They focused much of their scorn on the publicly visible menial workers, prostitutes, and saloon maids, who were probably older, wore more revealing clothing, and led strenuous lives. Few Americans described elite Mexican women in such a way.

At times, however, a combination of bombastic enthusiasm and male chauvinism seemed to help Americans overcome their racial apprehensions. Some of them reveled in claiming that Mexican women preferred American men and viewed them as redeemers. They boasted that the war had begun in part because of the jealousy of Mexican men over the admiration Mexican women expressed toward the superior American men.[37] War correspondents commented that Mexican girls loved Americans "wildly and madly, as none but Spanish girls" and that they "yield[ed] to courting easily," and a soldier said that Mexican women loved them even if their brothers and husbands hated Americans.[38] The discourse of manifest destiny appears even in the descriptions of men who indicated an interest in formal romantic relationships. Some soldiers claimed that Mexican women spied for American soldiers because they believed Americans would deliver them from oppression.[39] Mexican women of all classes, a soldier explained, were fully aware of the superiority of American men and thus preferred them.[40] In some cases, narrators related how Mexican women openly expressed their preference for American men, especially if the men had demonstrated their valor, since, allegedly, Mexican women lamented that Mexican men acted cowardly.[41] Clearly, men who made these claims, arrogant as they were, exhibited more openness to entering into interethnic relationships.

The purported fascination of Mexican women for American men fit well within the theme of women as the spoils of victory expressed by Sam Houston. For example, an American soldier described his participation in the occupation of Mexico as a conqueror-conquered situation and averred that it must be "in order of Providence, that these women, so justly to be admired, are to become wives and mothers of a better race."[42] Triumph in the war, others declared, earned them women as the prize of conquest.[43] No one, however, expressed the sense of entitlement better than the editor of the Mexico City volunteer newspaper, the *American Star*. He gleefully captured the attitude of some soldiers toward their relationships with Mexican women when he described a recent interethnic wedding: "Hurrah for annexation! No more arguments on the policy of annexing Mexico, but go to work and annex her daughters."[44] One may disagree on territorial annexation but not on romantic conquests, these statements made clear. The *Atlas* of Cincinnati likewise suggested that if the nation believed in its "manifest and inevitable destiny to infuse Anglo-Saxon notions, liberty, and blood into the Mexicans," then marriages offered the best path to reaching that objective.[45] Echoing the latter position, a volunteer advised "all timid bachelors to go to Mexico at once."[46] Notably, these conceited proclamations praised formal marriages, not mere sexual encounters. The practice of intermarriage became visible during and after the Mexican war. Some Americans probably welcomed newspaper accounts that more than a dozen volunteers from a Pennsylvania unit had returned with Mexican wives, one of whom was described as "a beautiful girl, with long flowing black hair, [and] lustrous black eyes."[47] Others, however, might have reacted with alarm and disdain at the reality of interethnic relationships. But cordial friendships and long-term relationships did in fact take place during the war period.

An examination of the social mores that permeated American life in the nineteenth century sheds light on why some white men felt a physical attraction toward Mexican women. Victorian America understood the centrality of sex and thus tried to transform and redirect its eroticism toward a spiritual role within marital life. Public expressions of sexuality therefore represented a menace, particularly if they involved people who were already married. Cultural norms accordingly sought to prevent a series of events that could start with a leer and lead to immoral sexual activity (i.e., premarital, extramarital, or too much marital sex).[48] Women's clothes aimed to repress men's desire by effectively limiting what they could see, especially in public. Ironically, the clothing of Victorian women created greater curiosity precisely because it concealed and eroticized what men wanted to but could not easily see. The length and width of women's dresses and skirts continued to increase and, coincidentally, reached their peak during the period (1840s–1860s) when Americans first encountered the relatively lightly clad Mexican women.[49] Predictably, white men felt a particular attraction to the exposed body parts of the Mexican women they met—although, of course, most of these men never met the middle- and upper-class Mexican women who were more likely to conform to American and European mores and fashion standards. For various reasons—such as cultural practices and warmer climates—some of these women offered glimpses at body parts that American women would typically not display in public.

Not surprisingly, the feet of Mexican women became a leitmotif in the narratives of soldiers and travelers. No other physical feature received as much attention. Victorian dresses and skirts made the feet of American women virtually invisible, and when exposed, shoes and stockings still offered a level of protection. Predictably, the relative candidness of Mexican women promptly garnered attention. Some visitors commented that the beauty and manner of dress of Mexican women exceeded those of their American counterparts, who tended to disfigure their natural grace with rigid clothing.[50] In contrast, according to the elated descriptions of American travelers, women in Mexico exposed their feet openly. The custom of not wearing stockings or elaborate footwear—of even walking barefooted—drew the gazing eyes of men who rarely, if ever, saw women's feet in public in the United States.[51] Clearly, American men wrote primarily about the poor, but the feet of Mexican women elicited fervent comments also because they suited the Victorian ideal of femininity. According to numerous descriptions, they were narrow and small, characteristics considered refined, youthful, and erotic in the United States. These qualities must have appeared even more prominent because the accounts of white men evince that they held a predilection for young Mexican girls, a fondness that bordered on pedophilia.[52]

"CLEAR WHITE SKIN IS PREFERABLE": UNDERMINING MANIFEST DESTINY

During the middle stages of the Mexican war, as newspapers across the United States sought to satisfy the public demand for reports on battles and on the people of Mexico, a traveler from Illinois recounted his visit to New Mexico. He started by denigrating Mexicans but described women kindly: upper-class señoritas wore fine dresses, and "slippers and silk stockings adorn their small feet and ankles"; they are more intelligent than the men, he explained, and added that their complexions ranged "from snowy white to copper yellow." At that point, he began correcting himself and stated that brunette, not snowy white, better described the lighter extreme and added that they were "most awfully ugly." They do have *one* good quality, he wrote—their kindness—and he noted that many of them had beautiful dark eyes, glossy black hair, and fine voices that "flow on in liquid sweetness." His uneven account certainly lacks the quality that a professional reporter could have provided, but therein lies its historical value. The writer inadvertently communicates the inner struggles he experienced while describing—and likely while meeting—Mexican women. His obvious attraction to their physical features, character traits, and voices seems to outweigh his single sweeping remark regarding their purported ugliness.[53]

His narrative offers possible explanations for these contradictions. His comment on their looks came after his hesitation in describing their complexion and before he added that his *fair* American countrywomen were more beautiful—paralleling a race-beauty conflation many travelers made. The comment also came after he noted the dictates of fashion that he describe Mexican women as beauties, a likely indication that he had read favorable descriptions and was in fact trying to write a counternarrative. Finally, his last paragraph reveals a probable reason for his negative portrayal: he admits that a young and single man—and he was neither—might fall in love with a woman who possessed the qualities he had just described.[54] He, in other words, sought to observe the responsibilities of a married man who had a wife as potential reader. This account, precisely because of its vacillation, simultaneously promotes and undermines the discourse of manifest destiny. First, the chronicler adheres to its tenets by establishing a hierarchy where white women are superior to Mexican women, who, in turn, are superior to Mexican men. Second, although American expansion depended on the advancement of westering white families, his ambivalent depiction underscores that Mexican women might indeed appeal to incoming white men, thus sabotaging the idealized Anglo-Saxon domesticity.

Such ambivalence was not uncommon. American travelers often undermined the credence of negative depictions by contradicting themselves or the opinions of others. An early traveler to Mexican territory, for example, described Indians as "dull, stupid people, and far from comely," in spite of the assurances from local priests, who informed him that their native lore included knowledge of astronomy and that they demarcated the seasons by the movement of the stars.[55] Similarly, an army doctor, who ascribed physical and behavioral deficiencies to intermixture, retorted that mestizos certainly could not have the resistance to pain American soldiers had frequently described. He resolved this episode of cognitive dissonance by allowing his theoretical treatises to override the empirical observations of the soldiers. Furthermore, he also expressed ambivalence when he admitted that Mexicans repeatedly treated him with kindness, even though his scientific theories maintained that the mixed races possessed a ruthless nature. He expressed regret for stating a scientific fact, but he did not let his personal experiences alter his racialist views.[56]

The most revealing contradictions involved intratextual incongruities, especially when an observer qualified a predominantly favorable depiction with a negative—typically racial—statement. This form of inconsistency frequently affected the descriptions of Mexican women. For example, a lieutenant elaborated at length on the beauty of local women, particularly of young girls, but remarked that American women were better because "clear white skin is preferable."[57] Another officer asserted that he had confirmed the reputed beauty of the women of Veracruz, adding that they were graceful and "well developed," but he commented that they could not compare to American women, for they lacked their "fairness and freshness." He later recounted that his fellow soldiers engaged in friendly and romantic relationships with lower-class women, underscoring that they perhaps did not ascribe as much value to light complexions.[58] Others, he might have surmised, did not conflate race and beauty.

Some of these illuminating contradictions at once promote and undermine the discourse of manifest destiny. The descriptions of Rufus B. Sage, a trapper who passed through northern Mexico in the early 1840s, illustrate this inconsistency well. Sage employed almost every available stereotype to describe what he labeled as the mongrel race of New Mexico. His six-page diatribe depicted the local population as ugly, filthy, lice ridden, half naked, primitive, indolent, superstitious, treacherous, and profane—epithets frequently used against Mexicans at the time. The women, he explained, possessed an affectionate and caring personality, but they lacked virtue and chastity, while suffering from ignorance and superstition. His contemporary readers might have wondered why anyone would want to coexist, let alone cohabitate, with such a degraded people. Yet, Sage undermined his own scathing narrative by indicating that interethnic relationships predominated in the area. He proved, in other words, that some Americans were sabotaging the dominant racialist discourse and contradicting his narrative and those of other itinerant chroniclers. Sage first encountered intermarried families on the American side of the Arkansas River, where he observed that most of the dozen or so local Americans were married to Mexican women. Evidently, other Americans, if not the more discriminating Sage, viewed life among Mexicans as more than adequate.[59] Yet, Sage's chronicle, by virtue of its publication, unfairly overshadowed the actions and preferences of his voiceless intermarrying countrymen.

Some soldiers had an additional reason to express scorn toward Mexican women: they professed that they had no interest in pursuing a romantic relationship with anyone. Some of them were writing to wives and family, and consequently, they spoke negatively of the women they met. For example, after seeing a Mexican woman, a war volunteer wrote that he had "never seen any old Negro half so hideous and disgusting." One soldier described Mexican women as the "most revolting, forbidding, disgusting creatures in the world." Yet, both men were writing to their American wives and probably wanted to alleviate any distrust their spouses might develop. Another American explained to his wife that *other* soldiers engaged in love relationships with local women, but that he did not.[60] One volunteer went so far as to write to his wife that he had only seen one pretty girl during his time in Mexico. His efforts to ease his wife's mind, however, clearly failed when he proceeded to tell her that the girl had "beautiful large, dark eyes and such a graceful figure" and that he would have certainly pursued her had it not been for the accompanying chaperone. His playful overtones notwithstanding, his wife must have certainly wondered how much she could truly trust him.[61]

In general, although some Americans produced contradictory accounts and others wrote solely in negative terms, examples of more considerate descriptions often counterbalanced negative portrayals. These nuanced accounts typically originated from Americans who spent more time among Mexicans. For instance, certain kinds of behavior often elicited accusations of immorality by Americans, but occasionally, more understanding observers offered a different perspective. They, for instance, deduced that wearing lightweight clothing had to do with customs, and not with indecency, or that the practice of public bathing signified not that Mexican women were exhibitionists, but that they espoused a concern for cleanliness and health. Bathing was a passion for them, a soldier explained. A volunteer similarly noted that Veracruz women never left the house unaccompanied by a trusted chaperone, and a soldier in New Mexico warned that people should not assume that women at fandangos were representative of the entire population. He also attributed the affectionate farewell embrace of a Mexican woman to the friendly customs of the place, not to lasciviousness.[62]

Similarly, American women expressed some racism and cultural insensitivity, but when they interacted with Mexicans, they tended to develop an admiration for the new culture.[63] They noticed aspects of cultural practices that men usually overlooked, and they generally offset and sometimes explicitly criticized the negative depictions of less understanding chroniclers.[64] For example, unlike the men, who delightedly spoke of the loose, revealing clothing Mexican women wore, some female observers distinguished, for one thing, between the clothing for private and public occasions, for warm and cold weather, of lower- and upper-class women, and of younger and older women. Whatever the situation, an observer explained, their attire always exhibited scrupulous hygiene and modesty. That is, women understood that clothing choices depended on specific situations. Martha Summerhayes, who lived in Arizona as a military wife, acquired such a level of acculturation that when she visited San Francisco, her aunt admonished her regarding the dress styles she wore. It might prompt people to think she was Mexican, the aunt reasoned. Summerhayes expressed indifference toward the opinions of others and added that Mexicans were "the only people who understand the philosophy of living. Look at the faces of the women in your streets."[65]

Class frequently also helps one to discern the more favorable subtexts. The discourse of periodical editors and politicians promoted arguments that consistently advanced American expansionism. They made sweeping remarks about Mexicans, while the chronicles of travelers—at times even those of assigned correspondents—contained internal contradictions. This dissonance reveals that some Americans who came into contact with Mexicans did not adhere to racialist rhetoric. Thus, distinguishing among the various types of travelers illuminates why some embraced and propagated the discourse of manifest destiny, while others tended to undermine it. More important, there are fundamental differences between (1) the texts of leisured travelers and amateur ethnologists—broadly defined as those who planned their trips and recorded their observations, usually with the intent of publishing a narrative—and (2) the journals and accounts of situational travelers, like soldiers, the first wave of Americans to record a touristic gaze of Mexico and whose texts were originally not meant for publication.[66] The latter accounts, in other words, originated as reactions to a new environment and did not incorporate or justify a political agenda. Accordingly, although the dominant expansionist narrative of Anglo-Saxonism depicted Mexicans as an undesirable population, chroniclers from the latter group destabilized this vision when they described their experiences among Mexicans. Their more accommodating accounts were not as renowned as those of politicians and major publications, but they do help explain why white men so openly and frequently entered into relationships with Mexican women when massive western migration began after the Mexican war. Many of those western settlers, moreover, left no further record of their views on Mexicans than a marriage license or a census entry.

The number of sources that describe how Mexicans perceived Americans pales in comparison to the plethora of information Americans recorded, but there are indications that both interest and apprehension were reciprocal. Americans frequently became the focus of the gazing eyes of men, women, and children, and the differences Mexican women saw in Americans produced curiosity and astonishment.[67] Before the U.S.-Mexico War, local Mexicans in Texas and New Mexico had reason to dislike and distrust American visitors. For instance, they pointed out that Americans displayed great arrogance and disrespect toward men and women. Mexican officials complained that American immigrants, whom they described as lazy, acted with disregard for Mexican laws and disrespect toward magistrates.[68] Women, furthermore, certainly noticed the gazing eyes of American men. Traditionally, public bathing depended on the separation of the sexes, and the presence of men in the vicinity undoubtedly raised suspicion and alarm among local women. Similarly, although white men described the seemingly flimsy clothing of Mexican women as immoral, the latter clearly noticed and resented their voyeuristic looks. A woman in Santa Fe, for one, began to consider wearing American-style capes because she had qualms about going to the plaza with her neck exposed, since many American men frequented the area. Those practices and other cultural differences occasionally caused misunderstanding and conflict.[69]

The accounts of the daughters of the old landed elites, although often plagued by misplaced nostalgia for a purportedly idyllic past, also convey resentment and fear toward Americans. Life was perfect during the pastoral age before the American conquest, Guadalupe Vallejo of California wrote in 1890. Many Americans arrived and married well among the better families, but some of them deceived, stole, and took advantage of the trust these families placed in them, particularly by using the new and confusing American legal and economic systems or by outright dispossessing them without providing explanations.[70] The Mexican war and the concomitant territorial cession caused anxiety among some of the Mexicans who held Americans in contempt for actual and rumored atrocities.[71] A daughter of the Vallejo family in California, for example, maintained such disdain that three decades after the war, she still refused to learn what she called "the language of the invaders" or to allow her children to speak it in front of her.[72] Similarly, María de la Guerra recalled that she and other women warned Mexican men that they should not trust Americans.[73] She remembered witnessing numerous abuses, and decades later she still held contempt for the American invading forces—as opposed to she and other Californios not being bothered by the occupation, as a mistranslated and highly disseminated version asserts.[74]

Equivocality also complicates our understanding of the predominance of the discourse of manifest destiny. Depictions from politicians, boosters, and men of the nascent sciences seemed—and claimed to be—reliable but in reality lacked the acumen that direct contact could better provide. Speeches, essays, and treatises originated from politicians and specialized writers—most of them from the Northeast—who never visited the people and places they so confidently described. When they discussed the supposed degradation of the Mexican race and expressed their scorn toward the amalgamation of the races, they in fact spoke of a national abstract project in which Mexicans and intermarriage represented obstacles or nuisances. But visiting Mexican areas did not automatically eliminate biases. Indeed, the leisured traveler of the nineteenth century often developed an ethnologist persona and embedded a sense of superiority in his narrative, inscribing his subjects within his own worldview. He also professed expertise about the people he studied or observed.[75] Furthermore, visitors from the middle and upper classes generally ascribed to strict Victorian values regarding morality, propriety, and standards of personal hygiene.[76] The likely familiarity that affluent travelers acquired from periodicals and books on germane subjects—like economic growth, the Mexican war, and racial theories—also might have created presumptions they held before they even encountered Mexican inhabitants. Not surprisingly, many of their texts paralleled each other and reinforced the rhetorical vocabulary some travelers learned before heading west. These learned men, in other words, spoke the same language of derision. The repetition of common themes even led to accusations of plagiarism.[77]

Those narratives differed from the accounts, diaries, and letters of soldiers and poor migrants in important ways. Ordinary whites did not refer to national projects or employ scientific language. The fact that travelers from the lower social strata never made any references to the allegedly imminent extinction of the mixed races indicates their lack of familiarity with such theories. The voices of common visitors—not the rhetoric of expansionists—thus come closer to informing the reader of the direct impressions of average westering whites. A relatively similar dichotomy developed in Arizona.

THE MEXICAN QUESTION REACHES ARIZONA

In 1873 a reporter from the Prescott-based *Arizona Miner* recounted his journey through the southern part of the territory. His visit to Pima County led him to complain that Tucson's Catholics—i.e., Mexicans—irresponsibly resisted the adoption of public schools, but he made positive remarks about progress in the Americanization of government institutions. He also commented that Mexican women—whom he described as superior to the men—were kind, pretty, and highly pious and added that some of them were educated and thus difficult to fool. He lamented, however, that they tended to marry young, a practice to which he attributed their inaccessibility to his fellow Americans.[78]

Although he misinterpreted the situation—white men in Tucson in fact frequently married young Mexican women—his observations resonate with some of the themes American travelers and soldiers discussed during the

U.S.-Mexico War: the region's need for social improvement, the beauty and kindness of Mexican women, and their superiority over Mexican men. The article also raised two issues that affected white men from both periods: the lack of white women in the area and the value of Mexican women as potential wives for incoming Americans. The author refrained from any reference to racial and cultural differences and from mentions of manifest destiny or entitlement over Mexicans. His depiction thus paralleled the simple personal narratives of ordinary white men, rather than the organized, formal arguments of expansionist boosters and politicians. More important, his comments reflected a pragmatic concern with how to negotiate life on the frontier, not with the supposedly historic mission of Anglo-Saxons. This piece, nonetheless, appeared during a transitional time in Arizona history, when the territory had spent only twenty-five years as an American possession—less than twenty in the case of Tucson. The institutional and societal Americanization of Arizona had begun but would proceed gradually over the rest of the century, especially in the southern areas, where the white population increased more slowly. Tucson, in particular, still retained a primarily Mexican population, and the majority of local white men were married to Mexican women. Those white men undoubtedly shared the favorable sentiments that the reporter from the *Arizona Miner* expressed toward Mexican women.

The transitional period also produced a series of attacks against nonwhites, as some newspapers and politicians adhered to the discourse of manifest destiny and advocated for the annexation of Mexico and against miscegenation. Indeed, racial attitudes that targeted Mexicans in Arizona fit within the national discussion that had existed since the U.S.-Mexico War. Arizona followed the larger discourse but only to a certain extent. Mexicans in Arizona—like in every other state and territory—never became targets of miscegenation statutes, but their social whiteness was ambiguous at best. The territory witnessed several waves of hostility toward various groups, including Mexicans, but such intolerance did not target all groups uniformly and did not plague the entire area. Newspapers and politicians generally maintained highly antagonistic views toward the Chinese and Indian populations—and Mexicans often joined whites in those attacks. Yet, the voices that beleaguered Mexicans came primarily from the northern and central parts of the territory and from mining towns, especially from Phoenix and Prescott. Whites predominated in those areas, and their pursuit of economic and political power frequently involved denigration of nonwhites. Not surprisingly, they at times chastised Mexicans and opposed interracial relationships. Yet, whites in southern Arizona, especially in Tucson, often counterbalanced those aggressive positions. To some extent, their actions resembled the subtexts that undermined the discourse of manifest destiny of expansionists at the national level.

As occurred with the dominant narratives of the U.S.-Mexico War, racial attitudes also shaped some of the early descriptions of Tucson. Samuel E. Chamberlain, a war veteran whose vainglorious narrative paints a characteristically stereotypical portrait of populations throughout Mexico, found his way to Tucson in 1848. As one might expect from a man who held Mexico in great contempt, he wrote negatively about the town, which, after all, remained Mexican territory until 1854. Tucson, he averred, must border the headquarters of Satan, and he explicitly referred both to the high temperatures and to the purportedly questionable character of its people. He maintained that the two hours he spent in the sun as punishment from his superior officer practically turned him into beef jerky, and such a condition made him feel even worse when he saw "several dilapidated looking greasers" salivating. Tucson seemed even more dangerous, he explained, because it had the power to corrupt venturing whites. According to Chamberlain, the Texan Tom Hitchcock had lived in the area for so long that he had become a beastly figure: he wore Indian and Mexican clothing and spoke indistinct utterances that combined English, Spanish, and Chinook, along with animal sounds (crows, bellows, and howls). He had accumulated several layers of acculturation and no longer fit American society, as his inability to give directions to the American troops allegedly demonstrated.[79] Such was the fate that awaited Americans, Chamberlain seemed to warn.

Other American men who visited the Arizona-Mexico border region during the 1850s and 1860s also conveyed their racial attitudes in their depictions of Mexicans. They often cast Tucson's Mexican population as inferior and devious. For example, a writer from a San Francisco magazine described Mexican men as swarthy, indolent, and addicted to a life of dances, saloons, and bullfights. Mexican women also received the correspondent's scorn when he suggested that their vanity led their brothers and love interests to waste money on their whims.[80] Others referred to the area as "the land of tawny assassins and mongrel horse-thieves" and described Mexicans as members of a "very low class."[81] Arizona newspapers made references to purported Mexican bandits as mongrels and even applied pejorative epithets to children. When criticizing the largely Mexican population of Yuma for not having a public school, the *Arizona Miner* concluded that "Catholic greaser children" did not need schooling after all.[82] J. Ross Browne's visit to the Sonora-Arizona region—he did not distinguish between residents on either side of the border—produced a depiction in which Indians and poor Mexicans primarily formed part of the landscape, along with plants and desert animals. Browne held an acute contempt for Tucson. He compared it to Sodom and Gomorrah, as it offered refuge to fleeing gamblers, thieves, and murderers who lived "very much in the Greaser style."[83] He, as it turned out, thus described some of the white men who eventually cemented their local prominence when they founded the Society of Arizona Pioneers.[84]

Racial admixture attracted special attention. Phocion R. Way, who spent two years in Arizona in the late 1850s, described Tucson as a chaotic and deplorable place, full of Indians, filthy Mexicans, and half-breeds. Similarly, the *Arizona Miner* repeatedly referred to Mexicans as greasers and half-breeds.[85] Mexicans, the editor later asserted, possessed "the lying, snake-like character of mongrels," and—perhaps revealing the origin of his racial anxieties—he suggested that the only viable solution might involve bringing them under the supervision of the Ku Klux Klan.[86] Participating in racial mixing seemed unappealing to these men. Browne, for instance, disdained the abundance of children with interracial traits, which he attributed to the mongrelization that derives from mere idleness. He described the children as "an abominable admixture" prone to crime and immorality. He concluded that the descendants of these miscegenous couples "may now be ranked with their natural compadres— Indians, burros, and coyotes." He made further references to the purported racial deficiency of Mexicans and specifically warned against intermarriage, opinions the *Miner* frequently echoed.[87]

Arizona's version of the Mexican Question, the oft-explored topic of John O'Sullivan and his *Democratic Review*, received ample attention in the nascent newspapers. The *Arizona Miner* had established its scorn toward Mexicans almost immediately. Unlike the virulent editorial attacks on Chinese residents, which typically focused only on local residents, Mexican residents on both sides of the U.S.-Mexico border became targets, and newspapers rarely clarified where the people in question resided.[88] They were equally Mexican in the view of the editors. The *Miner* began its litany of articles on the Mexican Question rather benignly in 1866, with a call for solidarity with the "sister republic" and a warning to France to abandon its colonial ambitions in Mexico.[89] Its tone soon changed, however, when its writers reacted with elation to a rumor that predicted the annexation of northern Mexico. They qualified their enthusiasm by stating that it might be impossible to get along with "the mongrel revolutionary people" who lived there.[90] The Mexican Question soon became a primarily negative editorial feature in the *Miner*, as the paper frequently accused Mexicans of committing crimes against whites and called for punitive action. The paper even insinuated that white Arizonans might have to retaliate against prominent Mexican Americans for failing to control their countrymen—although it did not specify how nor whether the criminals were Mexican nationals or Americans of Mexican descent. The *Miner*'s most vitriolic language appeared in its editorials on the purported Mexican crime raids and in calls for American intervention and annexation. It eventually adopted the discourse of manifest destiny, with the editor claiming that God and nature had made Mexico for Americans. This antagonistic view of Mexicans blatantly accentuated the editor's racial concerns. He posited that annexation threatened American democracy because it would allow corrupt American politicians—who supposedly bought the votes of malleable and ignorant Mexican Americans—to acquire an even larger base in the "mixed populations of Sonora."[91]

But the reward apparently merited the risk. In 1871 the paper fully endorsed the acquisition of territory and asserted—replicating the expansionist rhetoric of the 1840s—that the better classes of Mexico actually clamored to join the union and eagerly awaited "the day when 'manifest destiny' will place them under the government of the United States."[92] Over the next three years, the *Miner* repeatedly called for annexation, largely on the premise that Mexicans were committing crimes against Americans north and south of the border—since the writers viewed all people of Mexican descent as foreigners and thus held Mexico accountable for their actions in either country. The paper accused Mexico of being incapable of controlling its quarrelsome population of "half-breed-Indian dogs," a people unfit for self-government. The *Miner* also echoed the arguments of John O'Sullivan when its writers claimed that annexation would in fact redeem Mexico, and when they alleged that the current wave of crimes simply augmented the long list of vicious actions by Mexicans that dated back to the independence of Texas and the U.S.-Mexico War. Like the *Democratic Review* in the 1840s and 1850s, the *Miner* concluded that the mixed heritage of Mexicans had led them to their current state of ruin. The paper again revealed its southern racial attitudes when it compared Mexicans to the recently emancipated black population. As one writer posited, annexation would soon occur, and Mexican criminals would thus yield to "the 'tender' mercies of ex officers of the Freedmen's Bureau."[93] Although these enunciations coexisted with anxiety about the ability of Americans to avoid the Mexicanization of their institutions, they also exhibited an unabated aggressiveness that focused on race.[94]

Yet, these attacks belonged to a larger, pragmatic agenda, because the treatment of Mexicans often paralleled their role in political and economic debates. Central and northern interests resented the presence of Mexicans in southern Arizona because, as eligible voters, they tended to support local candidates—Mexicans for local elections and whites for state and federal offices. Thus, editorials from the *Arizona Miner* and from other areas where Mexicans accounted for small percentages of the population frequently questioned Mexicans' republican virtue and accused political rivals of manipulating or outright buying their votes. In a ridiculous hyperbole, the *Tombstone Prospector* reported that a Mexican man had trained his dogs so well that they capably herded his goats without any assistance and even hunted their own lunch. The piece focused on the purportedly questionable character of the owner and stated that he was as lazy as other Mexicans and alleged that the dogs even cast ballots, for "certainly they have as much if not more intelligence than many Mexicans."[95] Such scathing comments about the lack of intellect and democratic values of Mexicans also appeared in the editorials of the *Arizona Miner*. The paper accused Governor Richard C. McCormick of stealing a congressional election by relying on the votes of ignorant mongrels from Pima County and the Mexican state of Sonora. Demagogues, the paper contended, deceived men, women, and children about the honest white men of the north, turning the democratic process into a fraud that could result in the peonization of white Arizonans.[96] Not voting for northern candidates, these men suggested, demonstrated the political incompetence of Mexicans and thus their unworthiness and danger.

Prescott politicians would express similar sentiments years later, but they would further demonstrate their duplicity by accusing the population of New Mexico of being too Mexican, while praising Mexicans in Arizona. In the 1850s, they had feared that Mexicans would counterbalance the incoming migration of whites in the northern part of the state and dreaded the possibility that joint statehood would bring white Arizonans—who, according to a misinformed representative to congressional hearings, accounted for 95 percent of the population—under the control of Spanish-speaking New Mexicans. They contended that such an arrangement would force whites to use Spanish in schools and courts.[97] After New Mexico and Arizona became separate territories in 1863, their concerns dissipated, and they depicted Mexicans in Arizona as Americanized people of good character, far superior to their New Mexican counterparts. Northern Arizona whites did not have much to fear by the turn of the century. The territorial capital moved from Tucson to Prescott in 1877 and then to Phoenix in 1889, and Mexicans rarely won statewide elections.

These attacks coincided with election seasons or disputed results, but the atmosphere had certainly changed in Tucson since southern sympathizers in the 1860s feebly attempted to draw a constitution that promulgated the expulsion of all Mexicans from Arizona for opposing their plans for slavery.[98] These tirades now emerged to a large extent from political agendas—usually appearing during political campaigns of the first three decades of Arizona under the American flag.[99] The political motivation of these attacks became clear, for instance, during the various failed attempts to achieve statehood. In those campaigns, the same political interests that typically denigrated Mexicans conveniently depicted them as a miniscule, highly Americanized, and productive population.

The candid antagonism of central and northern whites did not, however, pervade the entire territory, particularly not Tucson, where Mexicans remained a majority into the 1890s, a long period when most local white men were married to Mexican women. The local *Arizona Weekly Star* also published stories of banditry along the border, but these reports often derived from reprinted articles from other newspapers. They furthermore recounted that Mexican authorities actively searched for the criminals. The paper even balanced its occasional coverage of Mexican fugitives with reports of *American* criminal incursions into Mexico and admonished that the American government should guard against such activities. Failure to act, the editor warned, might lead Mexican nationals to cross the border to retrieve their property and thus prompt other papers to complain of Mexican lawlessness.[100] The *Weekly Arizonian*, from nearby Tubac, argued what the *Star* would echo years later, that the federal government should secure the border to protect Mexicans, in this case against Indian attacks.[101] Similarly, when the *Star* addressed the prospect of annexation, it simply republished news bits from other states, reporting, for example, of rumors that the United States might acquire parts of Mexico or that New Orleans was promoting the idea of intervention to stimulate its local economy by serving as a base of operations.[102] The most aggressive language the *Star* published during this period of Mexican instability actually came from a letter to the editor and from an editorial that vaguely suggested that the United States should intervene to protect Mexicans from their despotic government.[103] Not surprisingly, political figures from Prescott responded with contempt for those white Tucsonans who opposed an aggressive policy toward Mexico.[104]

The *Star* went even further and refuted the assertion of expansionists that educated Mexicans desired annexation. It printed an excerpt from a Sonora newspaper that warned that international railway connections marked merely the beginning of an encroachment that would end in annexation, because "[r]ich and beautiful Sonora has excited the hungry cupidity of the nasal-voiced Yankee."[105] These sentiments were in fact widespread in northern Mexico.[106] Similarly, a reprinted article from Texas—which the *Star* called a sensible editorial—suggested that annexation might indeed work but only if both nations decided it was in their best interest. The *Tucson Citizen* added that annexation schemes lacked logic and that the country could better fulfill its mission by developing its own resources.[107] Furthermore, the *Star* explicitly called on Americans to stop the rumors of annexation and the conspiracies of reckless adventurers because they only worried patriotic Mexicans and incited feelings of distrust toward Americans.[108] Clearly, Tucson-area newspapers viewed the Mexican Question differently than did newspapers from central and northern Arizona, whether they genuinely empathized with Mexico or only sought to maintain stable relations with the local Mexican population and with trading partners in both nations. The *Weekly Arizonian* frequently encouraged the migration of Mexican families to Arizona so that the men could work in the mines and the women could bring stability to the camps—a sentiment shared by other mining interests.[109]

Mexican women did, in fact, receive more favorable treatment, but racism often permeated some of these comments. Depictions of Mexican women in Arizona largely paralleled the national pattern. Traveler Phocion R. Way opined that women in Tucson lacked virtue, but he noted that young girls were pretty and definitely preferred Americans to "greasers." The only white woman in town elicited great relief, he maintained, after seeing "so many swarthy faces."[110] But another visitor to Tucson noted that Mexican women were far superior to the men and that they naturally refined life in the frontier due to their Catholic upbringing and their great ability to run households.[111] Arizona newspapers occasionally employed the discourse of manifest destiny to describe the purported appeal of white men, but there was no explicit reference to the U.S.-Mexico War or to the role of women as spoils of victory. For example, in 1874 the *Arizona Weekly Miner*, which often depicted Mexicans as foreigners, maliciously implied that a religious celebration in Yuma primarily involved "senoritas, whisky and gambling," and later posited that the increasing crime in California was partly due to the jealousy of Mexican men over the preference Mexican women exhibited toward white men.[112] The *Tucson Citizen* even made a general invitation for whites to enjoy their time in town, although it clearly expressed partiality toward white women: "[L]et the eyes of

FIGURE 3. Alexander Levin, a Jewish immigrant from Prussia, and Zenona Molina, from Sonora, Mexico, c. 1870. The Levins operated a brewery in Tucson. Arizona Historical Society/Tucson, AHS Photo Number 69497.

the enamored youth explore the fathomless depths of dark Spanish or sweeter Saxon maidens."[113] These comments—their sexism notwithstanding—lacked the vitriolic disdain of the discourse of manifest destiny that had permeated American scientific and political narratives of the 1840s and 1850s.

CONCLUSION

Admonishments against intermarriages resurfaced repeatedly after the U.S.-Mexico War period, as pseudoscientists, expansionist politicians, and journal editors frequently deprecated Mexicans to suit larger agendas. But these men were discussing women they had yet to or would never meet. They furthermore expected westering men to play their assigned role in spreading the territorial domain and protecting white domesticity. But just like the ever-present examples of more open-minded subtexts, marriage practices after the incorporation of the Tucson area in the mid-1850s would demonstrate that white migrants made their own reflections and decisions regarding interracial relationships. They had their own future and happiness in mind, not the visions of an abstract national project. These men belonged to cohorts that spent enough time among Mexicans to assess their character and customs. Some of them eventually chose to form families with Mexican women. Their actions undermined the discourse of manifest destiny because they expressed the type of openness that facilitated intermarriage. Thus, although the voices of expansionism primarily ostracized Mexicans, the actions of the westering white men who actually carried out the expansion often proved more accommodating. In 1929 a California eugenicist visited southern Arizona and expressed great alarm at what he called the degraded and racially indistinguishable children of white-Mexican couples. He blamed white men for participating in these relationships and warned against a possible danger to white purity.[114] The admonition came more than seven decades too late. Whites had been consistently marrying Mexicans since the 1850s. In a way, as the next chapter explains, the practice had actually increased over that period, occurring primarily among working-class whites and Mexicans.

3

INTERMARRIAGE IN TUCSON, 1860–1930

BY THE EARLY 1890s, Tucson had changed significantly since its annexation to the United States in 1854. The Americanization of the commercial, political, and educational institutions was proceeding steadily, and the city, like the whole territory, had witnessed considerable demographic changes: the completion of the railroad and the pacification of Indians in the 1880s eventually led to increases in the white population of the city. The 1900 census would in fact mark the first time Tucson had more white than Mexican residents.[1] Even more indicative of the new type of migration, nuclear white families now outnumbered their Mexican counterparts.[2] But the ethnic background of the city's population extended beyond a simple binary of white and Mexican residents. The number of black residents had increased from only 9 in 1870 to 99, and the town now had 181 Chinese, whereas none resided there in 1870. The populace had also changed in other, more subtle ways.

For example, on November 26, 1892, William C. Brown married Katie McKenna. The proximity of the wedding to Mexican enclaves in all likelihood would have signified the presence of Mexican guests due to local networks. But in this case, they attended because they shared a familial kinship with the couple. Indeed, Brown's and McKenna's surnames obscured the fact that both had Mexican ancestry: the groom's father came from New York, while the father of the bride was born in Ireland. Both men had migrated to Arizona and married Mexican women more than two decades earlier. Furthermore, baptismal records identify the groom's given name as Guillermo Carlos and the

FIGURE 4. Everyone in this theatrical production at Tucson's Safford School (c. 1895) was directly connected to intermarriage. Top: Sofía Levin and José M. Ronstadt; middle: Guadalupe "Lupe" Dalton, Hortense Dalton, and Luisa Baffert; bottom: Frecia Montoya and Adelina "Lily" Goodwin. Sofía, daughter of Alexander Levin and Zenona Molina, married Juan García in 1905. Luisa, daughter of Frenchman Pierre "Pedro" Baffert and Isabel Torres, married Albert García in 1903. In 1902 Frecia, born in Mexico, married Aubrey Lippincott, a colonel in the U.S. Army from New York. In 1903 Lily, daughter of Charles Goodwin, from Georgia, and Petra Moreno, married Thomas Healy, from Minnesota. Arizona Historical Society/Tucson, AHS Photo Number 40587.

bride's as Catalina, and both had Mexican godparents. One can safely assume, moreover, that because white men of their fathers' generation typically arrived in Tucson as detached bachelors, the couple most likely had only Mexican relatives in Tucson. In other words, the Brown-McKenna wedding was primarily a Mexican affair, with a reception teeming with an ethnic ambience: filled with conversations in Spanish and capped by Mexican food and music.[3] The young spouses were but two of the hundreds of descendants of the white-Mexican couples who had married in the 1860s and 1870s. Marriages among partners of mixed ancestry were becoming increasingly widespread by the end of the nineteenth century.[4]

These relationships help illustrate both a continuation and a transformation of marriage patterns and family life in Tucson. Intermarriages between white men and Mexican women were taking place even more frequently by the turn of the twentieth century, but their decreasing representation in the growing population obscured their significance and their extent. By then, relationships among people of mixed ancestry were rising considerably. These young descendants of the early interethnic couples almost always had Euro-American surnames, and their marriage choices revealed much about local culture and class. Black and Chinese men continued to marry Mexican women, and by the early 1900s, white women began to enter into unions with Mexican men in small but meaningful numbers. This chapter discusses the development, extent, and significance of interethnic unions in Tucson, focusing primarily on white-Mexican unions, which occurred extensively and remarkably regularly between 1860 and 1930. It argues that class, more than race, consistently shaped the practice of intermarriage. An important contribution of this study involves the use of quantitative evidence to recast important misconceptions about intermarriage in the West. The chapter first presents a synoptic view of intermarriage in Tucson, a summary that resembles previous histories of white-Mexican relationships in the Southwest. Next, it provides a more detailed account of the same story to underscore important nuances. Finally, it offers a reexamination of the historiographical tenet that white-Mexican intermarriage became rare due to the increasing presence of white women. The case study of Tucson reveals that white men did not simply redirect their attention away from Mexican women when sex ratios improved.

INTERMARRIAGE IN TUCSON: THE USUAL STORY

Scholarly accounts of white-Mexican intermarriage in the Southwest in the nineteenth and early twentieth centuries largely emphasize the following narrative. Relationships between white men and Mexican women occurred rather frequently during early contact. Mexican elites and westering whites sought social, economic, and political advantages and thus entered into strategic networks via marriage. The practice declined, however, as the new power players (whites and their white-Mexican descendants) replaced the old elites. Strategic or accommodating relationships therefore became unnecessary. But by far, the biggest factor in the decrease of intermarriage involved the arrival of white women. Mexican women, their financial and political cache already diminishing, began to lose their matrimonial appeal. White men, qualitative and quantitative studies maintain, now shifted their focus to white women primarily because of racial affinity. The narrative fits well within the larger history of abuses and manipulation that characterized white-Mexican relations. Overall, this historiographical view portrays Mexican women as pragmatic tokens or, at best, as temporary substitutes during the transition from Mexican to white predominance in the Southwest. Their role supposedly lost importance, diminishing from sorely needed to irremediably unnecessary.

At first glance, Tucson largely parallels that general framework. Largely devoid of the natural resources of California and the farming and grazing land of New Mexico, southern Arizona still attracted a few thousand white settlers in the nineteenth century and many more in the early twentieth century. As in other parts of the Southwest, the initial western migration primarily involved white men, and they intermarried extensively with Mexican women. Unlike patterns in other western regions, a few—very few—of these marriages involved what one might consider elites, Mexican families that owned land or practiced trade. Census records demonstrate both the substantial exogamy rates among white men in the 1850s and 1860s and their steady decline into the 1920s: between 1860 and 1870, roughly 80 percent of the slightly more than one hundred white men in relationships had a Mexican partner; that number decreased to 39 percent by 1880, 15 percent by 1910, and a mere 7 percent by 1930. The decline in the number of intermarriages as a share of all white marriages leaves the impression that white-Mexican unions became rare as the white population, and especially as the number of white women, increased. Tucson therefore seems to resemble other southwestern locations. Yet, as this chapter explains, a quantitative analysis demonstrates that the perception of intermarriage becoming rare or declining is highly inaccurate in the case of Tucson—and most likely in other parts of the region as well.

INTERMARRIAGE IN TUCSON: A CLOSER LOOK AT THE USUAL STORY

Married life lay beyond the grasp of large segments of transplanted residents of the nineteenth-century Southwest. Whether arriving from east of the Mississippi, Europe, or China, migration typically resulted in unbalanced sex ratios in the former Mexican territory. For whites, Texas and California offered the most balanced populations, but even there female migration occurred gradually. For instance, by 1850, thirty years after large American settlements first appeared in Texas, the state still had 123 white men for every 100 white women, a number that included Mexican women. The gold rush allowed California to match Texas's population in a mere two years, but such rapid growth came at a cost. In 1850 white men totaled an incredible 1,223 for every 100 women. These ratios improved steadily in both states, but population balance still eluded them by the turn of the twentieth century. Nearby states and territories fared much worse. In Colorado and Nevada, white men outnumbered white women by about 50 percent into the 1890s. By far, however, these population imbalances paled in comparison to the situations African American and Chinese men encountered. With the exception of Texas—where slaveowners clearly brought male and female slaves in equal numbers—the Southwest offered rather poor prospects for black men. They regularly outnumbered black women by 2 to 1 and 3 to 1 in the 1860s and 1870s, and the imbalance decreased very slowly into the next century. Chinese men, on the other hand, would have envied the skewed ratios of blacks and whites. They faced incredibly slim chances of finding Chinese wives far into the twentieth century. Although the situation had been much worse in the 1860s and 1870s, Chinese men still exceeded their female counterparts by at least 12 to 1 in every southwestern locale as late as 1900, and the ratios worsened the farther they ventured from California.[5]

Arizona witnessed highly similar population imbalances for these three groups. The territory had approximately 250 white men for every 100 women in 1870 and 1880, and the ratio still stood at roughly 150 to 100 in 1900. As in New Mexico, these numbers tell only part of the story, for they include the largely balanced Mexican population. The example of Tucson discussed below illustrates that white women arrived very late in certain areas. Blacks in Arizona never enjoyed sex ratios below 2 to 1 in the nineteenth century, and they at times exceeded 6 to 1. Chinese men, meanwhile, found a far worse situation. By 1900, when conditions had vastly improved, men still outnumbered women by a ratio of 43 to 1. These imbalances meant that unmarried men from these three groups essentially had two options to marry endogamously: (1) wait for women of their ethnic groups to arrive; or (2) travel to an area with a balanced population. Nineteenth-century travel conditions, economic restraints, and distance, especially for Chinese men, considerably limited both possibilities. To varying degrees, however, all three groups demonstrated the desire and openness to form relationships with Mexican women. Blacks and Chinese, as discussed in the next chapter, faced additional challenges, but they and whites discovered that Mexicans in Arizona welcomed them into their families in remarkably high numbers.

Intermarriage in Tucson occurred quite frequently during the first two decades after its acquisition by the United States in 1854. The first American census (1860) revealed that endogamous Mexican families, of course, predominated in the population, but intermarriage clearly stood out. The Euro-American community remained small, composed primarily of approximately 150 white men, and very few of them belonged to family units. Only eight of them had white wives, and twice that many had formed families with Mexican women. No single white women resided in Tucson at the time, a situation that would improve very slowly over the next six decades (see table 1).

The early mythology of local white pioneers greatly celebrated the birth of the first white child in Arizona. It attributed the distinction to one-time Tucson residents William H. Kirkland and Ann Bacon, whose daughter Elizabeth was born in 1861.[6] The claim obviously rests on the racially contingent premise that neither the children of Mexicans nor of white-Mexican unions deserved the recognition. Interethnic families nonetheless existed in Arizona well before the 1860s. In Tucson alone, eight white-Mexican couples had children born in the 1840s and 1850s. Tucson's 1860 census thus corroborated the presence of the interethnic families that travelers had described in the 1850s, as the practice of intermarriage had actually preceded the arrival of the American flag in 1854.[7]

African Americans in Tucson also formed interethnic relationships from the beginning. The 1860 census included two rarities: black-white relationships. Mary M. Bell, a white woman from Louisiana, was married to Isiah Bell, a black carpenter from Georgia; and a white cook from the East Indies was married to a mulatto woman from Louisiana. Black-white unions would almost never reappear on the city's census manuscripts over the next seventy years. Chas Cooper, the only other black resident, lived with Inés Bernal, a Mexican woman. It is unclear where these couples married, but those marriages were already illegal under the prevailing New Mexico law—which even prohibited interracial cohabitation—and Arizona would outlaw them soon after it gained territorial status in 1863. These three unions shared a common characteristic: whereas some families listed estates of thousands of dollars, and most could claim at least a few hundred dollars in assets, these three couples had no

TABLE 1. Population, couples, and single residents, Tucson, 1860–1880

YEAR	POPULATION	ENDOGAMOUS AND INTERMARRIED COUPLES			SINGLE RESIDENTS 16 YEARS OLD AND OVER		
		WHITE	MEXICAN	WHITE-MEXICAN	WHITE MEN	WHITE WOMEN	MEXICAN WOMEN
1860	940	6	104	16	137	0	40
1864	1,568	2	150	22	203	2	98
1870	3,224	15	397	54	332	6	221
1880	7,007	149	461	97	1,168	40	291

SOURCE Derived from a database created by the author based on census schedules.

possessions whatsoever. Their occupations—carpenter, laborer, and cook—further reinforced their working-class status. The trend in the economic situation of intermarrying partners of all races would not change much over the next seventy years. The men from all ethnic groups were mostly laborers, and the women who stated their occupation primarily held menial jobs, such as laundress or seamstress.

Two realities characterized family life in Tucson before 1880: very few single white women lived in town, and the majority of marriages for white men involved Mexican women. Single white women first appear in Tucson records in 1864, when the imbalance for white residents was extremely high at 203 men to only 2 women. It had not improved much by 1870, when single white men still outnumbered their female counterparts 332 to 6. Although 40 single white women lived in Tucson in 1880, the male-to-female ratio remained terribly skewed because more than 1,000 white men now resided in town. The city's ratio of single white women to the overall population would improve but continue to fall far below the national average as late as 1920.[8] The dearth of white women and the prohibition on marriages with Indian women left only Mexican women as potential wives for incoming white men. Census forms did not always list marital status, and cohabitation did not necessarily mean that a formal marriage had taken place. In some cases, white men might have viewed their relationships informally, whereas Mexican women might have perceived them as analogous to marriages.[9] In Tucson, however, families in the deeply rooted Mexican communities most likely viewed both formal and informal unions as legitimate relationships.

However they were regarded, the number of interethnic couples rose steadily. In 1864 twenty-two white men lived with Mexican women, and by 1870 the number had increased to fifty-four. More important, the ratio of these relationships to endogamous white unions clearly underscored the significance of Mexican women in the formation of family life in Tucson. Indeed, Mexican women accounted for nearly 70 percent of all partners for white men in 1860, 92 percent in 1864, and 79 percent in 1870 (see table 2). These high percentages would not reappear in later decades, but Mexican women remained a significant marrying group for whites. For some cohorts of white men, as discussed below, highly similar data prevailed into 1930.

Marriages between Mexican men and white women did occur, but only occasionally. The 1880 census indicates that Santiago Aínsa, a justice of the peace born in Mexico, was married to Jeannie Aínsa, a woman from New York. Prominent

TABLE 2. Mexican, white, and white-Mexican unions per census year, Tucson, 1860–1930

YEAR	COUPLES			INTERMARRIAGE RATE	
	WHITE	MEXICAN	WHITE-MEXICAN	FOR MEXICANS (%)	FOR WHITES (%)
1860	6	104	16	13	67
1864	2	150	22	13	92
1870	14	386	54	12	79
1880	149	461	97	17	39
1900	453	394	132	25	23
1910	945	757	172	19	15
1920	1,946	1,142	228	17	11
1930	3,519	1,563	283	15	7

SOURCE Derived from a database created by the author based on census schedules.

men, like Epifanio Aguirre and Miguel Otero, also married white women.[10] In 1900 J. A. Legarra, a store clerk, was married to Edith, also from New York, and in 1910, Ramón Salcido, a blacksmith, was married to Mary, born in Missouri.[11] The number of these unions barely reached eight in 1920 and twelve in 1930. In 1930 these marriages involved women from Kentucky, Michigan, West Virginia, Wisconsin, Germany, and Norway. These relationships occurred primarily among working-class people.

Although the rate of interethnic unions continued to decline, the increase in the overall population meant that white-Mexican intermarriages were actually occurring more frequently. That is, more interethnic couples were marrying, but the number of white couples was increasing more rapidly. The railroad reached Tucson in 1880, and one might expect that its arrival would dramatically increase the number of white immigrants. But the economic recession of the 1880s halted migration and actually led to a decrease in Tucson's population.[12] It declined from over 7,000 in 1880 to under 5,200 in 1890, barely rebounding to 7,500 by 1900. White families drove the recovery in the population, and of note, the number of endogamous white families increased considerably, from 149 in 1880 to 453 in 1900. The practice of intermarriage also climbed, from only 97 in 1880, to 132 by 1900. Thus, despite the growth in the white population, interethnic unions still accounted for nearly one of every four relationships for whites. The larger southern Arizona region resembled this pattern. Pima County records reveal that between 1875 and 1900, more than one of every six marriages involved interethnic partners, a total of 415 couples.

These results contradict the contention of several scholars that the completion of the railroad signaled the decline and even the end of intermarriage by facilitating the arrival of white women.[13] Census and county records indicate that intermarriage consistently increased in number and accounted for a significant percentage of all marriages in Pima County until 1930, well after the railroad arrived in Tucson in 1880. Railroad companies stressed their role in bringing civilization and prosperity to the West, but social order remained elusive in many areas. Large cities grew, but small towns stagnated, and their expectations of economic development did not materialize.[14] Tucson's early history followed that pattern. It experienced population and economic growth *before* the arrival of the railroad, but the departure of the military along with the national economic recession of the 1880s actually produced a decline in population. Only the turn of the century, coinciding with copper booms and economic

FIGURE 5. Beatriz Ferrer, Jesús Barceló, and Sofía Hughes (c. 1890s). Beatriz married Hedley Soderberg, from Sweden, in 1902. Jesús married Robert Rusk, son of Theodore Rusk, from Kentucky, and Concepción Telles, in 1895. Sofía, daughter of Frederick Hughes, from England, and Sofía Barceló, married George W. Pickett, from Iowa, in 1901. Arizona Historical Society/Tucson, AHS Photo Number 72172.

diversification in southern Arizona, witnessed the arrival of more white families and single white women.[15]

Pressures on the population did affect the practice of intermarriage, but in a different way: demographic changes increased the rate of interethnic marriage for the Mexicans who remained in Tucson. In 1880 intermarriage accounted for 39 percent of all unions for whites but only for 17 percent for Mexicans. By 1900, however, the percentage for whites had declined to 23 percent, a rate that Mexicans actually surpassed at 25 percent. These changes stemmed from the demographic transformation that occurred between 1880 and 1900. When the population rebounded from its 1890 plunge, its ethnic composition had changed significantly. Although the number of endogamous white couples more than tripled, from 149 to 453, the number actually declined for Mexicans. Mexican immigration, as has occurred historically, paralleled economic conditions, and like the economy, it would begin to recover in the early 1900s. Four factors combined to raise the share of intermarriage among Mexicans: (1) single white women remained scarce until the 1920s; (2) white men now represented a larger segment of the population and boosted the pool of bachelors for Mexican women; and (3) white-Mexican couples would typically not retreat to Mexico when the economy contracted; but (4) many Mexican families likely moved to Mexico or to other parts of the Southwest, and the share of intermarriage thus increased for Mexicans who stayed in Tucson.

Mexicans were clearly benefiting from the availability of a more diverse populace with the addition of white, black, and Chinese men to the balanced sex ratios among the Mexican population. Exogamous practices for Mexicans peaked at 25 percent in 1900 and declined gradually into 1930. But even then, more than one in every seven relationships involving Mexicans was interethnic. By 1930, however, these interethnic unions extended beyond the white man–Mexican woman pattern of the 1860s and 1870s. Men and women of mixed ancestry dominated intermarriage from 1910 on, and Mexican men were also intermarrying more frequently. Intermarriage for whites as a share of all their unions significantly declined during the first three decades of the twentieth century, slowly but steadily dropping from 23 percent in 1900 to only 7 percent by 1930. Yet, intermarriages were increasing in absolute numbers. County records indicate that almost five hundred interethnic couples married between 1891 and 1910. The practice continued to increase into the 1920s. In fact, more people entered into exogamous unions from 1911 to 1930 than in the previous four decades combined. The increase after 1900 is even more significant since the data no longer include the southern area that became Santa Cruz County in 1899 (see table 3).[16]

The continuing practice of intermarriage maintained several consistent features. For example, sizeable age differentials characterized interethnic couples of the second half of the nineteenth century, and although these differences decreased gradually in the early twentieth century, they still remained higher than for endogamous couples. These early unions frequently involved white men over thirty years of age and Mexican women in their teens or early twenties. Men were, on average, at least ten years older than their partners until 1900, but the difference becomes more conspicuous when one compares it to endogamous marriages. For instance, in 1870, intermarried men were an aver-

TABLE 3. Marriage licenses involving interethnic partners, Pima County, 1872–1930

	TOTAL MARRIAGES	INTERMARRIAGES	INTERMARRIAGE RATE (%)
1872–1880	416	102	25
1881–1890	659	127	19
1891–1900	1,454	220	15
1901–1910	2,088	260	12
1911–1920	3,949	502	13
1921–1930	5,054	535	11
1872–1930	13,620	1,746	13

SOURCES Decennial census enumeration schedules, 1880–1930. Floyd R. Negley and Marcia S. Lindley, *Arizona Territorial Marriages, Pima County, 1871–1912*, and *Arizona Marriages, Pima County, Marriage Books 5–10, February 1912 through December 1926*; Marriage Licenses, Pima County, 1927–1930, SG 8 Superior Court, History and Archives Division, Arizona State Library, Archives and Public Records, Phoenix.

age of twelve years older than their wives. Endogamous white marriages, on the other hand, were more likely to have spouses of similar ages, and the men were older than their partners by an average of only five years. Age differentials declined over time for all interethnic unions, and by 1930, almost half of all couples involved partners within five years of age of each other. Some women were older than their spouses, but age equality had clearly not completely arrived for these couples. One can note that men in these relationships were still an average of eight years older than their partners, far above the differences among endogamous couples for whites (4.1 years) and Mexicans (5.1 years). One can interpret age disparities as beneficial to both partners. As these patterns and the narratives discussed in chapter 2 illustrate, white men held a fondness for young Mexican women. But, from the perspective of Mexican women, these men stood out above all Mexican men and all men their own age. Women had a larger pool of men, and their marriages to older men must have brought benefits that they deemed important, such as maturity and stability.

The historiographical emphasis on renowned families has left the impression that early intermarriage in the Southwest occurred primarily between enterprising white men and the daughters of the old Mexican elite as attempts by both groups to secure economic and political power. Those marriages did occur but were by far the exception. For one thing, situations in the various regions of the Southwest certainly developed differently. In Santa Fe, for instance, intermarriage occurred primarily among working-class people, and religious compatibility best explains why certain groups, like Irish men, intermarried with Mexican women.[17] Tucson definitely followed the pattern of its old territorial cousin, as census data strongly indicate that local intermarriage primarily involved working-class couples. One must wonder, given the high number of interethnic unions among the working class in the city, if a similar situation did not occur in more parts of the Southwest.[18] Even in the 1860 census, before the arrival of the federal and state governments and when occupations such as trader and merchant made up a large segment of the economically active population, the most common classifications for men in these relationships involved low-wage jobs, occasionally as carpenters and blacksmiths, but primarily as laborers earning less than fifteen dollars per month.[19] Repeatedly, between 1870 and 1930, working-class men represented almost two-thirds of all intermarried men. Merchants and ranchers/farmers consistently combined for under 20 percent of the total—not that they were amassing great fortunes. Finally, intermarriages involving white-collar workers, a professional class that developed slowly in Tucson, oscillated between 5 and 14 percent.

Although interethnic couples consistently belonged to the lower classes, their composition did change. White men's place of origin greatly correlated with their incidence of intermarriage in Tucson, a trend that becomes particularly noticeable after 1900. The most recurrent intermarriage in the nineteenth century involved white men born outside the West and Mexican women. Into the twentieth century, however, two groups of men increasingly entered into interethnic unions. As white families continued to settle in the region, white men born in the West, especially in Arizona, began to marry Mexican women in large numbers. Similarly, as the number of white women increased, Mexican men, too, entered into intermarriages in higher numbers. By 1930, men born in the West accounted for two-thirds of all intermarrying men, and the percentage of intermarriages involving Mexican men (15 percent) far exceeded those involving men from the Northeast (4.5 percent). Migration, of course, had not decreased—on the contrary. Rather, intermarriage proved appealing to migrating white men in the nineteenth century and to local men in the early 1900s. The background of the typical intermarried partners had certainly changed since the second half of the nineteenth century, when foreign white men and men from the Northeast represented anywhere from one-half to four-fifths of men involved in interethnic unions.

The new intermarrying white men were most frequently the descendants of those early migrants and of the ever-increasing midwestern families. Demographic patterns attest to the role of the Midwest as a migration hub. Men from that region typically migrated with their wives, and for that reason, they accounted for less than 15 percent of all intermarriages during every census year between 1864 and 1930. As early as 1910, only 5 percent of all local white men from that region married nonwhites. Their share of endogamous white couples, on the other hand, was simply extraordinary, as a great majority of those marriages included at least one partner born in the Midwest. The sizeable increase in the number of white families from that region has contributed to the misconception that intermarriage practices declined precipitously.

Perhaps the most noticeable change in the evolution of intermarriage involved the emergence of relationships that diverged from the white man–Mexican woman norm of the 1860s and 1870s. As discussed in the next chapter, Mexicans frequently entered into relationships with black and Chinese partners between 1860 and 1930. Also, by 1900, white women participated in 4 percent of all intermarriages, and Mexican men in 7 percent. Of note, partners of mixed ancestry were now involved in almost 33 percent of all intermarriages. These three groups gradually increased their levels of participation: by 1930, Mexican men were involved in 15 percent of interethnic unions, white women in 7.5 percent, and people of mixed ancestry accounted for 52 percent. Clearly, changes in the population facilitated higher interaction between some white women and Mexican men and thus led to more interethnic relationships. White women were evidently also interested in marrying outside their ethnic group and not merely serving as the wives of white men. Quantifying these unions, however, can be problematic since relying on surnames alone—as one frequently must when studying marriage licenses—can produce incorrect tallies.

For example, by 1920, the number of intermarriages among the children of white-Mexican couples had increased significantly. That year, approximately ninety marriages involved at least one descendant of interethnic couples.[20] The census offers proof of these unions, but using other sources can lead to an overreliance on the Euro-American surnames of partners of white-Mexican ancestry and on some Anglo-phonic surnames of Mexicans. An earlier study of county marriage records maintains that more than sixty white women married

Mexican men in the early 1900s.[21] A close examination of the census, however, reveals that a very high percentage of those women almost certainly were not white. Anglo-sounding Spanish surnames, like Martin, and common Euro-American surnames of Mexicans, such as Bartlett, can mislead. For instance, census records prove that Beatrice Jordan (Jordán), who married Juan Reyes in 1907, was Mexican, while Mabel Jordan, who married John Knagge in 1919, was white. Both marriages were endogamous.[22] But there is a simpler explanation to the apparent high number of white woman–Mexican man marriages. Census schedules provide information, such as birthplace, maiden name, parents' birthplace, native language, and year of entry if foreign born. Such data reveal that in 1910, there were only three Mexican men married to white women in Tucson, where most county residents lived.[23] A large percentage of the seemingly white women must have been of white-Mexican descent with the Euro-American surnames of their fathers. Indeed, marriages between Mexican men and women of mixed ancestry were highly frequent after 1900. Also, as the opening example of the Brown-McKenna marriage illustrates, an apparent white endogamous union that is actually one of mixed white-Mexican ancestry would in fact produce children with 50 percent Mexican ancestry and, importantly, two Spanish-speaking Mexican grandmothers. Surnames and racial categories can thus obscure the rich ethnic background of descendants of mixed ancestry.

The marriages of people of mixed heritage are illuminating in other ways as well. One should not assume that the descendants of white-Mexican couples naturally leaned toward relationships with specific ethnic groups. They married across the three plausible categories in sizeable numbers, and their marital choices at the turn of the twentieth century reveal important trends regarding race and class. They married partners who were also of mixed ancestry at very consistent levels between the 1890s and 1920s, regularly accounting for at least 25 percent of all unions for these men and women. Yet, data suggest that women of mixed ancestry benefited from a larger pool of potential spouses. The reason lies in the ethno-demography that prevailed in Tucson since the 1850s. White-Mexican marriages occurred primarily among working-class partners in highly Mexican neighborhoods: always in and nearby the downtown area, then as the city expanded, in the west and southwest sections as well (see figure 1). As time went on, intermarried couples—and thus their children of mixed ancestry— were increasingly more likely to live in districts with high concentrations of Mexicans and substantial numbers of whites but very few single white women. Therefore, women of mixed ancestry regularly interacted with three groups of

INTERMARRIAGE IN TUCSON, 1860–1930 87

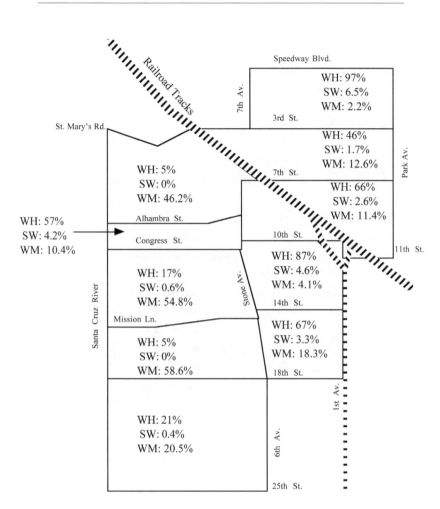

FIGURE 6. Tucson, 1910. Endogamous white households (WH) and intermarried white-Mexican households (WM) as percentages of all households in the district, as well as single white women sixteen years of age and over (SW) as a percentage of the population in the district (nationwide for whites: 5.3 percent).

men: Mexicans, whites, or men of mixed ancestry, all largely from the working class. Not surprisingly, these women married among all three groups in highly similar percentages. For men of mixed ancestry, however, the low number of white women in these districts left only two primary groups of potential spouses: Mexican women and women of mixed ancestry. Not surprisingly, they married into both groups at roughly the same rate. In sum, these men and women of mixed ancestry married among the widespread groups in their neighborhood. Therefore class, not race, better explains why women of mixed ancestry married whites at higher rates than their male counterparts did.

Between 1854 and 1900, almost the entire population, which never included Indian areas, lived near the original site of the old presidio, and interethnic couples resided uniformly throughout the small city. As late as 1900, intermarriage accounted for approximately 14 percent of all unions in each of the three census districts. All along, intermarriage had and would continue to follow a consistent pattern: it occurred frequently in areas with high concentrations of Mexican residents or with racial diversity but rarely happened in white neighborhoods. The census helps to illustrate a logical explanation to both patterns.

Although a close link between class and intermarriage existed from the beginning, the city's expansion made it seem like race influenced both the creation of ethnic enclaves and lower rates of intermarriage. The Gadsden Purchase of 1854 meant that people who migrated to Tucson in the 1860s entered an area where very few whites resided. As the town grew in the last decades of the nineteenth century, some areas continued to resemble the old Tucson, and others became ethnically diverse; yet intermarriage pervaded both. During the first three decades of the twentieth century, however, Tucson's population more than quadrupled (from 7,531 to 32,506), and settlement patterns occurred primarily along ethnic lines: whites settled largely in the north and northeast, and Mexicans and other minorities in the southwest, while the downtown area remained balanced. As population growth occurred, Mexican immigrants settled almost exclusively in the Mexican parts of town. They benefited from familial and ethnic networks and, especially, from affordable housing. Incoming whites, on the other hand, migrated primarily from the Midwest and largely lacked the types of networks that would make them gravitate toward Mexican enclaves. One can further identify two groups among these westering whites: (1) those who had some financial resources and migrated as entire families, and (2) others, predominantly single men, who were poor and primarily traveled alone. The first were able to rent or purchase residences in the expanding subdivisions in the eastern and northern sections of town, while those with fewer resources settled in the older and poorer neighborhoods, where Mexicans lived. These two groups negotiated greatly different racial spaces. Some of them rarely saw nonwhites, whereas others interacted with them daily. Intermarriage among the latter group followed that class-defined contact.

This development of ethnic enclaves became increasingly noticeable by 1920. That year signaled an impending transformation: conditions not only resembled the patterns of the early years but also pointed to the significant changes that would coalesce further. Tucson included areas where whites accounted for more than 80 percent of the households. In some parts, virtually no Mexicans resided. The next few years would see additional consolidation of these white enclaves, while areas in the southwest and, especially, in the downtown area still maintained higher levels of diversity because of their substantial number of poor whites, high numbers of interethnic families, and the presence of African American and Chinese residents. The demographic boundaries solidified to such an extent that only 3 percent of all Mexican households lay north of the railroad tracks and east of Third Avenue, an area where whites predominated almost completely over other groups. In fact, only approximately one hundred of the more than three thousand households included residents of Mexican descent. Not surprisingly, intermarriage in white districts fell well below the city average. For instance, in the three predominantly white districts, intermarriage represented less than 4 percent of all marriages. This pattern became even more pronounced in 1930, when the eight predominantly white districts had intermarriage levels that ranged from 0 to 3 percent.

But an old pattern did persist everywhere: the resident group in the minority, whether Mexican or white, exhibited high levels of intermarriage. That is, in enclaves where whites were a significant majority of the population, the few people of Mexican ancestry who lived there formed interethnic unions very frequently. Similarly, in areas where Mexicans outnumbered whites by large margins, white residents belonged to interethnic unions in high percentages. These relationships either cemented the acceptance of the incoming spouses into the area or served as their introduction. For instance, in 1920, in districts where whites accounted for less than 10 percent of the total households, their levels of intermarriage as a percentage of all their marriages ranged from 51 to 78 percent. In a way, whites who moved into those neighborhoods entered demographic spaces that largely resembled the Tucson of the 1860s and 1870s, when high levels of intermarriage were prevalent throughout town. In other words, more than sixty years after annexation, remarkably, as many as eight out of ten married white men in some Mexican areas had a wife of Mexican descent. A similar situation occurred in districts where Mexicans accounted for small fractions of the population. For example, in the four districts where Mexicans made up approximately 10 percent or less of all households, their levels of intermarriage as a percentage of all their marriages ranged from 33 percent to 48 percent. This trend makes sense because by 1920, the number of Americanized, economically and culturally adapted Mexican Americans had increased, as had their interaction with the young white population.

By then, single white women finally represented a significant percentage of the population, some seven decades after white men began to migrate into the area. But one should not automatically correlate their increase in the population to the decrease in interethnic couples as a percentage of all marriages. Such an assumption ignores important demographic and cultural facts. White women migrated primarily as members of larger families or, to a far lesser extent, were born in Tucson. Accordingly, they accounted for extremely low numbers in the Mexican parts of town. Furthermore, their representation in the city always trailed the national average. Yet, in predominantly white enclaves, they consistently matched or exceeded national rates. Their presence in these areas would continue to increase over the next ten years. By 1930, the city included seven districts where single white women sixteen years of age and older accounted for at least seven percent of the population (see figure 2). In three of these districts, their proportion (9.6 percent, 10.3 percent, and 21.4 percent) far surpassed the national average of 5.2 percent and the city's average of 4.7 percent. Unquestionably, the number of single white women increased every decade, and conversely, interethnic unions consistently decreased as a percentage of all unions for white men after 1880. Yet, interdecennial data prove that the increasing presence of white women had no significant effect on intermarriage rates.

To suggest otherwise improperly emphasizes only the role of white men by assuming (1) that they alone made marriage decisions, and (2) that they preferred white women and thus began to disregard Mexican women, who were no longer coveted or needed. The rate of intermarriage relative to the general population definitively declined over time, but one constant offers insight into why that statistic obfuscates as much as it illuminates. From 1860 to 1930, rates of intermarriage between white men and Mexican women remained consistently high in Mexican enclaves and low in white districts for one primary reason: geographic proximity frequently involved class parallelism and promoted familiarity and marriage. In Tucson, the areas where residents from the various ethnic groups interacted contained the highest number of intermarriages. But white women lived predominantly in areas where very few nonwhites resided. Just like white men who lived in Mexican areas married extensively with

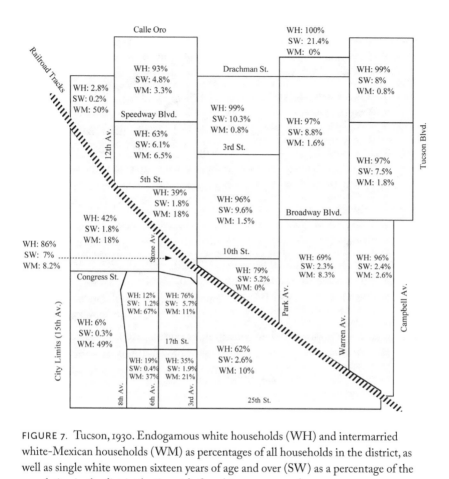

FIGURE 7. Tucson, 1930. Endogamous white households (WH) and intermarried white-Mexican households (WM) as percentages of all households in the district, as well as single white women sixteen years of age and over (SW) as a percentage of the population in the district (nationwide for whites: 5.2 percent).

Mexican women, when white women resided in Mexican enclaves, they logically, if perhaps surprisingly within the current historiography, married Mexicans more often than did their isolated female counterparts in white neighborhoods. After all, if white men did prefer white wives—and if preference alone produced marriages—they could have sought them in the east side of Tucson.

But all nineteenth-century Tucsonans lived under the limitations of their inherited cultural norms and historical reality, both of which circumscribed and guided their decisions. White men and women most likely viewed racial affinity as only one of several factors when making marriage decisions. From that perspective, white endogamous marriages faced potential obstacles. For instance, some white men might not have found religious compatibility among the mostly Protestant, midwestern white population of the east side and thus would have preferred Catholic wives. Just as likely, white women might have preferred American or Protestant men over the foreign or non-Protestant men who resided on the west side. Class probably played a role as well. Single white women belonged to families that were relatively stable financially, whereas white men from western parts of Tucson tended to belong to the working class. Just as important, age considerations might also have directed some white men toward exogamy. Intermarried men were consistently older than their Mexican wives, while endogamous partners were closer in age. Yet, in 1920, single white women were, on average, twenty-seven years old, and almost one-third of them exceeded thirty years of age. Some white men might have preferred younger Mexican women to older white women. Furthermore, although one can assume that some white men sought racial or cultural homogeneity, others perhaps favored heterogeneity. That is, white men might simply prefer Mexican women or women of mixed ancestry. In other words, they inherited an agency that limited their options.[24] These possibilities complicate the old contention that intermarriage became rare as white men redirected their attention toward the arriving white women. But a simpler explanation persuasively recasts that longstanding tenet.

INTERMARRIAGE IN TUCSON: A REASSESSMENT OF THE OLD STORY

The key to reassessing the common explanation that the arrival of white women negatively affected intermarriage rates rests in focusing on the fundamental difference between whites who were (1) married and (2) marriageable. The historiographical explanation on why the practice of intermarriage began to dwindle originates from a misinterpretation of demographic transformation. The first noticeable change in the composition of white families occurred in the 1870s. Tucson experienced a brief economic boom in that decade, and its population more than doubled.[25] The number of intermarriages increased considerably from fifty-four to ninety-seven, and it would continue to increase every decade. But the following change creates confusion: the number of intermarried households for whites *as a percentage of all white households* declined from

79 percent in 1870 to 39 percent in 1880. The two figures do not contradict each other: the increase, of course, refers to the total number of intermarriages, and the decline refers to their representation among all marriages for whites. Scholars, however, have thus far emphasized only the latter. A closer analysis reveals the limitations of that approach. One must examine the nature of white migration during these years. White men began migrating as members of families as well as, but no longer primarily, bachelors. Marriage involves a conscious decision based on, among other factors, available options. White men who migrated with their wives belonged to a pool of men who were already married and no longer had the option to marry in Tucson. Those who arrived alone, on the other hand, were marriageable and did have that option. The latter group consistently intermarried. Studies of intermarriage need to focus more attention on the marriageable and not on the already married or on the entire white population.

The following statistics shed light on this important distinction. Looking again at the data from 1870 to 1880, the number of intermarriages had almost doubled, from 54 to 97, but the number of endogamous white families had increased even faster, from only 14 to 149. This noticeable surge meant that white endogamous couples now outnumbered their white-Mexican counterparts for the first time, 149 to 97. Yet, although all 97 intermarried whites obviously at one point had the option to marry in Arizona, not all of the other 149 did. A great number of the latter actually migrated with their spouses. That is, they were not marriageable, and one cannot therefore conclude that these white men redirected their attention to white women. In a way, they had no attention to redirect. Focusing only on the men who arrived as bachelors yields remarkably revealing results. In fact, as explained below, the decline in interethnic marriages from 1870 to 1880 was barely noticeable.

The analysis that produces those results involves the following process. Using birthplace information for husbands, wives, and children allows for the creation of cohorts of whites based on the likelihood that they were either married or marriageable when they arrived or lived in Tucson. Whites who married Mexicans unquestionably had the option to marry in the West, but the following criteria place endogamously married whites in different groups. First, white couples whose children were born in a different place (state, territory, or country) certainly had formed a family before migrating to Arizona. These partners (Cohort A; see below) did not have the option to marry locally, and one can safely eliminate them from intermarriage rates. Second, one can further remove couples if both partners originated from the same place (Cohort B). Highly skewed sex ratios before the 1920s make it extremely unlikely that a white bachelor would manage to find eligible white women in Tucson, let alone one from his very same birthplace. Third, the same lack of single white women in the area allows for the informed elimination of another group that very likely arrived already married. In these couples (Cohort C), at least one, but usually both, of the partners originated from what one might call a migration entrepôt, say New York, Ohio, or Illinois. Migrants from farther away (e.g., Ireland or Massachusetts) likely married during a phase of a larger migration that culminated in Arizona (more on this category later). Fourth, some couples involved partners whose demographic information did not place them in or out of Arizona at the time of their marriage. They might have married elsewhere but certainly belong to a group in which spouses perhaps met in Arizona (Cohort D). Finally, men born in Arizona or who married white women born in Arizona certainly lived in the area as unmarried (Cohort E). They thus belong to the same cohort as those who intermarried. In sum, one can classify the likelihood that whites in endogamous marriages lived as single in Arizona as follows:

> Cohort A: Virtually nonexistent: spouses almost certainly migrated with their partners because their oldest child was born outside Arizona.
> Cohort B: Highly unlikely: both spouses were born outside Arizona and in the same place (state, territory, or foreign country).
> Cohort C: Improbable: spouses likely met in a migratory entrepôt, like Missouri or Ohio.
> Cohort D: Probable: no evidence places the spouses inside or outside Arizona before marriage.
> Cohort E: Virtually certain: at least one spouse was born in Arizona.

The implementation of these criteria produces the following results for the change in marriage patterns from 1870 to 1880 (see table 4). Including all marriages for whites, as historians have always done, yields an intermarriage rate that decreases from 79 percent in 1870 to 39 percent in 1880. But removing whites who belong to Cohort A, whose children, after all, place them outside Arizona at the time of their marriage, raises intermarriage rates to 92 percent in 1870 and 51 percent in 1880. Further removing Cohort B (those who were born in the same place as their spouses) brings the rates to 96 and 58 percent, respectively. Eliminating Cohort C (entrepôt marriages) increases rates to 100 percent

TABLE 4. Intermarriage rates for whites based on certain scenarios, Tucson, 1860–1930

	COUPLES		INTERMARRIAGE RATE				
YEAR	WHITE	INTERMARRIAGES	IF ALL WHITE COUPLES INCLUDED (%)	SCENARIO 1: IF COHORT A EXCLUDED (%)	SCENARIO 2: IF COHORTS A AND B EXCLUDED (%)	SCENARIO 3: IF COHORTS A, B, AND C EXCLUDED (%)	SCENARIO 4: IF COHORTS A, B, C, AND D EXCLUDED (%)
1860	6	16	73	76	80	94	100
1864	2	22	92	100	100	100	100
1870	14	54	79	92	96	100	100
1880	149	97	39	51	58	92	99
1900	453	132	23	34	39	84	97
1910	945	172	15	23	28	69	80
1920	1,946	228	10	18	22	59	73
1930	3,519	283	7	12	15	41	57

SOURCE Derived from a database created by the author based on census schedules.

in 1870 and 92 percent in 1880. Discarding Cohort D (those who probably met in Arizona) is unnecessary at this point for 1870, but it would increase the 1880 intermarriage practice to 99 percent. For 1880, in other words, taking into account only the white endogamous marriages that almost certainly took place in Arizona means that only 1 percent of whites married endogamously. The rest married Mexicans. Even including those who probably met in Arizona (Cohort D) leaves the white endogamous rate at only 8 percent. In either case, intermarriage was by no means becoming rare for those who had the option to marry.

Assessing the probability that whites possessed or lacked the ability to marry in Arizona is rather straightforward when dealing with all groups, except Cohort C (entrepôt marriages). Yet, even in that case, census records leave little doubt about the suitability of viewing specific states as migration entrepôts. White migration to Tucson by far involved men and women from midwestern states and from California and Texas. Couples in which both partners originated from the same state largely migrated from those two states and from Illinois, Indiana, Missouri, and Ohio, and to a lesser extent, from Iowa, Kansas, Michigan, and Wisconsin. Those families almost certainly migrated together and accounted for approximately 20 percent of white couples from 1900 to 1930. But their effect on the demographic composition of Tucson was much more pronounced, because in another 70 percent of endogamous white marriages, at least one partner came from one of those ten states. A typical entrepôt couple involved a person from a state whose population grew rapidly in the nineteenth century, like Illinois or Texas, and a spouse from a place father north and/or east, like Connecticut for Illinois and Louisiana for Texas. But entrepôt unions could also involve partners from other states, like Minnesota for Canadians or New York for Irish immigrants. Similarly, some marriages involving Texans or Ohioans did not qualify as entrepôt unions when the other partner came from a place like Oregon or Idaho. One cannot soundly speculate where those couples met—and they thus belong to Cohort D (probably meeting in Arizona). California is the only entrepôt state that does not necessarily lie between Arizona and the original place of origin of the other spouse, but it qualifies as a meeting space because it functioned as a rebounding area. Census data suggest that migrants frequently tried their fortune there and ultimately settled in Arizona. The composition of families from Cohort C highlights the role of these entrepôt areas. The wives, much more than the husbands, were born in these states, making it clear that men originally settled in those places, wed, and eventually continued their migration to Arizona with their family. The fact that more than 70 percent of the oldest children of all endogamous white couples were born in those states further cements their designation as migration entrepôts.

This reassessment of intermarriage rates still results in steady declines over time, but the changes become much less dramatic than previously understood. For instance, in 1910 intermarried families were only 15 percent of *all* marriages for whites. Yet, the total increases to 28 percent when one removes Cohorts A and B (those who most likely married before settling in Tucson). But one can safely discard the group of whites whose birthplace combined with that of their spouses place them in an entrepôt state at the time of marriage (Cohort C). The early 1900s, after all, witnessed a sharp increase in the migration of families from the Midwest. These entrepôt couples most likely arrived together, and removing them further raises the intermarriage rate for the remaining whites to 69 percent. This figure is a fairly accurate baseline estimate of how common intermarriage remained for whites who actually had the option to marry. The previous exclusions leave only two cohorts in the pool of whites who had the option to marry in Tucson. Some (Cohort D) probably met their spouses in Arizona, for no evidence indicates whether they knew each other before arriving in town. If one were to remove them, then the intermarriage rate would include only Cohort E, couples with at least one spouse born in Arizona, and the rate would rise to a substantial 80 percent. Remarkably, counting only the marriages that almost certainly took place in Arizona leads to the following conclusion: more than fifty years after the United States annexed Tucson, up to eight of every ten people of white ancestry who wed locally chose partners of Mexican descent.

Foreign whites frequently intermarried at higher levels than their native-born counterparts. Not surprisingly, eliminating those who lacked the option to marry in Arizona yields an even higher incidence of intermarriage for them, too. Their intermarriage rates were extremely high in the 1880s, but birthplace analysis reveals the continuation of high exogamy into the twentieth century. In 1910 their frequency of intermarriage climbs from 12 percent, if one includes all their marriages, to as high as 89 percent, if one includes only the group that certainly married in Arizona (Cohort E). Thus, it is likely that, as late as 1910, almost all the foreign whites—all men, in this case—who lived in Tucson and whose marriage took place locally, married partners of Mexican ancestry. The same process of elimination raises the intermarriage rates for foreign whites from 10 to 82 percent in 1920 and from 7 to 75 percent in 1930. These statistics prove significant because the number of couples with at least one foreign white spouse increased by roughly 100 every decade starting in 1900, reaching 450 by 1930. Yet, focusing only on the marriageable cohorts produces intermarriage rates above 55 percent from 1860 to 1930.[26] In other words, more white foreigners were moving to Tucson, but almost all of them came with a family. The ones who migrated alone intermarried at remarkably high percentages.

The reexamination of intermarriage rates also proves useful when analyzing ethnic enclaves. Just like specific geographic areas in 1930 Tucson indicated a correlation between demographic composition and the practice of intermarriage, applying the process of elimination increases the incidence of intermarriage for whites both in Mexican enclaves and in ethnically diverse areas. Although this was 1930, demographically speaking, the two large areas in question resembled the Tucson of decades earlier. What one might refer to as a newer version of the Tucson of the 1860s and 1870s involved the southwestern corner of the city. Mexicans in this quadrant accounted for 72 percent of all households, and whites for only 12 percent. Interethnic relationships there represented 37 percent of all marriages for people of white ancestry. As high as this intermarriage rate already seems, the elimination of Cohorts A, B, and C would raise it to 84 percent—and up to 91 percent with the elimination of Cohort D. One can only state for sure that a mere 9 percent of local marriageable whites definitely entered into endogamous marriages. Figures in the ethnically diverse area that included the entire downtown area are lower but still considerably high. Whites there outnumbered Mexicans by only 45 to 38 percent of households, and many blacks and Chinese resided there. Sixteen percent of married people of white ancestry were intermarried, but the number climbs to 74 percent after removing the cohorts that likely wed elsewhere. Only 26 percent of married whites undoubtedly married endogamously. These two large areas accounted for 44 percent of the city's population, and they functioned as the intermarriage hub in 1930, a role the entire town had played in the second half of the nineteenth century.

CONCLUSION

Until recently, historians have promoted the argument that white-Mexican marriages occurred primarily between prominent white men and the daughters of Mexican elites. A few marriages in Tucson did follow that pattern, but they were the exception and primarily occurred during the early years of territorial status. The high number of intermarriages—more than 100 in every decade, and approximately 1,800 between 1860 and 1930—indicate that intermarrying was never exclusively, or even significantly, a prerogative of elites only. Census data suggest that these relationships occurred as whites—and to a lesser extent, Asians and blacks—entered predominantly working-class Mexican spaces and interacted with Mexican residents. By 1930, the nature of intermarriage in Tucson had undergone various transformations, but several forms of continuity persisted. The changes were clear. There was a decline in the rate of intermarriage as a percentage of all marriages, not quite because the number of single white women increased, but primarily because entire white families started to arrive in higher numbers. Thus, into the twentieth century, a lower percentage of white men were married to Mexican women in Tucson because a higher percentage of them already had wives when they migrated. Those who migrated alone continued to intermarry in high percentages. The white man–Mexican woman intermarriage that prevailed during the second half of the nineteenth century had also given way to other types of interethnic unions. The men and women of white-Mexican ancestry accounted for most intermarriages after 1900, and Mexican men and white women also began to marry at higher, if relatively modest, rates.

The continuities coincided with the most significant change in the ethno-demography of Tucson—the development of white and Mexican enclaves. Although intermarriage for whites *appeared* to decline into 1930 as ethnic enclaves coalesced, it remained relatively consistent for people of Mexican ancestry, averaging 16 percent between 1860 and 1930. Its regularity is rather logical. Practically all Mexicans lived in Mexican or racially diverse areas, spaces where ethnic interaction and intermarriage always occurred at high rates. The most revealing continuity involves those areas where intermarriage remained frequent into the twentieth century, especially for certain groups. Ethnically speaking, whites who moved into these neighborhoods were in some way entering twentieth-century versions of old Tucson. These areas demographically and culturally resembled the Tucson of the 1860s and 1870s and likewise replicated the high levels of intermarriage of the early years. In other words, the ingredients that repeatedly facilitated ethnic interaction and intermarriage still predominated in some parts of the city. The analysis that eliminates specific cohorts of whites reveals that intermarriage remained high at least through 1930, particularly for foreign and working-class white men and especially in Mexican areas, at rates of 70 percent or higher. In this significant way, intermarriage had clearly not declined more than seven decades after the United States took possession of the Southwest. Mexican enclaves where intermarriage remained high after 1900 thus continued to serve as a central component of the western experience for migrating white men.

Whites, of course, lived throughout Tucson in large numbers. Blacks and Chinese, on the other hand, resided almost entirely in areas with high and extremely high percentages of Mexicans. Like westering men of the 1850s through the 1870s, black and Chinese cohorts into the 1920s suffered from considerably skewed sex ratios—more so, in fact. But whereas white men in Arizona could legally marry any of the few white women as well as any from the larger pool of Mexican women, black and Chinese men could not. Nonetheless, for blacks and Chinese, relationships with Mexicans—both formal and informal—were important components of their community formation in southern Arizona, as the next chapter explains.

4

"THE WOMAN IN QUESTION IS NOT A WHITE WOMAN, BUT A MEXICAN"

Relationships with Blacks and Chinese

MANUEL AHLOY AND ISABEL ESCALANTE traveled two hundred miles from Tucson, Arizona, to Silver City, New Mexico, in August 1891. They undoubtedly rode on the recently completed railroad line that connected towns from California to Texas along a southern route. Although the eight-hour train ride represented some inconvenience and expense—the roundtrip tickets alone cost the working-class partners nearly one hundred dollars—venturing by horse carriage, as travelers had done just a decade earlier, seemed almost prohibitive. That ten-day journey would also have incurred significant lodging costs and would have proved particularly strenuous in the midst of southern Arizona's summer temperatures, which typically surpass one hundred degrees Fahrenheit.[1] In the couple's view, however, the trip merited both cost and effort, for they were visiting Silver City to enter into marriage.[2] Manuel Ahloy was actually born Fô Loy in Hong Kong and could not legally marry Isabel in Arizona.[3]

This chapter locates the marriages of Mexicans with African Americans and Chinese within the history of racial attitudes in southern Arizona between 1860 and 1930. It argues that these intermarriages occurred primarily because blacks and Chinese entered the racially ambiguous space Mexicans occupied in the Southwest, an area characterized by both racist attitudes and racial fluidity. Frequently, time and location—more than legal restrictions, definitions, and categories—determined which interethnic unions could legally take place.

Some of these couples actually obtained marriage licenses in Arizona, while others traveled outside its borders to circumvent the miscegenation law (1865–1962). This study briefly addresses the manifestations of racism—such as laws, rhetoric, and violence—but underscores the relative forbearance with which these couples managed to form families. Their intermarriages demonstrate that individuals capably adapted to the legal, social, and cultural realities of the Southwest as they sought the benefits of family life and the protection and recognition of legal marriages. The chapter focuses on three subtopics: (1) the great difficulty black and Chinese men experienced in their pursuit of family life in the West; (2) the ability of interethnic couples to marry inside and outside Arizona; and (3) the racial fluidity surrounding the identity and classification of people of mixed racial ancestry.

The existence of these marriages indicates that miscegenation laws were strict yet porous. It also reinforces the argument that the construction of Mexicans as a racial group positioned them between whites and nonwhites. The proliferation of miscegenation laws in the second half of the nineteenth century stemmed from state and territorial efforts to codify white supremacy and to establish firm distinctions between whites and nonwhites. Accordingly, in the 1860s, western legislatures began to prohibit certain marriages. Yet, they never banned unions among nonwhites, for instance, between blacks and Chinese, because their marriages did not threaten white purity.[4] The racial in-betweenness of Mexicans thus proved important because their official classification as white in the nineteenth century coincided with their social construction as nonwhite.[5] In their position as an intermediate group, Mexican elites sought to establish their whiteness by separating themselves from blacks, Chinese, and Indians. But poor Mexicans frequently faced the same obstacles and ostracism as nonwhites and were not in a position to pursue social whiteness. Their racial ambiguity meant that some interethnic couples could escape the grip of miscegenation laws by convincing local officials that neither partner was white or by traveling to evade the law. Mexicans, several studies have demonstrated, were thus often able to marry nonwhites.[6] Their relationships with blacks and Chinese in Tucson followed a similar path.

Men like Fô Loy could hardly expect to marry when they immigrated to the United States after the mid-nineteenth century. In the early 1880s, he arrived in Tucson, where he met his future wife, Isabel, a recent immigrant from the neighboring Mexican state of Sonora.[7] Born only one generation after the United States obtained half of Mexico's territory in the U.S.-Mexico War

(1846–1848), the future spouses partook in the migratory wave that settled in the burgeoning American Southwest. As part of the Americanization process in the acquired lands, the new state and territorial governments swiftly imposed legal codes that reflected, among other things, American racial prejudices. In the case of Arizona, this transformation included an immediate ban on marriages of whites to blacks, Chinese, and American Indians. The couple thus decided to make the long and expensive visit to Silver City to evade the law.

THE PROSPECT OF PERMANENT BACHELORHOOD

Intermarriage in the Tucson area was particularly important for black and Chinese men because economic conditions, cultural biases, legal barriers, and imbalanced sex ratios largely limited their marriage prospects in the West before the early twentieth century—even longer for Chinese men.[8] Discrimination and abuse against black and Chinese residents pervaded the region. Most notoriously, Chinese residents lived under constant harassment and vilification by the dominant white population in major towns in California and in nearly every mining town in the West. Verbal attacks ranged from claims that they refused to Americanize to allegations of dealing drugs, spreading disease, and practicing polygamy, but physical violence typically erupted only in small work camps, such as those in Idaho, Oregon, Washington, and Wyoming.[9] Blacks, meanwhile, did not fare much better in the West. Both groups experienced malicious newspaper campaigns and labor segmentation and exclusion. But whereas the worst of anti-Chinese expressions came in violent episodes, blacks suffered systematic discrimination and segregation that often resembled the patterns of the South. Several states and territories specifically targeted blacks in law and practice to deny them equal access to voting, schools, residential areas, and, of course, marriage. Not even African American buffalo soldiers managed to escape this type of treatment.[10]

Chinese immigrants also endured violent treatment in northern Mexico, where they arrived in significant numbers primarily after the United States restricted their immigration in 1882.[11] They experienced increasing physical attacks, including the massacre of more than three hundred Chinese residents in Torreón, Coahuila, in 1911. In Sonora, the state that has historically sent the highest percentage of Mexican immigrants to Arizona, local populations accused Chinese men of taking their jobs and their women, 166 of whom had married Chinese men. In 1923 the Sonora legislature unanimously approved a law to forbid marriages between Chinese men and Mexican women, and in 1931 the state enacted a law to deport Chinese immigrants altogether.[12]

Arizona exhibited the vitriol of California, the violence of the mining towns, and the hostility of northern Mexico, but it proved to be better than those places. Chinese men had to deal with local covenants that restricted mining sites to whites only, and in some towns, they faced de facto anti-Chinese leagues and were forbidden residence in certain neighborhoods.[13] They endured constant negative press throughout Arizona, although actual violence took place primarily in the mining areas of Clifton, Flagstaff, Prescott, and Tombstone, among others. They fared better than in other states, but at least fifteen Chinese men died in such episodes.[14] Likewise, the treatment blacks received in Arizona highly depended on where they resided. The territory enacted discriminatory and segregationist laws from its creation, but mining camps and the Phoenix area displayed more antagonism than did other towns. These places generally adopted residential, labor, and school segregation sooner and longer than other towns. Conditions deteriorated as the African American population of Arizona increased from 155 in 1880 to 1,848 in 1900, and to 8,005 by 1920.[15]

In addition to the antagonism black and Chinese residents encountered—and as a manifestation of it—Arizona's miscegenation law greatly limited their ability to form families. As explained in chapter 1, the newly formed Arizona Territory wasted no time in encoding racial barriers. The First Arizona Territorial Legislature (1864) approved a ban on "marriages of white persons with negroes or mulattoes." The very next year, the territory added Indians and Chinese to the list of people who could not marry whites.[16] The law recognized marriages that took place legally in other states or territories—including interracial marriages—regardless of their legality in Arizona. Although in 1901 the legislature made it illegal to leave the territory purposely to circumvent the law, Arizona couples could still, in theory, secretly visit another state or country, marry, return to Arizona, and enjoy the legal protections of valid marriages.[17]

Racial segregation and the presence of minority groups usually correlated with the enactment of bans on interracial marriage, yet the Arizona law and its amendments anticipated, rather than responded to, such circumstances.[18] The census indicated that no Chinese resided in Arizona in 1860, and that only twenty had moved in by 1870. In fact, Arizona's Chinese population never exceeded 1,700 between 1870 and 1930, when it had decreased to 1,110.[19] The

African American population was similarly miniscule at the time the law was adopted. Merely twenty-one blacks lived in Arizona in 1860, and twenty-six a decade later.[20] Arizona lawmakers were most likely codifying attitudes they had learned in or from other locations.

But the Arizona legislature went even further in 1887 when it amended the statute to prohibit marriages of "persons of Caucasian blood *or their descendants* with Africans, Mongolians *and their descendants*."[21] The new law greatly curtailed intermarriage options by forbidding people with any trace of black, Chinese, or Indian ancestry from marrying people with any percentage of white ancestry—anticipating the one-drop laws that would appear in other parts of the United States in the early twentieth century. Thus, if one went with a racial definition of Mexican—rather than with their legal whiteness—mestizos would find it difficult to marry. As partially white, they could not marry non-whites, and of course, as partially Indian, they could not marry whites. Ridiculously, a strict enforcement of the law would mean that multiracial people could effectively marry no one, not even another multiracial partner—an unintended effect of legislation that only sought to restrict marriages to whites. In sum, as early as 1865, Arizona had adopted a miscegenation law that exceeded those of most western governments, and by 1887, it had surpassed most legislatures in the country by encoding strict racial prerequisites.

In addition to having to negotiate miscegenation laws and racist attitudes in the West, black and Chinese men faced considerably limited prospects of a married life in Arizona because of the highly disproportionate sex ratios that plagued their communities. Two factors combined to produce a high probability that black and Chinese men would find it difficult to form families. First, the great majority had migrated either as married men traveling alone or, more frequently, as single men. Second, relatively few black and Chinese women moved into the Southwest before the turn of the twentieth century, and in the case of Chinese women, before the 1940s. Indeed, the situation looked especially troubling for Chinese men. Nationally, they outnumbered Chinese women by a ratio of 21 to 1 in 1880, and by a still high 4 to 1 in 1930. They fared even worse in Arizona, where the ratio was 52 to 1 in 1880, 20 to 1 in 1910, and a significantly better yet unbalanced 3 to 1 in 1930.[22] In Tucson, only one unmarried Chinese woman sixteen years of age or older resided from 1860 to 1910, and between 1880 and 1930, single Chinese men always outnumbered their female counterparts by a ratio of at least 10 to 1 (see table 5). Black men, meanwhile, faced a better situation but still suffered from skewed sex ratios. The presence

TABLE 5. Unmarried black and Chinese residents sixteen years of age or older, Tucson, 1880–1930

YEAR	BLACK MEN	BLACK WOMEN	CHINESE MEN	CHINESE WOMEN
1880	3	0	98	1
1900	24	4	54	0
1910	18	10	116	0
1920	39	16	64	6
1930	124	60	71	7

SOURCE Derived from a database created by the author based on census schedules.

of soldiers temporarily distorted the calculations, but blacks in Arizona only approached a balanced population by the early twentieth century. In Tucson, however, black men outnumbered potential black female partners by approximately 2 to 1 into 1930.

A close look at census data reveals that these unbalanced ratios took a particularly heavy toll on the domestic lives of Chinese men. A great majority of those who migrated to Tucson between 1870 and 1930 faced the high probability of living in long or even permanent bachelorhood. For instance, whether single or as absentee husbands (married but living apart), Chinese men who settled in Tucson consistently migrated to the United States when they were approximately twenty years old. Focusing solely on older residents leads to a dramatic conclusion. Absentee husbands had lived away from their wives and families for approximately thirty years—although men with financial resources probably made trips to China (see table 6). The typical single man over forty years of age, on the other hand, became progressively older, and his length of residence increased every decade. In 1900 the average bachelor of that cohort was forty-seven years old and had lived in the country for twenty-five years. By 1930, these long-time bachelors were on average fifty-eight years of age and had resided in the United States for an extraordinary forty-three years. Evidently, large numbers of Chinese men never managed to marry in the United States or to make marriage trips to China. Although male relatives formed strong bonds, and single men often joined adopted families, sadly, these men had arrived as

TABLE 6. Chinese men forty years of age and older, by marital status, Tucson, 1880–1930

YEAR	MARRIED LIVING APART			SINGLE		
	TOTAL	AVERAGE AGE IN YEARS	AVERAGE YEARS SINCE MIGRATION	TOTAL	AVERAGE AGE IN YEARS	AVERAGE YEARS SINCE MIGRATION
1880	4	50.5	No data	9	44.3	No data
1900	54	47.9	28.4	34	46.9	25.4
1910	38	48.9	27.1	90	50.9	29.5
1920	63	54.0	33.2	33	54.7	35.8
1930	17	50.6	28.5	32	57.5	43.3

SOURCE Derived from a database created by the author based on census schedules.

young laborers, spent more than two-thirds of their lives in the American West, and faced the tangible possibility of dying as old bachelors, a sentence further complicated by racist attitudes in the region.[23]

"DESCENDANTS OF INDIANS AND MOORS": BEATING THE ODDS IN THE ARIZONA BORDERLANDS

Racist attitudes in the American West and in northern Mexico, a strictly worded miscegenation law that preceded the arrival of most Chinese and blacks to Arizona, and extremely skewed sex ratios in their communities all combined to create almost insurmountable odds against the formation of families. Therefore, the number of relationships these men formed with Mexican women, although comparatively small relative to their total populations, proved to be even more significant. The fate of men who never married—and locally only two black men and one Chinese man formed relationships with white women—attests to the importance of these relationships. The abusive treatment blacks and Chinese faced in the West would suggest that Tucson, with the presence of whites and a large percentage of Mexican immigrants from Sonora, might portend difficulties. Such was not the case. Several circumstances combined to facilitate better interaction in Tucson, especially in Mexican enclaves.

Examples of ethnic antagonism clearly illustrate how Arizona resembled other parts of the West, but significant factors demonstrate conditions that fostered forbearance in Tucson. Two dichotomies help explain the fluidity of race and the variability of race relations in the seemingly intolerant territory. First, as chapter 2 explains, there were effectively two Arizonas, one where whites predominated over other groups and controlled political and economic power and another one where they did not. Second, there were two kinds of whiteness in Arizona, social and legal (Anglos possessed both and Mexicans only the latter, if inconsistently). Consequently, blacks and Chinese—and Mexicans, for that matter—encountered hostility more in central and northern Arizona and in mining towns than in Tucson, and in cases of interethnic relationships, black and Chinese men experienced contempt only when they pursued relationships with white women. Thus, local whites functioned as enforcers of racial divisions even when the miscegenation law failed to serve its purpose.

Most likely because of their relatively low numbers, Tucson's black and Chinese residents did not encounter the type of harassment they faced in other regions and in Arizona mining towns, although their local experiences were far from idyllic. Tucson officials often linked prostitution to the Chinese community and excessively targeted the few opium dens in town, but no violent anti-Chinese campaigns occurred in the city. Furthermore, the city never had to deal with the creation of Chinese brothels—a source of great antagonism from the white population in San Francisco. Most Chinese resided within a small radius that lay within the larger Mexican enclave, and one can barely describe the area as a Chinatown (see figure 8). It did, however, offer comfort and security: most local Chinese had migrated from the same province, and they could peacefully gather and perform their cultural rituals. Verbal attacks did exist, but the efforts to segregate Chinese businesses did not receive enough support in Tucson to take effect by law or custom. In 1893 the Tucson City Council rejected a proposal to restrict Chinese settlement to certain areas, thus granting them the freedom to escape the types of enclaves that existed in other Arizona towns, for instance, in Phoenix, Prescott, and nearby Tombstone.[24] The situation was worse for blacks. As in other towns in Arizona and throughout the West, they faced segregation in Tucson. Initially churches and recreational places separated them from whites or excluded them altogether. As opposed to other areas, however, school segregation in Tucson arrived late and ended immediately after the *Brown* Supreme Court decisions in 1954 and 1955.[25] Furthermore, although the local Spanish-language newspaper occasionally expressed contempt toward Chinese merchants' purportedly unfair tactics, the black and Chinese labor forces never became large enough to represent threats to Mexican and low-skill white workers.[26]

In Tucson, black and Chinese residents lived in predominantly Mexican enclaves.[27] In a way, a combination of race and class served as a segregating factor for the entire sector and precluded the need for residential ordinances. Evidence suggests that, in general, blacks and Chinese interacted peacefully with other groups. They often catered to the white and Mexican communities as grocers, launderers, barbers, and laborers and learned Spanish and/or English. The very few black and Chinese who lived in white neighborhoods worked as either cooks or servants. Their presence therefore did not threaten or undermine the class and racial status of whites in those areas. Editorial attacks occurred occasionally in town, but papers from central and northern Arizona and from mining towns expressed far more hostility and did so more frequently than their Tucson counterparts.[28]

The story of Samuel Bostick illustrates how the special circumstances of the borderlands allowed a former slave from the Deep South the opportunity to form a household in the Southwest. In 1854 President Franklin Pierce

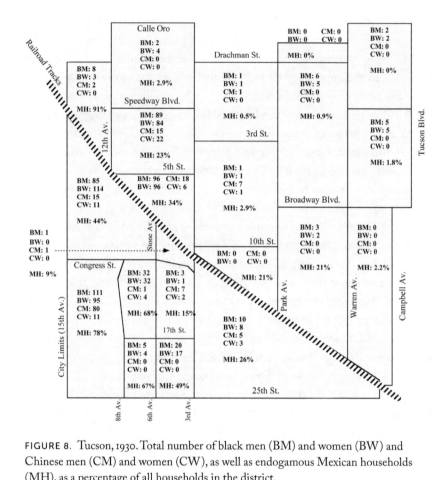

FIGURE 8. Tucson, 1930. Total number of black men (BM) and women (BW) and Chinese men (CM) and women (CW), as well as endogamous Mexican households (MH), as a percentage of all households in the district.

appointed Rush Elmore, a lawyer from Alabama and a veteran of the U.S.-Mexico War, to the supreme court of the Kansas Territory. During his first two years in office, Elmore found himself in political turmoil and experiencing economic difficulties, and he allowed one of his fourteen slaves to purchase his freedom. That decision would affect the lives of a twenty-three-year-old slave, a then-three-year-old girl from Sonora, and several generations of southern Arizonans who into the twenty-first century still combine the English surname of their slave ancestor with Hispanic first names.[29]

Samuel Bostick was born in 1833 on the plantation of the Elmore family.[30] Thanks to the entrepreneurial abilities that would characterize his eventual life in Tucson, Bostick managed to accumulate enough money to obtain his manumission from Elmore in 1856. He found his way to Tucson in the late 1860s and soon became the proprietor of a barbershop. Bostick's business prospered, but his race eventually became the focus of an editorial exchange between Tucson's competing newspapers. In the midst of Reconstruction politics in 1870, Bostick and other business owners removed their advertisements from the *Weekly Arizonan* after it endorsed Democratic candidates. Pierton W. Dooner, the editor of the paper, responded by defaming his former clients, including Bostick. He wrote long, vitriolic depictions of J. E. McCaffry, asserting that his respect did not "amount to a row of beans," and of Esteban Ochoa, whom he characterized as a "goose of a man." Dooner, however, did not deem Bostick worthy of an elaborate characterization. He limited his attack to a succinct, racially charged sentence: "Sam Bostick is a barber of 'African persuasion.'" In his view, Bostick's race sufficed to condemn him. The editor of the Republican-leaning *Tucson Citizen* soon responded to these comments. He stated that Bostick possessed "good, manly traits" that Dooner could never match. Yet he also ascribed negative qualities to Bostick's race, although not to the barber himself: "Sam," he wrote, "is a well behaved, trustworthy citizen, albeit he is dark skinned." Thus, while Bostick's foe attributed implied flaws to the barber's race, his defender suggested that he was a person of good character *in spite of* being black.[31]

Bostick's defender, while not enlightened, did underscore the barber's position in the community, which was due in part to his wife. Bostick had married Albina Barraza in 1869, and the couple would have at least nine children between 1870 and 1890, some of whom also became barbers.[32] Samuel and Albina enjoyed a good reputation within the town's economic establishment. The couple frequently purchased basic and luxury goods on credit, bought and sold city lots, claimed land, and received loans from prominent white men who had also married Mexican women. They clearly enjoyed personal and commercial interactions with whites and Mexicans, and Samuel even ran for the position of public administrator in 1870.[33] The family moved to Florence, Arizona, in 1877, where he once again opened a barbershop. They left on good terms, however, maintaining property in Tucson until 1880.[34] Thus, even with the underlying racism that surrounded the Bosticks, their relationship and their family seem to have enjoyed an otherwise peaceful and gainful experience in town.

Tucson differed in another important way from areas that antagonized black and Chinese residents. Intermarriage of various forms characterized the multiethnic space they entered in southern Arizona in the latter half of the nineteenth century. These interethnic unions became commonplace in Tucson immediately after its acquisition by the United States in 1854. As discussed in chapter 3, the town's first U.S. census (1860) revealed that, in addition to the preponderant endogamous Mexican families, the few white men who resided in town were twice as likely to live with Mexican women as they were to live with white women. These white-Mexican intermarriages continued to increase in total numbers for the next seventy years. Tucson society therefore lacked the clear separation between whites and nonwhites that existed in the South and in most of the West. As blacks and Chinese arrived, they actively participated in the continuance of this pluralistic and multiracial community.

Decennial census schedules reveal the existence of several black-Mexican and Chinese-Mexican couples between 1860 and 1930. They begin to appear soon after American annexation in 1854. The first American survey of 1860 indicated that Charles Cooper, a black laborer from Delaware, lived with Inés Bernal, born in Mexico. Although the census does not indicate if they were married, they still fell under the purview of the miscegenation law of New Mexico because the still-intact territory (until 1863) forbade both marriage and cohabitation between blacks and whites.[35] Overall, eight unique black-Mexican unions appear on the census between 1860 and 1930. Chinese-Mexican couples, meanwhile, first show up in census records in 1900, when Charles Lee and Manuel Ahloy were listed as married to Mercedes Gálvez and Isabel Escalante, respectively. Five more Chinese-Mexican couples would appear over the next three census canvasses. Nonetheless, census schedules offer only a partial account of the practice of intermarriage among these groups. After all, some people might have lived in town for several years only to depart without leaving a local census record.[36]

Although census enumerators often failed to indicate if a couple was married, civil records reveal that these partners had some success in marrying legally in Arizona despite the standing miscegenation law. Officially sanctioned Chinese-Mexican unions are significantly difficult to find. Only Jew Lee and Francisca Valdez, who married in 1910, and Dong Yet and Rosario Ramírez, who wed in 1924, obtained licenses and married legally in the Tucson area. The earliest black-Mexican marriage in Tucson, meanwhile, occurred only four years after the territorial miscegenation law went into effect. As noted previously, Samuel Bostick married Albina Barraza in 1869. The couple remained in Tucson for the next five years. In 1872 Emmett Woodley, a former buffalo soldier from Virginia, and Leonicia Terrazas also obtained a legitimate marriage in Tucson. Four years later, Peter Thomas married Refugio Suárez, and in

1893 Luke Harrison, from Texas, married Juana Darío. Finally, in 1917, Henry Ransom, from Arkansas, and Guadalupe Ramírez obtained a marriage license, although it appears they never filed it. They were trying to legitimize their long relationship. In 1900 they informed the census enumerator that they had married in 1894, but there is no record of a civil or religious marriage. It is unclear why they might not have completed the marriage process. County clerks ultimately decided who merited access to the institution of marriage, and couples could not bypass them, but the Ransoms had already overcome that obstacle. At that point, they needed only a justice of the peace or a religious officiant to perform the ceremony. Whatever their legal marital status, they remained together for another twelve years (thirty-three total), until her death in 1929.[37]

The Bosticks and the Woodleys complemented their civil marriages by celebrating religious weddings. The Bosticks wed at Saint Augustine Catholic Church six months after their civil ceremony had taken place. The priest, addressing his primary concern, recorded the fact that the couple practiced different religions but made no reference to Samuel's race. The county clerk had written "colored" after Samuel's name, perhaps to conform to the practices of civil record keepers or as an ineffective effort to absolve himself of any legal ramifications.[38] The priest, nonetheless, most likely understood the legal implications of the territorial miscegenation law. He wrote "casados por lo civil" (married in the civil, i.e., legal, way) on the registry, an annotation he did not make for other marriages. In other words, the priest underscored that his ceremony held only religious significance and, thus, that it did not constitute a violation of the law. After all, the priest also expressed ambivalence when he married Emmett Woodley and Leonicia Terrazas three years later. As with the Bosticks, he noted the difference in religions, but with Emmett, the priest actually wrote "colored man" next to his name. He even wrote it in English, whereas he almost always used Spanish or Latin in such documents. It is unclear why he would take such a step to record his own violation of the law. Perhaps he sought to follow the lead of the county official who granted the marriage license. These annotations notwithstanding, both the county clerk and the priest broke the law by solemnizing these marriages. The potential punishment for officials and spouses included prison sentences of up to ten years and fines of up to ten thousand dollars.[39]

The priest broke no law when he married You Cang, from China, and Esperanza Fraijó, from Sonora. The couple wed at Saint Augustine's in 1896, but the priest indicated that the couple had already obtained a civil marriage in

Lordsburg, New Mexico—the nearest New Mexico town connected to Tucson by rail. Thus, his ceremony held only religious, not legal, implications. The priest probably did not know that the legislature had recently repealed the punishment for solemnizing such ceremonies. By the late nineteenth century, however, racial cataloging certainly formed part of the marriage process, even for the Church. Although a justice of the peace had already married Cang and Fraijó in New Mexico, the Tucson wedding was not superfluous. Esperanza had already given birth to the couple's first child two months before their trip to Lordsburg, and the religious ceremony legitimized the relationship in the eyes of the Church and the community.[40]

Like the Cang-Fraijó wedding indicates, these couples acted with persistence in their efforts to form families. For example, a divorce record suggests that some Chinese-Mexican couples were indeed marrying elsewhere even if living in southern Arizona. Such was the case of Lee Kow and Mercedes Chávez, whose divorce in 1920 is the only legal separation of a Chinese-Mexican couple in Tucson between 1860 and 1930—and records indicate that no black-Mexican couples divorced during this period. They stated that their marriage had taken place in 1916, but no license or certificate of it exists in Pima County.[41] Residents moved in and out of the area, and census canvasses could only record them if their time of residency coincided with the decennial enumeration. Some couples might have married in Mexico or New Mexico, returned to Tucson, and moved away, all between census counts. Others might have married outside Arizona before settling in Tucson, making their unions perfectly legal but leaving no traces of a marriage license locally. Thus, the dissolution of the Kow-Chávez union indicates that their marriage definitely took place, but one can only offer conjectures on where and, more important, on how many other couples' situations resembled theirs.

The travails of Wong Qui Cio and Pascuala Nava in the American Northwest offer insight into the high mobility of some couples and their experiences in pursuit of legal marriages. The couple met during Wong's twenty years of residence in Mexico, where he became fluent in Spanish. He pursued a romantic relationship with Pascuala after her first husband died. She and Wong soon migrated to the United States. In early October 1916, the clerk in Spokane County, Washington, began receiving telegrams from Helena, Montana. In his first message Wong asked whether Washington state law would allow the marriage of a Chinese man to a white woman. The state had long ago repealed its miscegenation law (1855–1868), which had only banned black-white marriage, so the clerk replied that Chinese-white marriages could indeed take place. Undoubtedly aware of local racial attitudes, however, the clerk accordingly warned that "it would be difficult to get a license here, or to get any one to marry them." The persistent Wong immediately replied and succinctly explained: "[T]he woman in question is not a white woman, but a Mexican." This clarification perplexed the clerk, and he decided to consult the local prosecutor. Wong and Pascuala received an affirmative reply and made the three-hundred-mile journey from Helena over the weekend. They easily obtained a marriage license and married at the Spokane courthouse. Two Chinese friends accompanied them and served as witnesses. The entire process—inquiry, biased rejection, clarification, bewilderment, counsel, assent, train ride, obtaining a license, and marriage ceremony—took Wong and Pascuala merely five days and a long, expensive trip.[42]

The newspaper account left important facts unexplained, but one can safely reach several conclusions. The resourceful Wong, who had also mastered speaking and writing in English, had already exhausted all efforts to marry in Montana, including making the argument that Pascuala did not meet the legal definition of whiteness. The couple undoubtedly considered and inquired about marrying in Idaho and Wyoming, both of which lay closer to Helena but also forbade Chinese-white marriages at various points. The couple most likely relied on ethnic and legal networks to ascertain if the prohibition on Chinese-white marriages existed in Washington. But three racialist preconceptions clearly stand out from the telegraphic exchange. First, initially the Spokane clerk effectively denied a license for a Chinese-white marriage that his state had never banned. His explanation of the unlikelihood that anyone would marry such a couple reveals much about local racist apprehensions, definitely his. Second, he most likely had not seen many Mexicans, but his indecision indicates that he did not assume they were white. Third, somewhere between their departure from Mexico and Wong's clarification that Pascuala was not white, the couple had learned that she lacked social whiteness in the United States. Yet, the fact that they could not marry in Montana clearly indicates that she also legally qualified as white, where Helena officials apparently adhered to strict interpretations of whiteness. Her racial in-betweenness therefore hurt her in Helena but not in Spokane. The experiences of Wong and Pascuala illustrate how black-Mexican and Chinese-Mexican couples in Arizona could have discovered that they might sometimes benefit from local racial ambiguities. When they could not, they, too, like Wong and Pascuala, crossed into the nearest jurisdiction that would allow them to marry.[43]

One such situation occurred in Tucson, where residents undoubtedly knew that marriages were taking place outside Arizona. In spite of the names, the case almost certainly refers to the marriages of Manuel Ahloy to Isabel Escalante and Jim Lee to Concepción Moreno. In 1891 the *Tucson Citizen* reported that Lang Kim and Ah Loy requested marriage licenses to marry Mexican sisters with the surname Moreno and, when rejected, maintained that the women were not Caucasian but "descendants of Indians and Moors."[44] The probate judge dismissed the argument by explaining that Mexicans were Caucasians. The headline, "Mongolian Love Laughs at the Barriers of the Law," aptly captured how the couples circumvented the law: they traveled to Silver City, New Mexico, married there, and returned to Tucson, where, as the *Los Angeles Times* reported later, they "lived happily ever afterwards."[45] Although Mexico was more than one hundred miles closer, it appears that New Mexico became the preferred destination for both Chinese and blacks. Perhaps couples ascribed more validity to an American than to a Mexican marriage certificate, even though Arizona law recognized domestic and international marriages equally. Resistance to Chinese-Mexican marriage in northern Mexican towns might have also dissuaded some couples. Chinese-Mexican couples, however, decided on New Mexico for a simple reason: the 1882 Chinese Exclusion Act made return trips from Mexico highly problematic. Although no additional details exist about the legal travails of these two Tucson couples, the experiences of Fong Ling and Teresa Morales in Phoenix provide insight into the type of situation they faced.

Fong intended to marry Teresa in 1912. Wedding plans ran into trouble, however, when the sixteen-year-old Teresa absconded, and a friend informed the police that "an attempt was being made to marry a white girl to a Chinaman against her will." Local authorities immediately prohibited the union on two grounds: the apparent unwillingness of the girl and the ban on interracial marriage. Teresa, they stated, fell "within the definition of the term 'Caucasian.'" The *Arizona Republican* even claimed that she had a white father and a mother of Spanish descent—both were actually Mexican, according to census records. The couple had already obtained a license because the girl's mother had signed a parental consent for the minor, and Fong's lawyer had argued that Teresa was in fact ethnologically "mongoloid." A confused clerk, unsure of what the term meant, issued the license because he thought it meant "mugwump" (mixed). Although Fong explained that Teresa had actually approached him with the idea of marriage, the legal complications convinced him to call off the wedding. Authorities clearly concentrated on both age and race, but the conspicuous headline accentuated only the latter: "Cupid Loses Bout with Eth Nology [*sic*]." Fong certainly grasped the focus on race, for he and Teresa married in Lordsburg, New Mexico, three years later. Teresa was by then of legal age but still as racially different as before, an obvious motivation to travel more than 240 miles to obtain a marriage license.[46]

In all likelihood, accounts of successful wedding trips to New Mexico influenced the decisions to employ that tactic. Indeed, New Mexico legal records reveal the frequency of the practice and the existence of networks among interethnic couples. One can safely assume that this recourse formed part of the conversation among interethnic couples that could not legally marry in Arizona, as dozens of couples made visits to New Mexico in the ensuing years. A couple could offer both moral support and valuable information to prospective spouses. For example, in 1920 Manuel Samaniego and María Lee—daughter of a Chinese-Mexican couple—traveled from Tucson to Lordsburg. The children of Chinese-Mexican couples do not seem to have encountered major problems in securing legal marriages in Arizona, but Manuel and María must have deemed it necessary. Their wedding proceeded smoothly, and they evidently informed María's sister of their success, for one year later, Isaura Lee and Harry Williams Nelson also found their way to Lordsburg. A certain apprehension might have prompted Isaura and Harry to opt for New Mexico. She had previously married a Chinese man legally in Arizona, and although the law forbade divorced residents from remarrying within one year of the dissolution, her first husband, Tong Yee, had actually died in 1919. Perhaps she feared that even though local officials allowed her to marry a Chinese partner, a marriage to a white man was a different matter. She might have been unaware that both marriages were equally illegal in Arizona, but the marriage to Harry must have seemed like more of a violation, so the couple opted for New Mexico.[47]

Black men also used the recourse of traveling to New Mexico. In 1895 a black man and a Mexican woman applied for a marriage license in Tucson but had to travel to New Mexico after a judge refused their request.[48] Another black-Mexican couple from Tucson made the trip in 1929, when two similar couples from nearby Nogales also made the long journey to Lordsburg.[49] It appears that couples could simply return to Arizona and live unperturbed. The acquiescence of local communities, however, does not necessarily prove that they condoned the marriages of blacks and Chinese to whites—which Mexicans technically were—but demonstrates, rather, that Mexicans epitomized a racial ambiguity that facilitated the occurrence of these marriages. As far as southern Arizonans were concerned, these ethnic groups were racially compatible.

Couples could also exchange information with friends. For example, the aforementioned Ahloys made their wedding journey in 1891 in the company of Jim Lee and Concepción Moreno, another Chinese-Mexican couple from Tucson, all in pursuit of legal marriages. The four friends had most likely discussed and planned their trip together, for they married on the same day and served as witnesses to the others' ceremony.[50] Similarly, Charles Lee and Concepción Chávez married in Lordsburg in early 1898. Four months later, and certainly after sharing information about the opportunity to obtain a legal marriage across the territorial line, they accompanied and served as witnesses to Hi Wo and Emeteria Moreno when they, too, made a marriage trip to Lordsburg. In all likelihood, lying to the local authorities formed part of the advice, for both couples falsely claimed local residency.[51] Their deception reveals a real but unnecessary apprehension. Until the legislature closed the loophole in 1901, Arizona law allowed extra-territorial marriages regardless of where the couple resided at the time of the ceremony.

For the most part, however, these brides and grooms openly declared that they lived in Arizona.[52] Evidence indicates that Arizona couples deliberately visited New Mexico as a strategy to escape the purview of the miscegenation law. In total, at least thirty-two interethnic couples from various racial groups made such wedding trips between 1891 and 1929. Most of them came from Tucson or from places located closer to it than to any New Mexico town, but some traveled from as far as Phoenix. Only seven couples made the journey before 1910, but the numbers increased in the 1910s and 1920s, as the combined Chinese and black populations, although still small, grew considerably. Although traveling convenience meant that endogamous couples from Arizona towns bordering New Mexico frequently crossed into Silver City and Lordsburg to marry, the interethnic couples in question made trips that ranged from 110 to 270 miles, clearly inconvenient distances and expenses to cover if they could otherwise marry locally. The ethnic backgrounds of these couples leave little doubt regarding their intent to circumvent Arizona statutes: thirty of the thirty-two couples involved Asian or black men, and they primarily married Mexican women.[53] They all knew—or, at least, feared—that they could not marry legally in Arizona.

FIGURE 9. Hi Wo (back), and from left to right, Felicia Wo, Soledad Wo, Emeteria Moreno-Wo, and José Wo (c. 1900). Felicia and José were Hi Wo's children from his marriage to Loreto Moreno, Emeteria's sister. Loreto had died by 1898, when Hi and Emeteria traveled to Silver City, New Mexico, to marry, circumventing Arizona's miscegenation law. Arizona Historical Society/Tucson, AHS File MS1242F73_AI.

Class partially explains why some Chinese-Mexican and black-Mexican couples made marriage trips to New Mexico but others did not. Including all couples, regardless of whether or where they married, these men and women had arrived in the area recently. Chinese immigrants frequently resided in several parts of the West before settling in southern Arizona, and African Americans primarily came from the South. Nearly all the Mexican women they married had relocated from northern Mexico. Census takers almost never listed occupations for women, but of their partners, Chinese men were usually involved in commerce, and African Americans in the service industry. The men in these marriages were, on average, older than their wives, but age differentials were similar among those who traveled to New Mexico and those who did not. Yet, age, especially when combined with the specific jobs men held, does indicate how class might have influenced the decision to make wedding trips.

In the case of Chinese-Mexican couples, the men were older than their partners by an average of nineteen years in traveling couples and twenty in the rest. Yet, while men in nontraveling couples averaged thirty-nine years of age and women nineteen, the numbers increase to forty-three years for men and twenty-four years for women in couples that traveled. The data suggest that the difference proved meaningful. For instance, the decisions of women who eventually married in New Mexico were grounded not only in more maturity, but perhaps also on previous relationships. They could better assess the qualities they valued in a partner, the most important of which probably involved financial stability. To start, the cost of the trip, at more than one hundred dollars, made the journey more unlikely for laborers, who, even if employed the entire year, might barely earn enough for the train tickets. And indeed, the occupations of men who traveled to New Mexico indicate that they had achieved some financial stability. The available data—for sixteen couples only—reveal that although only five of nine owned their home, eight either owned or managed a business, and the only one employed as a laborer had previously co-owned a restaurant. In comparison, only one of the six men who did not make the trip managed a business, while the rest worked in lower positions and lived as renters.

The records do not indicate the social class of the Mexican women before marriage, but the relatively older age of the traveling brides suggests that they had access to enough resources to be independent—for instance, through their labor—or that their families could afford to support them. Furthermore, it seems reasonable that established Chinese men would take the financial situation of potential brides into account. A final connection between class and wedding trips to New Mexico involves economic pragmatism. A legal marriage conveyed rights and privileges to both spouses and to their children, such as inheritance and financial support in case of separation. Legal marriage also conferred legitimacy on the children, a significant step for both legal and sociocultural reasons. Arizona recognized all these New Mexico marriages before 1901, and even after that year, a union received validation unless courts could establish that the couple intentionally circumvented the law. Consequently, couples with assets to safeguard had additional motivation to acquire the legal protections that a formal marriage could bestow. Although economic concerns did not significantly influence the decisions of Mexican women to enter into relationships with Chinese men, financial resources definitely determined who decided to travel to New Mexico to pursue a legal marriage.

The circumstances of wedding trips by black-Mexican couples differ in important ways from those of their Chinese-Mexican counterparts. Black-Mexican couples apparently encountered fewer difficulties in obtaining marriage licenses in Arizona. Six of the fifteen couples married locally, and another five traveled to New Mexico. The other four couples might have remained unmarried—because unions banned by the miscegenation law did not convert into common-law marriages—or perhaps these couples married in Mexico. Maybe officials viewed Mexicans as more racially approximate to African Americans than to Chinese. After all, as chapter 2 explains, the discourse of manifest destiny often compared Mexicans to blacks and mulattoes. These African American men had not achieved substantial upward mobility, but neither were they poor. Half of them owned their homes and were an average of ten years older than their Mexican wives, very similar to the age differentials for white-Mexican couples. Occupation and time may partially explain the wedding trips of these couples. Three of the men were teamsters, three soldiers, three barbers, two cooks, and only two worked as low-skill laborers. Three of the five men who traveled to New Mexico with their future wives were stationed at nearby army posts in Nogales and Douglas in the 1920s. As soldiers, these men could count on steady incomes to finance the trip but had yet to establish the local roots and networks that perhaps gained other African Americans favorable treatment from court clerks and thus the ability to obtain marriage licenses locally. Finally, although they did not encounter as many potential obstacles returning to the United States as Chinese-Mexican couples did, they still decided not to marry in Mexico, perhaps aware of the stricter immigration enforcement of the late 1920s.

Economic concerns also seem to explain the only intermarriage involving a Chinese woman. Chinese women entered into interethnic relationships extremely rarely, even with the descendants of mixed families. Records reveal only one marriage between a Mexican man and a Chinese woman. In 1920 John Low, a Chinese storeowner in downtown Tucson, expended considerable resources looking for his missing daughter, Yoke Shem Low. Searches in Tucson, nearby towns, immigration facilities, and even in Kansas City—where they found the body of a Chinese girl—produced no results. Two weeks later, the parents located the eighteen-year-old in Los Angeles. The father's anguish, however, only turned into anger when he learned that his daughter had in fact eloped and married a young Mexican. John Low refused to comment publicly, but friends explained that the daughter had acted against Chinese tradition by marrying a "foreign devil."[54] (See note 54 for an explanation of two purported Mexican man–Chinese woman unions that actually did not occur.)

Marriages with black women were just as rare. As discussed in chapter 1, Joe Kirby, of white-Mexican descent, married Mayellen Conner in 1914. In another case, Miguel Bostick, the son of Samuel Bostick and Albina Barraza, was the only descendant of a black-Mexican couple to form a union with a non-Mexican. In 1920 he lived with Gertrude Bostick, a black woman from Texas. They obviously viewed their relationship as a formal arrangement since they declared they were married, and she took his surname. No record of a license exists, however, and the couple had separated by 1930. By that year, Miguel, too, had formed a relationship with a Mexican woman.[55]

The local Chinese and black populations could ill afford to lose any women to exogamous marriages. At such a young age, Yoke Shem was one of only six unmarried Chinese women in Tucson. This marriage therefore might have cost her merchant father an opportunity to cement connections with other Chinese businessmen. The African American population was not as skewed, but few single black women lived in town. Black residents certainly reacted with less apprehension than did the angry father of Yoke Shem Low, since Miguel Bostick was half-African American.[56]

The children of interethnic couples experienced more success in their pursuit of legal marriages in Arizona. Altogether, twenty-six of thirty relationships of partners of mixed ancestry involved Mexicans (see table 7). Although all the marriages of these descendants were technically illegal in Arizona, at least twelve of them actually received licenses and married locally, and two more circumvented the law by traveling to New Mexico. Of course, the absence of a

TABLE 7. Unions of Mexicans or mixed ancestry with blacks or Chinese, 1880–1930

MAN	WOMAN	NO LEGAL RECORD	ARIZONA LICENSE	NEW MEXICO LICENSE	TOTAL
Chinese	Mexican	6	3	15	24
Mexican	Chinese	1	0	0	1
Chinese-Mexican	Mexican	5	1	0	6
Chinese-Mexican	Chinese	1	0	0	1
Chinese	Chinese-Mexican	0	1	0	1
Mexican	Chinese-Mexican	8	2	1	11
White	Chinese-Mexican	0	1	1	2
Black	Mexican	5	6	5	16
White-Mexican	Black	0	1	0	1
Black-Mexican	Mexican	1	6	0	7
Mexican	Black-Mexican	0	1	0	1
	Total	27	22	22	71

SOURCES Decennial census enumeration schedules, 1880–1930. Floyd R. Negley and Marcia S. Lindley, *Arizona Territorial Marriages, Pima County, 1871–1912,* and *Arizona Marriages, Pima County, Marriage Books 5-10, February 1912 through December 1926*; Marriage Records, Grant County, Clerk's Office, Silver City, New Mexico; Marriage Records, Hidalgo County, Clerk's Office, Lordsburg, New Mexico.

NOTE The only Mexican man–Chinese woman relationship refers to the elopement by Yoke Shem Low described in this chapter.

license does not mean that the couple remained unmarried. Given the ease with which these marriages apparently took place, other, similar couples most likely married in Arizona as well. They remained highly mobile, and their marriages might have taken place away from Pima County. Others might have resided in Mexico and married there.

Thus, a combination of census, civil, legal, and church records yields a more accurate account of the number of unions of Mexicans with blacks and Chinese. Including all couples with and without marriage licenses, in the Tucson area alone, at least forty-one unions took place between Mexicans and either blacks or Chinese, and another twenty-nine involved the descendants of those kinds of couples. As occurred in intermarriage with whites, Mexican women entered into exogamy much more frequently than did Mexican men, participating in fifty-three of these relationships, whereas Mexican men were in only thirteen. Twenty-four of these unions occurred between Chinese men and Mexican women, and sixteen between black men and Mexican women. Almost three-quarters of these two types of unions (twenty-nine of forty) received legal sanction in Arizona or New Mexico. For their part, Mexican men primarily married women of Chinese-Mexican ancestry. Although these numbers seem relatively small, one must keep in mind that at no point from 1880 to 1930 were there more than twenty endogamous Chinese couples in Tucson. Similarly, the number of black couples only surpassed ten by 1910, more than five decades after African Americans first arrived in the area. Consequently, although relatively few in number, interethnic unions with Mexicans held a significance that became most apparent when those relationships ended and these men once again found themselves disconnected from familial ties.

Take, for example, the case of Charles Embers. He died of heart disease on November 27, 1935, at the Southern Methodist Hospital in Tucson. He had resided at the facility for more than three years and suffered from senility during the last few months of his life. His degenerative condition and the fact that no one claimed his body combined to produce inaccuracies in his death certificate. Relying on limited records, the hospital staff listed him as a single sixty-year-old laborer with an unknown birthplace and a thirty-year residence in Arizona.[57] This paucity of biographical information unfairly obscured the richness of Embers's life in the West, with experiences that rivaled those of some of the city's renowned pioneers—such as the Hugheses and the Bradys. He was in fact eighty-six years old, a gold rush baby of former slaves from Tennessee who had followed the migration to California, where Embers was born in 1849. He moved to Arizona in 1866 after hearing about mining opportunities. He never left. More than a common laborer, he had served as cook in Arizona during most of his life, working for mining entrepreneur and frontier chronicler Charles D. Poston in the 1860s and in various hotels in Tucson.[58]

Neither was Embers a single man. He had settled in Tucson in the early 1870s, and like so many incoming American men who arrived between 1860 and 1930, he formed a relationship with a Mexican woman. Although a few black-Mexican couples managed to marry in spite of Arizona's miscegenation law, his relationship with Dolores Salcido most likely became formalized in Mexico or remained an informal union, as they apparently never obtained a marriage license in Arizona or New Mexico. Census records nonetheless indicate that Charles and Dolores viewed their relationship as a marriage, because in 1900, they declared that they had been married since 1876. They had one child and lived together for fifty years, until Dolores succumbed to a long battle with thoracic cancer in 1925. In 1933, at the age of eighty-four, Charles proudly stated that he was the oldest living person who had migrated to Tucson.[59] With over six decades of residence in the city, he was probably right.

Although some form of senility might have already been plaguing Embers when Dolores died—he established her age at 103 years, rather than the actual 70 years—he still managed to provide essential information about his late wife. He knew that she had migrated from Mexico around 1870, since she had apparently already lived in Tucson when he arrived. He could not remember the names of her parents, but he did recall the small town where she had been born. It is thus likely that he visited Ures, Sonora, perhaps even for their wedding. He almost certainly spoke Spanish, for she did not speak English as late as 1900, and he was familiar with the formal Hispanicized married name she used, identifying her as Dolores Salcido de Embers.[60] His own death might have occurred in obscurity, but he ensured that hers did not.

IN THE BORDERLANDS OF RACIAL CLASSIFICATIONS

The fact that some black-Mexican and Chinese-Mexican couples managed to marry in Arizona while others could not highlights the fluidity of the region's racial attitudes and, in particular, the racial ambiguity of Mexicans. Government documents clearly illustrate the vacillation of officials in ascertaining the meaning of racial designations, frequently giving contradictory classifications to the descendants of interracial couples. For example, civil, legal, and vital records identified descendants of white-Mexican ancestry as mixed, Spanish,

Latin, or even as Latino-Saxon, in addition to the predominant classifications of white and Mexican.[61] Census enumerators also demonstrated ambivalence when classifying interethnic families. When the census bureau adopted *Mexican* as a racial category in 1930, it provided clear instructions on how to classify Americans of Mexican ancestry. But census enumerators in Tucson, ignoring the guidelines from Washington, listed almost two-thirds of the approximately 1,700 second-generation Mexican Americans as *Mexican*, and not as the instructed *white*, demonstrating an unwillingness to grant them statistical whiteness. Their racial attitudes thus contravened the racial fluidity that the census bureau sought to institute. Local enumerators essentially conveyed their opinion that these American citizens had not ascended the racial hierarchy. They were too Mexican to be white.[62]

The children of couples involving Mexicans and nonwhites also experienced inconsistent racial classifications by census enumerators and government officials. In their case, however, the variance could signify the difference between whiteness and nonwhiteness. For example, Emmett Woodley and Leonicia Terrazas married in 1872 and had six children. In 1900 the census classified them as "negro" and white, respectively, and their daughter, Manuela, as white, although census guidelines instructed that she fell under the category of "black" for being any percentage of "Negro descent." (The 1900 census did not include a separate category of "mulatto.")[63] Yet, when the Woodleys' son, Frank, and his wife, María Martínez, had a child in 1909, the birth certificate listed Frank as "Negro + Mexican"—a precise if not official classification. Frank later remarried (now to Dolores Villa) and moved to Buckeye, Arizona, where numerous census and vital records always classified him and his children as either white or Mexican, but never as black or mulatto.[64]

An explanation of these discrepancies lies in an analysis of geographic spaces and racial proximity. An illuminating comparison involves the Woodley children and Henry Ransom, Jr., the son of Henry Ransom, a black man from Arkansas, and Guadalupe Ramírez, born in Mexico. When Henry, Jr., lived with both parents, the census listed him as white in 1900, even though, as with Manuela Woodley, he should have been listed as black. But although Frank Woodley was incorrectly classified as white in 1920 and as Mexican in 1930, Henry was correctly classified in both years, as "mulatto" in 1920 and as "negro" in 1930.[65] The difference lay in the people who surrounded them and the towns where they lived. The enumerators based the racial designation of these two men of identical black-Mexican ancestries on the whitest relative present, the opposite approach of census designers, who placed the emphasis on the darker relatives. Thus, when these Mexican mothers were around, census takers probably found it illogical to classify their children as black. Their racial attitudes illustrated a perception of the Mexican population as distinct from whites but, apparently, more distinct from blacks. They might have viewed the children of these women as too Mexican to be black, a nuanced distinction other states did not make.[66]

The absence of their Mexican mothers shifted the focus to other relatives. Thus, Frank remained white or Mexican on census and vital records because he lived and had children with Mexican women. That is, he maintained close proximity to Mexican residents, not just his family, but to a larger Mexican community that inhabited an unincorporated area described as Mexican Town. Even if he had a dark complexion, it would have seemed illogical to classify him as black because his nearest peers were all Mexican. Unless he declared it himself, civil officials would have found it difficult to ascertain the race of his African American father. In Henry's case, the presence of his Mexican mother between 1900 and 1920 had somehow qualified him as white or mulatto. By 1930, however, she had died, and when father and son shared a home, the enumerator accurately followed census instructions and listed both as "negro." His father's race made him and his son equally black.[67]

That label notwithstanding, Henry, Jr., apparently felt quite comfortable in his self-identity when returning to the United States after accompanying his mother to her birthplace in Sonora, Mexico, in 1917: he identified himself as an English-speaking Mexican named Enrique. When he died in Phoenix in 1955, the hospital could only find out the name of his father and the maiden name of his mother, and with no other information regarding his race, the staff listed him as "Negro-Mexican." In an era when government agencies frequently demonstrated uncertainty regarding racial categories, such a classification somehow seemed as appropriate as any other.[68] It coalesced the mixed ancestry he embodied—and undoubtedly understood—and the labels he must have heard throughout his life.

Location and racial proximity also produced inconsistent racial classifications for the descendants of Samuel Bostick and Albina Barraza-Bostick between 1900 and 1930. When six of their children lived alone in the largely Mexican town of Florence, Arizona, in 1900, the census taker correctly listed them as black. Yet the seeming acumen of the enumerator might have instead conveyed certain racialist views, because he mistakenly identified as black Carmen

West, a Mexican woman married to the only black resident, Simon West from Tennessee.[69] In 1910 the four siblings who still appeared on the census were correctly listed as mulatto. By 1920, Miguel Bostick was again accurately classified as mulatto when he was living with a black woman listed as his wife. That year, his two sisters, Claudia and Luisa, and Luisa's daughter were sharing a home, and all were classified as black, even though the girl was three-fourths Mexican. Although none of the Bostick children was ever listed as white between 1900 and 1920, the 1930 census clearly illustrated the ambiguity and fluidity of racial classifications. In all likelihood, when the only options were "white," "black," and "mulatto," census takers held apprehensions about classifying the Bosticks as white—which Mexicans technically were—even though they listed Spanish as the native language of some of the Bostick children. Yet, the adoption of the category "Mexican" in the 1930 census evidently assuaged such reservations, allowing the six descendants of the Bostick-Barraza marriage (two children and four grandchildren) who appeared on the 1930 census to be listed as Mexican. That is, once *Mexican* became a separate and inferior category of white, the Bosticks technically acquired whiteness, at least in census statistics.[70]

The classification of the descendants of Chinese-Mexican couples also revealed inconsistencies. For example, the death certificate of María Ahloy—daughter of Manuel Ahloy and Isabel Escalante—classified her as Mexican. Conversely, the child of a similar couple—Dong Yet and Rosario Ramírez—was recorded as Chinese. To complicate matters, the Board of Health registered one child of Heng Lee and Ernestina Ayala as white, while one of their other children received the vague designation of "light." José Wo, son of Hi Wo and Loreto Moreno, was classified as white in his birth certificate and in later documents as Chinese, Chinese-Mexican, Mexican-Chinese, and white.[71] Census canvasses also returned various results. Because the 1900, 1910, and 1920 censuses did not provide instructions for the classification of children of Chinese-Mexican couples, enumerators could list them as white or Chinese. Not surprisingly, they used them both. In 1900, the children of two Chinese-Mexican families were classified as Chinese and those of two others as white. Similarly, in 1910, one couple's children were classified as Chinese and another's as white. In 1920, all twelve children of Chinese-Mexican ancestry, by three couples, received a classification of "white."[72] The 1930 census suffered from similar discrepancies. That year, ten people of Chinese-Mexican ancestry lived in Tucson, belonging to six different families. Because all descended from Chinese man–Mexican woman couples, census instructions required their classification as Chinese. Nonetheless, enumerators adhered to the guidelines in only five cases, recording the other five as Mexican.[73]

Although the above classifications held no legal ramifications, the racial attitudes of civil officials and census enumerators hint at why black-Mexican and Chinese-Mexican couples found social acceptance and sometimes legal forbearance. The children of these relationships undoubtedly understood their mixed ancestry. The very combination of Hispanic given names with non-Hispanic surnames reminded them of their diverse heritage, and they constantly identified the place of origin of their parents, whether in Arizona or nearby Mexico, or farther away, in the American South or China. Without their self-reporting, census and vital records would have lacked the necessary information to establish race, since Mexico has historically comprised many different ethnicities. Yet, even with that information, hospital staffs, medical personnel, and census takers could not consistently agree on the racial designation of people of mixed ancestry because their own racial attitudes and assumptions circumscribed their ability to classify multiracial people. In other words, not all members of these multiethnic societies understood their complexities. Such vacillations became highly important because the enforcers of miscegenation laws—city clerks, justices of the peace, and religious figures—also wavered when deciding whether a couple was indeed interracial and whether they met the racial requirements to marry in Arizona. If the racial proximity of Mexicans to blacks and Chinese frequently conveyed that they belonged in close enough categories to form families with each other, the qualifications of people of mixed ancestry to marry anyone proved even more difficult to assess. Of course, some clerks exercised stricter judgment, and occasionally, partners who looked too dissimilar received no licenses, even when lawyers cited the purported Moorish ancestry or Mongolian traits of Mexicans. Yet, the fact that intermarriages involving Mexicans almost never encountered social opprobrium illustrates that, as far communities were concerned, those relationships made sense.

CONCLUSION

The relative infrequency of marriages of Mexicans with either blacks or Chinese does not diminish the significance of the relationships to these partners. Their experiences illustrate the complexities of interethnic unions in the

Southwest at the turn of the twentieth century. These marriages certainly received more acceptance than black-white and Chinese-white couples could have experienced in Arizona. In this important way, the presence of a large Mexican community in Tucson was undeniably beneficial, especially to uprooted black and Chinese men who formed families with Mexican partners. To start, they avoided the lives of bachelorhood that plagued their migrant communities. Some even obtained legal marriages in an era of strict miscegenation laws, and those who could not marry in Arizona had the recourse of securing a New Mexico marriage and returning to southern Arizona to live in peace, a comfort not available to blacks and Chinese who tried to or did marry whites. Furthermore, the kinship networks of their Mexican wives allowed these men to connect to the larger Mexican and white communities. Most important, these unions brought domestic and international migrants a sense of rootedness and belonging that so many of their peers never found.

The stories of these African Americans, Chinese, and Mexicans aptly exemplify the experiences of thousands of immigrants who arrived in the Southwest during the late nineteenth and early twentieth centuries and eventually entered into interethnic unions. They, like so many domestic and foreign migrants meandering around the West, ultimately decided to settle down in Tucson and form a family. For many of them, the city became their final destination indeed because they died there, far removed from their birthplaces. One can only imagine how many white, black, and Chinese men perished in the West in complete anonymity, leaving their parents and siblings without any news about their lives and deaths. Although more closely connected to the Mexican communities of southern Arizona, the migratory experiences of Mexican women did not differ greatly. Whether viewed as El Norte by Mexicans, as the West by Americans, or as America by Chinese, the region signified risks and uncertainties for nineteenth-century settlers, and therein lies one of the strongest links between migrant men and the Mexican women they married, many of whom had recently migrated from the border states, especially from nearby Sonora. Both groups saw the world through the eyes of transplanted men and women, and intermarried couples undoubtedly found much comfort in their shared experiences and in their hopes for a better future. Such connections probably outweighed any apprehensions they might have had about cultural and racial differences.

For these interethnic couples, a successful trip to the county clerk, whether in Tucson or in New Mexico, marked the culmination of overcoming obstacles and making calculations to find family life in the West. African American and, especially, Chinese men faced overwhelming odds. They had to negotiate racist attitudes, miscegenation laws, skewed sex ratios, and cultural apprehensions. In Tucson, however, they benefited from fluid ethnic spaces and from the racial ambiguity of Mexicans. But their unions with Mexican women did not stem from mere good fortune. They had to convince their potential brides that a suitable future awaited them. After all, Mexican women could and did marry extensively with whites and, of course, with Mexicans. In other words, they had marital options that black and Chinese men lacked. In forming families with each other, these groups stood to gain: the men beat the odds and were able to marry, and Mexican women achieved familial stability and some social mobility that, while keeping them in the lower classes, improved their lives. Local marriages only numbered in the few dozens, and three couples separated several years later—although only one of them legally divorced—but the Tucson area offers merely a glimpse of the larger picture. Several barriers made these interethnic marriages highly improbable. But it is very likely that hundreds of other similar couples also managed to form families in the U.S.-Mexico region. As chapter 5 illustrates, the great majority of all interethnic unions in Tucson enjoyed both longevity and stability. But regardless of the duration and relative happiness of these families, intermarried partners—whether black, Chinese or white—experienced a profound immersion into the Mexican culture of the Arizona borderlands.

5

MARITAL EXPECTATIONS IN THE BORDERLANDS

HIRAM S. STEVENS became a successful businessman and a popular member of Tucson society during the more than thirty-five years he spent in Arizona. Born in Vermont in 1832, he was among the first Euro-American men who settled in Tucson after its annexation to the United States via the Gadsden Purchase (1854). Like so many of those early white settlers, he entered into marriage with a Mexican woman. He wed Petra Santa Cruz in 1858, when he was twenty-six years old and she was only fourteen. Among his many accomplishments, Stevens belonged to the Pima County Board of Supervisors at the time of his death and had previously served as mayor of Tucson and as territorial delegate to the U.S. Congress. The town's lore remembers him as a founding member of the Pioneers' Society—"the pioneer of pioneers," according to local newspapers that reported his death—and as the man who introduced the locally renowned Sam Hughes to his eventual wife, Atanacia, Petra's younger sister. But while Sam and Atanacia enjoyed a long and happy marriage that included ten children, the Stevenses' relationship came to a tragic end. On March 21, 1893, Hiram returned from a trip to Nogales, shot his wife twice, and then went into another room and shot himself in the head. The bullet did not kill him instantly, most likely because of the poor condition of the gun, and his wife's wounds to the head and hand were not life threatening. He never regained consciousness, however, and died two hours later, while Petra recovered and lived another twenty-three years, dying at the age of seventy-two.[1]

The Stevens marriage stands out because it experienced the stability and longevity that most of Tucson's interethnic families enjoyed but also the discord that plagued some couples. As husband and wife, Hiram and Petra lived through the regional uncertainty and insecurity of the three decades that preceded the pacification of Indians and the completion of the railroad in the 1880s. They formed important personal and economic ties to other prominent Tucsonans and had thus accrued social and financial capital. The economic downturn of the 1880s and early 1890s nonetheless brought difficulties to the family finances, and Stevens became reticent as he tried to remedy the situation over several months. His anguish evolved into violence on that fatal day in March. Although newspaper accounts attributed his actions to, among other things, domestic troubles, "a fit of mental aberation [*sic*]," and even to severe bowel trouble, his friends and wife recognized the link between the financial strife and his uncharacteristic dejection. His actions had not come entirely unexpectedly to them, as his wife had recently confided to her sister that she feared her husband. In all likelihood, the potential loss of status played a role in prompting Hiram to attempt murder-suicide as a solution to his problems. The popularity of the Stevens family became evident during the highly attended wake and funeral procession, with crowds that had no precedent in the town's history.[2]

The Stevens marriage and the legal cases of others offer insight into sources of problems and frustration but also into the obstacles that other couples managed to avoid or overcome. This chapter explores some of the experiences that characterized members of interethnic families. It discusses the highly Mexican nature of family life for interethnic couples, the importance of property, the role of personal networks, and the incidence and causes of divorce. The chapter argues that class and culture largely framed not only the success and failure of interethnic couples, but also how they dealt with marital dissatisfaction. These experiences evince that the sociocultural nature of southern Arizona, a fluid Mexican borderlands region, shaped the worldviews and expectations of the wives and informed how interethnic couples interacted and even why and how they separated.

FAMILY LIFE

The preponderance of the Mexican population, the relative unavailability of many women from other ethnic groups until the late nineteenth century, and

the openness with which Tucson residents intermarried combined to make local family life a markedly Mexican experience. Men from other ethnic groups
usually adapted to the Hispanic traditions of the Mexican women they joined
in marriage or cohabitation. For instance, whatever the beliefs of the husbands
before marriage, interethnic households predominantly conformed to the Catholicism of the Mexican side of the family. Some of the white men came from
Catholic backgrounds—most evident were the cases of men born in France,
Ireland, or Italy—but virtually all weddings took place at Saint Augustine's regardless of the faith of the husband. Therefore, non-Catholic men underwent
a form of initiation into the religious world of their wives when they entered
into a union with a Mexican woman. Although some men chose to convert to
Catholicism before marrying, for two groups of men, their ability to marry a
Catholic bride rested on certain requirements.[3]

Religion was an important but surmountable obstacle. Correspondence
from the vicar apostolic of Arizona suggests that Catholic priests sought to
spread Catholicism among Protestants and non-Christians and to ensure its
primacy among Mexicans. They constantly worried about the presence of Protestant missionaries and public schools in southern Arizona.[4] Mexican families
even established a private school so that their daughters did not have to at-
tend classes with Protestant children. Not surprisingly, therefore, intermarried
Mexican women often took measures to ensure the preeminence of Catholicism in their families.[5] They required their prospective spouses to sign an affirmation that acknowledged the authority of the Catholic faith in two areas:
the document stipulated that no other wedding ceremony—e.g., in a Protestant church—would take place and that the husband would not interfere in
the teaching of Catholicism to the children. Interfaith marriages took place
outside church property, for instance, in a private residence, but they received
equal recognition within the Church.[6] White men, it seems, willingly complied
with these preconditions. Jewish men who resided in nineteenth-century Tucson lacked a strong sense of religious ties and were traditionally predisposed
to grant their Mexican wives complete control of the religious upbringing of
the children.[7] Therefore, almost universally, the children of interethnic couples
were baptized and raised according to Catholic traditions. As late as the 1940s,
most descendants of interethnic unions, regardless of the combination of faiths
among their ancestors, remained practicing Catholics.

Black and Chinese men also adapted to the Catholicism of their Mexican partners. Protestant and Jewish men only had to recognize the primacy of

Catholicism. The Church, on the other hand, viewed non-Christian Asian men as infidels, and they frequently had to convert to Catholicism before receiving the wedding sacrament. For example, Fô Loy underwent conversion just before his marriage. He was baptized at Saint Augustine's in 1890, receiving the Christian name of Manuel that he would carry until his death. Soon after, the neophyte Manuel married Isabel Escalante. The couple would return to the church on many occasions to baptize and confirm all their children, as did many other Chinese-Mexican couples. Black-Mexican couples were more mobile, but the Bosticks and the Woodleys also baptized at least eight of their children at Saint Augustine's. Mexicans from the working class served as godparents for nearly all these children, leaving both sets of parents united as compadres. Not surprisingly, the children adhered to Hispanic culture and married in Catholic ceremonies.

The socioreligious tradition of compadrazgo formed part of the larger process of integration into the Mexican areas of Tucson.[8] In a way, the presence of Mexicans in southern Arizona facilitated the acceptance of new arrivals into the well-established Mexican community. These bonds commonly involved the connections of Mexican wives and their complex interracial communities.[9] These networks proved especially beneficial to blacks and Chinese, who tended to have few members of their own ethnic group nearby. The women they married, even recent Mexican immigrants, maintained kinship ties with their extended transnational families, the Mexican and non-Mexican spouses of their relatives, and the black and Chinese relatives and friends of their husbands. Baptisms thus provided these couples the opportunity to establish or cement local connections. For instance, in 1874, Emmett and Leonicia Woodley chose as godparents Barney Dublin, a black friend who lived with the family, and Manuela Uzarraga, who perhaps had a relationship with Barney but was most likely a friend of Leonicia.[10] When the Woodleys baptized their second child, they called on Hiram Stevens and Petra Santa Cruz Stevens to serve as godparents.[11] To obtain the favor from such a prominent family illustrates the good reputation of the Woodleys, who almost certainly relied on the local acquaintances of Leonicia. By far, however, most compadres of interethnic couples belonged to the lower classes and were almost always Mexican. But in a working-class town like Tucson, being able to count on the support of these networks, whatever their social status, could prove highly valuable. These connections undoubtedly helped black and Chinese spouses negotiate their daily lives.

Men who intermarried also adapted to the Hispanic linguistic tradition of their Mexican wives. To start, census records reveal that the Mexican women in these relationships generally did not speak English, an indication that intrafamily communication most likely occurred in Spanish—at times to the chagrin of fathers. Furthermore, men who originated from European cultures often adopted Hispanicized versions of their names, while Chinese men frequently received Hispanic names—typically names of saints—when they converted to Catholicism, or as they interacted in the Mexican communities, where most of them resided. Not surprisingly, in the second half of the nineteenth century, the children of interethnic couples from all backgrounds almost always received Hispanic names. For example, the children of Manuel and Isabel Ahloy received names like Antonio, Francisco, and José Manuel, while Samuel Bostick and Albina Barraza used names like Miguel and Francisca. (This custom greatly facilitates the identification of people of mixed ancestry because of the abundance of residents with Hispanic first names and non-Hispanic surnames, such as Carlos Lee, José Ong Woo, Manuela Woodley, and Santiago Bostick.) The tradition of giving Hispanic names declined but remained remarkably common into the twentieth century. In 1930 most children of interethnic families still received Hispanic names (like Margarita, José, and Juan) or bicultural names (such as Laura, Clara, and David). In sum, whether saying their children's names, talking to their wives, or indeed hearing their own names, these men who grew up in China or, in the case of whites and blacks, primarily east of the Mississippi River, were surrounded by the Spanish language.

Perhaps the most significant manifestation of the Mexicanized experience of these interethnic couples involves the marital choices of their children. For instance, although the children of white-Mexican couples married extensively among their three major cohorts (Mexicans, whites, and people of white-Mexican ancestry), the descendants of black-Mexican and Chinese-Mexican couples almost universally formed families with Mexicans. Their choices were likely an indication of their Mexican cultural upbringing, particularly the importance of religious and linguistic affinity—all due primarily to the roles and influence of their mothers. For instance, sixteen of the nineteen children of Chinese-Mexican couples married Mexicans. Likewise, all eight descendants of Tucson's black-Mexican couples formed relationships with Mexicans.[12] Between 1880 and 1930, only one of the marriages of these descendants involved a white spouse, but the existence of that marriage demonstrates the fluidity of racial classifications in the borderlands. In 1914 Alexander MacMinn, from Scotland, married Rita Lee, the daughter of a Chinese man and a Mexican

Flin Sisters-Monica, Frances, Louisa, Lydia

FIGURE 10. Mónica, Francisca, Luisa, and Lidia Flin (c. 1918). They were daughters of Jules Flin, a stonemason from France, and Carlota Brunet, from Mexico. Mónica, Francisca, and Lidia married Mexican men. Luisa married Ferdinand Baron Tully, founder of various short-lived newspapers in Spanish. He was the son of Carlos Tully, a white-Mexican man, and Adele Baron, a white-Mexican woman. Arizona Historical Society/Tucson, AHS Photo Number 64769.

woman.[13] They obtained a marriage license from the county clerk and wed at Saint Augustine's. Their union, although prohibited under Arizona's miscegenation law, occurred uneventfully, most likely because Rita, growing up in a Mexican neighborhood and speaking Spanish, could probably pass as Mexican. In the eyes of county officials, she was one of many Mexicans who resided in the area and could thus marry a white man.

LEGAL DISPUTES

A notorious divorce battle offers insight into the role of class, culture, and gender in the lives of interethnic couples. The marriage of María Bonillas and Giuseppe Coppola attracted much attention from the moment of their engagement in 1919 to the complicated end of their relationship in 1922. Giuseppe, a lieutenant in the Italian army, met María, the daughter of the Mexican ambassador, while serving as attaché in the Italian embassy in Washington, DC. The capital's press offered extensive coverage of their engagement and wedding in early 1919, including pictures of the bride and details on the prominence of the young couple. Reporters highlighted the grandiosity of the reception and the eminence of the diplomats in attendance, informing that the newlyweds would travel to New York for a few days before sailing for Italy. They depicted the couple as an idyllic match, "another of [Washington's] dearly loved international marriages."[14] The apparent fairytale would not last long: by May 1921, Giuseppe had arrived in Tucson and obtained a writ of habeas corpus to force María's parents to allow him to see his wife and sons. What happened between their departure for Italy and his arrival in Tucson would be highly contested in three legal confrontations.

Although María stated that she had instructed her father not to allow her husband to see her because she feared he might take her children to Italy, the court accommodated both parties by granting Giuseppe the right to visit his sons for one hour each day at the Bonillas residence, but only under the supervision of a probation officer. Evidently not satisfied with the extent of his access, one week later Giuseppe filed a $250,000 lawsuit against Ignacio and Mary Bonillas, María's parents, accusing them of the alienation of his wife, whom he had yet to see. "Coppola Sues for Quarter Million for Love of Wife," read a headline in the *Tucson Citizen*.[15] While waiting for the start of the trial, Giuseppe visited Italy, and María filed for divorce on charges of constant humiliation and extreme parsimony. Once the alienation trial began, Giuseppe focused his complaint on the purported intrusiveness of María's mother in an effort to convince the jury that the Bonillases were indeed capable of causing, and thus to blame for, the inaccessibility of his wife. María countered with an extensive explanation, underscoring that a pattern of mistreatment and neglect lay behind her own decision not to see her husband. In spite of this declaration and other denunciations by María, the jurors ruled in favor of Giuseppe. They apparently lent much credence to his overall complaint that the alienation of his wife derived from a simple fact: "too much mother-in-law."[16] The jury nonetheless limited the damages to $1,500. But even that attenuated victory would be short lived.[17]

The judge in the trial summoned all parties the next day and informed them that he had granted María a limited divorce—until divorce proceedings could take place. He gave her custody of the two children and ordered Giuseppe to cover her legal fees of $250 and to pay a monthly alimony of $125. He also placed a lien on the $1,500 the jury had awarded him. As if to convey to Giuseppe that the marriage had indeed ended, the judge instructed him to ship María's belongings from Italy at his own expense.[18] Giuseppe appealed the decision, however, and a new judge determined that the case merited a full trial because the original judge did not have the authority to grant limited divorces. In the new proceedings, María reiterated her previous declarations and recounted further experiences of abusive behavior and neglect. But Giuseppe denied these accusations and once again placed all blame on his mother-in-law, insisting that he treated his wife kindly; that she reciprocated and maintained a nice relationship with Giuseppe's mother and friends; and that he had even bought her a piano. He emphatically stated that he and his wife enjoyed "Very happy relations. Very happy."[19] As proof, he presented letters she had written him while he had made a business trip to the United States two years earlier. The judge cited those letters as his reason for dismissing all of María's allegations and refusing to grant the divorce.[20]

To a great extent, much of the discord between María and Giuseppe revolved around class issues. Divorce, already rare for interethnic couples, occurred even less frequently among families with substantial assets. The paucity likely resulted both from the relatively small number of upper-class interethnic families in Tucson and from the desire to avoid the division of assets. But this infamous divorce certainly demonstrates that elites had different prerogatives and could better defend themselves. To start, María cited both lack of financial support and humiliation as grounds for divorce, an indication that, coming from a family of affluence, she expected Giuseppe to offer a lifestyle and treatment suitable for a woman of her status. Her testimony in the three trials primarily underscored the discomfort and degradation she had experienced from the very start of her year in Italy. She explained that when she and Giuseppe settled there, they first had to live at his sister's home in "the foulest and dirtiest quarters" and later with his mother in an unsanitary one-room residence. She also declared that her husband berated her in front of his relatives and friends for her inability to haggle with produce vendors and that she had to use her own money to buy clothes, food, and medicine.[21] Giuseppe's supposed parsimony became an easy target for the Arizona press. "Italian Complains Wife Cost Him Three Cents a Day," read a headline from the *Arizona Republican*, referring to the money she could have saved by haggling. Giuseppe, María surmised, had clearly married her out of interest. She described his disappointment when learning that she had received no monetary dowry, leading her to realize early on that she had entered into a "mercenary marriage." He was a "Fortune Hunter Seeking Her Heart," the *Tucson Citizen* underscored.[22] In sum, the experiences she recounted sharply contrasted with the status and expectations of a woman the Washington press had identified as "Senorita Maria Bonillas, daughter of the Mexican Ambassador to the United States."[23]

Friction over behavior and intentions also revolved around the spouses' different cultural backgrounds. The most recurring motif in Giuseppe's testimony involved his conception of the roles of women. He described his own mother as friendly and supportive—referring to the same behavior María viewed as servile. His mother was the model Giuseppe expected María to follow, while María's mother embodied the antithesis. Not surprisingly, Giuseppe supported his claim of alienation by targeting the behavior of María's mother: she, he asserted, constantly eavesdropped on the couple's conversations while staying with them in Italy; demanded that mother and daughter sleep in the same room; and forbade her daughter from sitting on his lap and even from holding hands. Giuseppe further tried to cast his mother-in-law as vile and ungrateful by alleging that she despised the United States and "commonly referred to Americans as gringos and . . . expressed dislike for them frequently."[24] He and his wife, Giuseppe maintained, had enjoyed an excellent relationship until her mother showed up at their home in Italy. Aware of the cultural assault, María clarified that she and her family loved the United States. (Ironically, of all the four people involved in the trials, only her mother was a native-born American.) She also shifted the cultural argument by accusing Giuseppe of attempting to kill her faith even though he, as a Protestant, had signed an agreement to ensure that she and their future children would freely practice Catholicism. Notably, she never denied that her mother engaged in the behavior Giuseppe described. She simply did not see it as intrusive. María and her mother clearly assumed that a woman's family remained relevant after marriage. Giuseppe, on the other hand, expected to have no interference, not even from his wife, in dictating the direction of the marriage. These two worldviews could not coexist.

Beyond these broader class and cultural differences, disagreements over gender roles created much of the tension that circumscribed both the marriage and the trials. At the crux of the friction lay not only the presumed responsibilities of men and women, but also, and especially so, the extent of María's self-determination. María's decision to leave Giuseppe in Italy to move in with her parents indicates a willingness to release him of his financial obligations in exchange for her freedom. She allowed him not to meet the role of provider she attributed to a husband as long as she did not have to adhere to the submissive behavior he expected from a wife. That calculation conveyed the type of determination she would demonstrate in Tucson. From the start of the legal disputes, María repeatedly stated that she had decided not to see her husband, but Giuseppe still filed and continued to pursue the alienation lawsuit. In his view, she could not have made such an important decision, because only her parents and he could hold that level of autonomy over her. Those gendered attitudes had become clear while in Italy, as he demanded behavior that placed María in a subservient position: that she polish his shoes every day; that she wash his back; that she make a daily list of all expenses and account for every penny; and that she write to him every day, when apart, to recount her activities. Her frequent refusal to comply should have convinced him that she was capable of and willing to decline to see him once the situation arose.

Yet, when that scenario actually played out, Giuseppe still adhered to his views on gender hierarchies. After he claimed that her father had imprisoned her against her will, María's response that she had actually "expressed a desire never to see [Giuseppe] again" did not sway him.[25] She also explained her rationale: she feared that her husband would take the children to Italy if given the opportunity. The Bonillases even obtained from María's attending physician an affidavit that corroborated her affirmation. Notably, when she first decided to leave her husband and return to the United States, Giuseppe approved the trip only after she agreed not to return until she was "willing to accept [his] orders."[26] She agreed and never returned. He followed her to Tucson less than a year later. The judge who had ruled on the limited divorce believed that María

(1) truly desired to live apart from Giuseppe because (2) he mistreated her, two assertions the jury refused to accept even though she made them in person. In other words, beyond finding her credible, the judge—unlike Giuseppe and the men in the jury—cast María as someone endowed with the individuality to decide whether she wanted to see her husband. When the second judge ruled against María, Giuseppe finally accepted her resolve after she filed yet another divorce petition. He made a last visit to his two sons to say goodbye and gave them gold lockets with photographs of them and their father. The children grew up in Tucson with María and her family.[27]

As the following legal cases illustrate, the experiences of María and Giuseppe were both representative and unusual among interethnic couples in Tucson. Most significant, María and other Mexican women demonstrated that they did not enter their marriages alone. Their ability to call on local and even transnational networks became a valuable resource when their relationships failed. At times, those very connections led to marital conflict because white men resented the attachment of Mexican women to their families. It involved, after all, emotional and social capital most men could not match, often because of their recent relocation to the Southwest. Their wives, children, and in-laws were often the only family they had in southern Arizona or even in the West. Class differences signified that not everyone could count on influential connections for support, such as lawyers and doctors, let alone the political and legal contacts of a former ambassador. But that level of network was not always necessary. For instance, women who decided to run away from a bad marriage required only the type of shelter any poor relative or acquaintance could provide, in Arizona or in Mexico. Similarly, working-class friends and families often sufficed as witnesses when Mexican women sought to protect indispensable assets and to defend themselves against character attacks.

But the Bonillas-Coppola marriage also stands out because it differed from most interethnic relationships in the Tucson area. For example, the types of examples other women cited as grounds for divorce frequently extended beyond class-based humiliation. Some women endured actual verbal and physical attacks as well as degradation. Their responses often paralleled the actions María took, but the obstacles they overcame make their stories more remarkable. They negotiated an unfamiliar court system in what for them was a foreign language, and some of these women lacked literacy skills even in Spanish—all barriers María did not encounter. Their use of networks, therefore, proved more meaningful. The financial assets at stake generally paled in comparison to what María and her family possessed, but their relative value often carried more importance because of their modest circumstances. In the end, class separated María from most intermarried Mexican women, but they all benefited from their familiarity with the Arizona borderlands area and their connections to its Mexican inhabitants.

Relationships with whites inevitably placed Mexican women within the realm of the U.S. legal system following annexation. As widows and divorcées, they often faced serious obstacles, but they sometimes managed to defend their claims to property and financial support in the courts. Like the rest of the Southwest after the United States acquired the Mexican territory, Tucson abandoned the Spanish/Mexican legal tradition, in which the word of family members and acquaintances ensured protection of inheritances and property rights. Under Spanish and Mexican laws of the nineteenth century, laymen occupied the local courts, and they followed local customs and values. Their rulings seemed arbitrary to early American settlers but helped to maintain peace in the community.[28] After annexation, however, personal affidavits and the honor system did not always suffice in American courtrooms. Tucson residents had to adhere to formal wills, public announcements, petitions, lawsuits, and legal precedent to protect their rights and economic interests. Mexican women learned, nonetheless, that they could still rely on friends and family to support their claims. Thus, although white men initially held a better understanding of the legal process, Mexican women overcame their early disadvantage and increasingly demonstrated ample competence and determination when it became necessary to enter the courtroom.

During the first two decades under the American flag, Mexican women could face grave difficulties if their white husbands died intestate. They could summarily lose some or all of the assets the couple had accumulated. In the absence of a will, legal procedure dictated that local newspapers announce the death of the individual, the need for administrators of the estate, and a call for creditors and potential beneficiaries to file claims. From the outset, these cases signified several obstacles for the Mexican widows of white men. First, some of these relationships were in fact informal unions, lacking the automatic protection of legal marriages. Second, some husbands maintained property and assets solely in their names. Third, most intermarriages occurred among working-class people, increasing the probability that the couple would not be familiar with the importance of formal wills. Fourth, most intermarried white men migrated to Tucson as detached bachelors, and their widows lacked the support of their husbands' side of the family to inform them of the proceedings or to help establish their claims—or just as likely, a distant in-law might suddenly appear and dispute a judgment that favored the wife. Finally, during the early years, Tucson had only English-language newspapers. Even after Spanish-language papers appeared, the low levels of literacy among poor Mexicans—especially among women—made those sources of information practically inaccessible. These disadvantages signified that legal abuses could and did take place.

Familiarity with the American legal system thus allowed white men the opportunity to exploit the relative lack of awareness of Mexican widows. Not only were white men more likely to be literate, but they also belonged to circles of friends, coworkers, and business associates with whom newspapers and legal proceedings were topics of conversation. Opportunities to profit from legal ambiguities did not go unnoticed. For example, when Mahlon E. Moore died intestate in 1868, Charles H. Meyers and Edward N. Fish promptly responded to a newspaper announcement to administer his estate. The positions offered the men not only the accompanying remuneration, but also the task of appraising and distributing Moore's assets. The process advanced smoothly until the widow Dolores Moore appeared in court—most likely under the advice of an acquaintance who informed her of the proceedings. By then, she had managed to secure only the family house, the sole possession that the law excluded from the administrators of the estate. She apparently had remained oblivious to the appropriation of the family assets until then. She acknowledged receipt of the property by signing with a cross, an indication of her illiteracy and thus her susceptibility to such manipulation of the law.[29] One can see the type of opportunism that allowed Meyers and Fish to find local prominence in commerce and government and as founding members of the Pioneer Society. To women like Dolores Moore, however, they were simply the men who oversaw the dissection of the family's estate.[30]

The courts' inclination to appoint white men as administrators increased the likelihood that women would lose property, but Mexican women could sometimes overcome obstacles, such as illiteracy and lack of information, to recover at least part of their husbands' assets. Manuela Kennedy, also illiterate, signed with an X when she took steps to halt the carving of her property in 1870. The legal process lasted a long six months, as she repeatedly sought to establish her legal claim to the estate of her late husband, Hugh Kennedy. He had died during an Indian raid in March 1870. Manuela made a court appearance early in the process and proved that she was indeed Kennedy's wife. By that time, however, a judge had already appointed as administrator, W. W. Williams, a man who frequently answered newspaper announcements for such positions. The court instructed him to allocate an interim sum of fifty dollars per month as sustenance for the widow and the couple's child. Not only did Williams ignore the order, but the unexpected complications—such as Manuela's legal complaint that she had received no payments and her motion that Williams sell the estate and give her a fair share—also prompted him to resign. Manuela's persistence paid off. Despite her illiteracy, the court named her administrator of her husband's estate. Her involvement undoubtedly cost Williams and several purported creditors a potential windfall. Williams had originally appraised the entire estate at one thousand dollars. Yet, a later assessment determined that Kennedy's personal property alone exceeded four thousand dollars, and his real estate holdings reached almost ten thousand dollars. Williams's departure, however, only delayed the predatory actions of Kennedy's business associate, F. L. Austin. He convinced the court that Kennedy's assets should cover part of the debts their partnership had allegedly accrued. He managed to obtain sole title to Kennedy's San Pedro property and also received two thousand dollars from his personal estate. In the end, the family wealth had certainly diminished, but Manuela's determination and direct involvement ensured that she and her son could keep a considerable share of the estate.[31]

Divorce cases were the most frequent legal disputes over financial security. Various factors combined to make marriages particularly unstable in the West, especially during the second half of the nineteenth century. The difficulty and instability of migration produced a higher incidence of divorce in the West because of disruptions in family dynamics, religious life, social attachments, and kinship networks. Couples also had to negotiate financial problems associated with the boom and bust cycles of the nascent economies of the region. Protestant churches and laic associations developed slowly, and residents often lacked the moral support of established communities. Married men who traveled alone faced the additional strains of separation, economic uncertainty, and difficulties in transportation to reunite with their families—all potential causes of marital strife. Those factors and the more liberal divorce laws of the West meant that between 1890 and 1900, the divorce rate in western states outpaced the national average. In 1900, for example, fourteen of the fifteen states or territories with the highest rate of divorce lay west of the Mississippi River. That year, Arizona ranked eleventh in the nation.[32]

As in most of the West, socioeconomic conditions in Tucson remained highly unstable until the early twentieth century, and intermarriages faced other potential barriers. The United States officially took possession of Tucson in 1854, but the population stagnated until the 1870s. White families migrated in significant numbers only after the completion of the railroad in 1880. The population soon decreased, however, due to the economic recession of the 1880s and the departure of federal troops, only recovering by 1900. As transplanted men and women—a large percentage of Mexicans had also recently immigrated, typically from northern Mexico—intermarried partners had a proven ability to remove themselves from an unacceptable situation by leaving their spouses. Either partner could relocate to other parts of the Southwest, and Mexican women had the additional option of moving in with relatives south of the border. Logically, of course, intermarriage by definition involves the intermingling of differences, and several factors could further jeopardize the relationship. For one thing, interfaith unions, which were a large percentage of intermarriages, tended to end in divorce more frequently than religiously endogamous unions.[33] These couples, furthermore, typically had to overcome differences in language, culture, and race. Those and other factors could only exacerbate the already difficult conditions of the Southwest.

Yet, the divorce rate among local intermarried couples was actually lower than state, regional, and national levels. The sixty years surrounding the turn of the twentieth century—roughly the period covered in this book—witnessed a dramatic rise in the divorce rate in the United States, resting at about 16 percent in the 1920s. Neither conservative moral campaigns nor numerous legislative restrictions managed to impede the increase.[34] Thus, considering the potential pressures of racial and cultural differences that could logically complicate marriages already afflicted by the socioeconomic instability of western marriages, the divorce rate of Tucson's interethnic couples remained remarkably low between 1873 and 1930. It averaged slightly below 8 percent between 1873 and 1900, and roughly 5 percent between 1901 and 1930, both rates well below the regional and Arizona averages (see table 8).[35] The strict criteria on divorce by the Catholic Church might help explain the lower incidence of divorce among Tucson's interethnic couples. For instance, as a study of contemporary Los Angeles demonstrates, the divorce rate among Mexicans was lower than among whites.[36] Tucson couples might not necessarily have adhered to religious mandates, but their Catholic cultural upbringing certainly influenced their aversion to divorce. Other factors, such as the well-established Mexican community, the relative peace that prevailed after 1880, and the imbalanced sex ratios, all likely had a positive effect on marital longevity.

TABLE 8. Marriages and divorces among interethnic couples, Pima County, 1873–1930

YEARS	NUMBER OF NEW INTERMARRIAGES	DIVORCES	DIVORCES PER 100 NEW INTERMARRIAGES
1873–1880	87	9	10.3
1881–1890	127	10	7.9
1891–1900	220	15	6.8
1901–1910	260	9	3.5
1911–1920	502	24	4.8
1921–1930	535	36	6.7
Cumulative	1,731	103	6.0

SOURCES Decennial census enumeration schedules, 1880–1930. Floyd R. Negley and Marcia S. Lindley, *Arizona Territorial Marriages, Pima County, 1871–1912*, and *Arizona Marriages, Pima County, Marriage Books 5–10, February 1912 through December 1926*; Marriage Records, Grant County, New Mexico, Clerk's Office, Silver City; Marriage Records, Hidalgo County, New Mexico, Clerk's Office, Lordsburg; Clerk's Office, Pima County Superior Court, Tucson, Arizona; Marriage Licenses, Pima County, 1927–1930, SG 8 Superior Court, History and Archives Division, Arizona State Library, Archives and Public Records, Phoenix

When Tucson interethnic couples did file for divorce, they typically cited the same reasons as families in other parts of the West: desertion and failure to provide financial support were by far the most frequent complaints in these cases. Their pragmatic preoccupations and litigation over property demonstrated the normalcy of the lives of intermarried couples. Domestic violence did exist, but it rarely involved ethnic tension. As men and women faced marital discord, the use of networks and the cultural uniqueness of the Arizona borderlands played important roles. These forms of support proved especially significant in the burgeoning Southwest of the nineteenth century.

Concerns over property and financial support repeatedly arose during divorce proceedings. From the outset in the 1870s, Mexican women acted with resilience in their efforts to retain their share of the family assets. For instance, in 1873, María Jaime-Gay filed for divorce from her husband of five years, Mervin G. Gay. She accused him of excessive drinking and abusive language, but her primary complaint involved physical violence. According to María, her husband repeatedly attacked her—typically by hurling objects at her. She finally decided to end their marriage after he threatened to kill her. Her petition included the typical legalistic language of the period—undoubtedly attributable to legal counsel—that requested an "equitable and just" division of the "common property." But María left nothing to chance. She meticulously listed the quantity and value of all the assets the couple had accumulated, among them a lot in downtown Tucson ($500), 78 cows ($2,490), 30 calves ($150), 2 horses ($80), and 126 chickens ($60). It is unclear how much of the property she received in the settlement, but her direct involvement and awareness that she was entitled to a share of the family assets certainly helped her case.[37]

María Jaime-Gay was personally aware of the state of the family's finances, but women who lacked similar information often relied on the assistance of relatives and friends. The marriage of Joaquina and Charles Franklin was brief but eventful. They married in March 1871 and informally separated in May the following year. Joaquina filed for divorce one year later, citing failure to provide as her sole complaint against Charles. The timing of her petition coincided with a recent revelation from her network of relatives and friends that her husband had found employment several months earlier and had already accumulated one thousand dollars. She promptly demanded half the common property as compensation for two years of unfulfilled sustenance. Charles appeared before the court and denied the accusations. He said that he had neither a job nor the purported thousand dollars and that he had not failed to provide for his wife. In one of the very few examples of the otherization of Mexicans in divorce proceedings, Charles added that she had abandoned him by moving to a "foreign country" for more than a year—a simplistic effort to ostracize the well-known nation that lay less than seventy miles to the south. But he went even further by casting doubt on the reputation of his wife. During this time, he claimed, she maintained adulterous relations with one or more men. As proof, he stated that she had infected him with syphilis. Although such allegations implied serious imputations regarding the danger of Mexican women to unsuspecting white men, Joaquina maintained enough local networks to defend her reputation. The case thus evolved from a he said/she said squabble into a he said/ *they* said attack on Charles's credibility. Relying on court interpreters, Joaquina, her mother, and her uncle testified that (1) her trip to Mexico was for medical reasons and at Charles's suggestion; (2) he had only occasionally given money and provisions to his wife; and (3) her mother had offered her food and clothes, and the uncle had provided shelter. Charles failed to call a single witness, and

TABLE 9. Divorce petitions of intermarried couples, Pima County, 1873–1930

CAUSES GIVEN FOR DIVORCE	WIFE AS PLAINTIFF, N=58 (%)	HUSBAND AS PLAINTIFF, N=32 (%)
Desertion	47	53
Abuse	31	25
Failure to support	19	0
Drinking	2	0
Felony	2	0
Adultery	0	13
Other	0	9

SOURCE Clerk's Office, Pima County Superior Court, Tucson, Arizona.

the judge ruled in favor of Joaquina. Her local network had therefore furnished information about her husband's assets and helped her to secure her share in the divorce.[38]

As these cases illustrate, financial concerns repeatedly characterized divorce proceedings. Failure to support and desertion accounted for two-thirds of all causes intermarried women cited in their divorce petitions (see table 9). The Fairbanks divorce exemplified these legal hearings. Manuela Fairbanks filed for divorce in 1874, two years after marrying Benjamin D. Fairbanks. She accused him of neglecting to provide financial support despite earning a monthly income of one hundred dollars. Manuela also appealed to Mexican relatives and friends to buttress her case. They testified that Benjamin enjoyed good health and worked regularly but spent his money gambling and visiting houses of ill fame. They also informed Manuela that he had recently received five hundred dollars, either in cash or in "good promissory notes." Their testimony helped her obtain a divorce and five hundred dollars in annual alimony.[39]

White men also understood the importance of favorable testimony. Although most of them migrated as bachelors—thus possessing smaller pools of relatives and friends—they could effectively use networks in their legal cases. For instance, when Jacob Youstcy sought to end his two-year marriage to Dominga

Sosa-Youstcy, he called on several friends to support his claims. His wife had already abandoned him, but he based his case not on charges of desertion, but on adultery, asserting that some friends repeatedly told him that she was a "perfect street-runner" and that others said that she maintained a brothel. He also claimed that he had found an undressed man in his house and money in his wife's possession. Except for that accusation, most of his case rested on the testimony of a Mexican woman and a white man. She claimed to have witnessed Dominga committing repeated acts of adultery—once with a local African American the witness knew by name. The white man, meanwhile, reported that a prostitute had said Dominga was "spoiling the trade," but he did not explain what he meant. The questionable character of the witnesses notwithstanding, the court granted the divorce.[40]

Husbands who filed for divorce primarily focused on the dissolution of the marriage, but when they also wanted custody of their children, the testimony of relatives and friends increased in importance. In 1905 Thomas Potts accused his wife, Angela R. de Potts, of abandonment but based much of his case on her purportedly immoral character. He asserted that she drank excessively and that her disregard for their two young children made her an unfit mother. Thomas called on his brother and a friend to bolster his argument. Their account simply supported what he had already said but sufficed to secure custody of the children. Angela, however, had a recourse of her own. She never appeared before the court, choosing instead to abscond to Nogales, seventy miles south of Tucson. The fact that Thomas did not specify whether he meant the Nogales in Arizona or the one in Sonora, Mexico, illustrates how southern Arizonans viewed the two Nogales as essentially one town. Angela had previously moved in with relatives there, admonishing her husband that she might leave him permanently. She had returned then, but her second estrangement would be permanent. Thomas thus obtained a hollow legal victory in winning custody of the children because his wife could count on the support of relatives and the safety of geographic separation. Thomas persevered but later stated that all inquiries among his acquaintances had yielded no clues, although he probably knew few people in the predominantly Mexican Nogales area.[41] No court ruling could compete with Angela's resourcefulness in keeping her children.

Mexican women frequently sought comfort and help among relatives when facing marital problems. Discontented women resorted to desertion so frequently that abandonment accounted for 53 percent of all causes men cited in their divorce petitions.[42] The majority of these women probably moved in with nearby relatives or friends, but others appealed to their networks in Mexico.

MARITAL EXPECTATIONS IN THE BORDERLANDS 151

For instance, in 1883, Erasmus Wood filed for divorce and custody of his two children on the grounds of abandonment. Yet Palmira, his wife of ten years, ignored the court summons. Instead, she promptly took the children to Mazatlán, Mexico, almost seven hundred miles away, where her mother's relatives lived.[43] Eulalia Haynes most likely employed the same strategy when the court awarded custody of her son to the father. She never appeared in court, and all efforts to locate her failed.[44] Similarly, Mariana Youstcy—the second of the three failed intermarriages of Jacob Youstcy—remained in Tucson during the divorce trial, but when her husband won custody of their son, the court could not enforce its decision, since Mariana had already left the area. Neither Jacob nor court officials could find her, for she had most likely resettled in her native Mexico.[45] In sum, although litigation over custody generally favored wives, Mexican women aptly compensated when rulings did go against them. They relied on family and friends and on the well-wrought migration trails of the border region. The combination of networks and mobility aptly reveals not only the resourcefulness and determination of Mexican women, but also the porosity of the political border. Until somewhat stricter enforcement of immigration laws and the creation of the border patrol in the 1920s, crossers, especially Mexicans, could easily go back and forth between the two nations.[46] Mexican women could thus have access to networks in the larger borderlands area that encompassed both sides of the border.

Yet, relocating so far away from an estranged spouse did not always seem necessary. In 1892 James Brady obtained a divorce from his wife, Mariana. Although the couple had been married for two years, they had only lived together for thirty days. He claimed that he provided a good home and appropriate sustenance and that she told him that "she had no fault to find" with him. Instead, the problem lay with the location of his house. He lived in Pantano, thirty miles southeast of Tucson, and Mariana could not cope with the detachment from her family. After two brief sojourns in that house, she refused to return. She purportedly told James that "she would rather live in a prison than in Pantano."[47] She preferred to live near her family, and he would not consider relocating to Tucson. The divorce proceeded smoothly. A similar situation occurred with the marriage of Halim Karam, a Syrian immigrant, and Enriqueta Díaz-Karam. The thirty-year-old Halim wed the seventeen-year-old Enriqueta in 1917. They remained legally married for fifteen months, but she returned to her parents' house after living with Halim for only eight weeks. She definitely did not want to live with her husband and repeatedly refused the money he sent her. He filed for divorce, in part to secure visitation rights to see his young daughter.[48] These two cases illustrate the importance of having family networks nearby. In this regard, Mexican women certainly never felt isolated as they entered into marriage with men from other ethnic backgrounds.

The importance of extended families for Mexican women must have become quite evident to intermarried men, and like Giuseppe Coppola, some husbands found it unbearable. Francisco Gil might have been seeking to prevent a similar kind of meddling when he forbade his wife from visiting her mother and relatives. In either case, he understood the importance her extended family represented. The involuntary seclusion, the vulgar language with which he spoke of her family, and physical abuse finally prompted Sarah McDermott de Gil—her mother was Mexican—to file for divorce. The judge dismissed the case, but she proved her determination by relocating to her parents' home anyway. Francisco eventually accepted her departure and obtained a divorce two years later. He accused her of abandonment, for she never returned. In her view, however, the marriage had ended when she left his house.[49]

Men, too, often employed desertion to end their marriages. The use of this recourse is evident not only in the actual claims of abandonment, but also in women's citing failure to provide in their divorce petitions. While Mexican women could readily leave because they found comfort and support in their connection to people and places in southern Arizona and northern Mexico, white men perhaps found it just as easy to move away precisely because they did not maintain such attachments. Indeed, aside from their local wives and children, most intermarrying men lacked family roots that might keep them in town. The number of divorce cases filed by women that involved desertion (47 percent) or failure to provide (19 percent) suggests that the marriage had essentially dissolved by the time those cases reached the courtroom. Although two-thirds of all petitions by women cited desertion or failure to provide, the total number of husbands who did either (38) pales in comparison to the total number of intermarriages (approximately 1,700).

In some cases, the men simply moved to another part of town or to a nearby area, but other examples clearly illustrate the itinerant nature of some migrating white men. For instance, Luz Osuna-Houston ended her seven-year marriage to Ezra B. Houston in 1897. The couple had spent only four years together because after they had relocated to Hermosillo (in Sonora, Mexico), Ezra had abandoned his pregnant wife and returned to the United States. Initially, he remained in contact, writing letters from El Paso, Texas, but eighteen months of silence convinced her that the relationship had ended, and she filed for divorce after returning to Tucson.[50] The marriage of Faustina Gilliland (née Leon-

Aldrich) resulted in a similar dissolution. She traveled from Tucson to Kansas City to marry James Gilliland in December 1893. The couple then proceeded to Chicago for an extended honeymoon. But once Faustina realized that James constantly requested money from her, she refused to oblige. In response, he abandoned her in Chicago, stealing her clothes and jewelry. She looked for him but could never locate him. Her mother, Teófila, had to travel to Chicago to retrieve her penniless daughter.[51] Faustina easily obtained a divorce soon after. As in the Bonillas-Coppola divorce, she viewed her husband as a fortune hunter. In this case, however, he was the one who resorted to abandonment, prompting her parents to exercise their class prerogative by protecting their daughter's—and their own—family honor and vilifying the ex-husband.

Cases of abandonment, however, often concealed issues that extended beyond the actual desertion. Defendants in these proceedings almost never appeared before the court—probably because most had already left the area or because they assumed that the divorce would soon occur anyway. Therefore, the voices of those who decided to leave their spouses remain mostly silent, and one cannot quantify or qualify the factors that prompted their decisions. Yet, some clues do exist. For instance, 31 percent of women seeking a divorce cited physical abuse as the primary cause of their divorce petitions. But that number most likely represented only a fraction of the actual number of marriages that dissolved due to spousal abuse. Namely, recalling that more than half (53 percent) of petitions men filed involved abandonment by their wives, a significant number of those women probably decided to leave their husbands in response to some form of abuse. Men, too, were victims of abuse, although they cited fewer—if more scandalous—cases than women did.

Women who based their divorce petitions on spousal abuse typically limited their legal complaints to general accusations of "physical and verbal abuse" or "mental and bodily suffering."[52] Sometimes, however, they chose to elaborate, and their descriptions illustrated the extreme forms of mistreatment they—and most likely others—had endured, in some cases for many years. For example, Inez Tabor obtained a divorce after she accused her husband of attempting to choke her and constantly using vile language, even making death threats against her. She further accused him of causing great physical and emotional anguish by forcing her to travel to New Mexico barely two days after giving birth.[53] Other women also received death threats during episodes of physical and verbal abuse. In one case, Robert Fisher, who had married Joaquina Fisher only three weeks earlier, ordered her to obtain $1,500 from her father and threatened to kill both if she refused. She did go to her father's house but chose to remain there instead. She later rejected her husband's pleas to return to him, fearing that he would eventually follow through with his threats. She divorced him soon after.[54] Mexican women had a particular aversion to verbal abuse, especially if it occurred in front of their children or in public. Juanita Montgomery accused her husband, Donald, of physical and verbal abuse. She described the bruises and lacerations she had suffered and the vulgar language he had used toward her. Juanita emphasized what she called a deep public humiliation when, on one occasion, he beat her and insulted her in public, and on another, he paraded through the streets of Tucson in the company of other women. He, in turn, accused her of immorality, but his arguments did not prevail. Juanita further convinced the judge to send the couple's two children to live with Donald so that he would support them while she could visit them whenever she wished.[55]

Those marriages involved physical and emotional suffering but lasted a relatively short period of time—from three weeks to less than three years. The twenty-three-year marriage of María Urrea Van Alstine, on the other hand, included at least thirteen years of severe abuse. She even had to endure the last five years of her marriage without any financial support for her and her eight children. Her testimony recounted various episodes of violence—including her husband's flinging a chair at her when she was pregnant—constant accusations of infidelity against her, stalking, and death threats. For instance, in 1905, her husband assaulted her with a loaded gun, and in her estimation, only the intervention of her children prevented her certain death. She finally divorced him in 1910.[56]

Mexican women were not always on the receiving end of domestic violence. Some of them actually carried out the abuse themselves. Abuse accusations against wives accounted for the second highest number of complaints men filed (25 percent), trailing only abandonment (53 percent). Men primarily referred to lesser, if at times humiliating, offenses such as dish throwing, broom strikes, and cursing.[57] Some, however, accused their wives of more serious acts, like knife wielding, teaching their children to curse at them, allowing relatives to move in to aid in the abuse, and even threatening and eventually causing bodily harm, in one case by running over one of them with a car.[58] For example, Charles B. Harris tended to flee the house when his wife, Diega, entered into what he characterized as "spells of ungovernable temper." One day, however, he could not run fast enough. Diega caught up to him and slapped him on the streets of Tucson. Remarkably, Diega did not deny the allegations. Instead, she attempted to justify her actions by accusing her husband of failing to provide and of excessive drinking. She expressed particular contempt at having to use income from her own investment properties to support him and his gambling addiction. Although appearing as the defendant, she, too, demanded the dissolution of the marriage. The testimony evinced that neither spouse was living up to the gender expectations of the other. He resented her physical abuse even though he did not contribute to the household. She, on the other hand, emphasized that she provided all financial support, implying that he deserved the beatings she gave him.[59]

In an extraordinary case, the divorce of a Tucson couple reached the pages of the *Los Angeles Times*. Thomas Johns sought to end his marriage to Erminia Johns and to divide their common property, worth a substantial ten thousand dollars. What drew the attention of the *Times* was the nature of the accusation. Thomas claimed that his wife had poisoned him and thus left him incapacitated for two and a half years. He said that he still feared for his life because she wanted to kill him to get his money and that he had lately refused to eat and drink at home. Erminia—a "good looking Mexican woman," according to the *Times*—shrewdly avoided responding directly to the accusations. Instead, she explained that the doctors did not specifically identify the cause of his ailment as poisoning. She expressed love and concern for her husband but retorted that he could in fact work yet chose not to. She also claimed that Thomas physically and verbally abused her in public and that she had to take in roomers and to work as a laundress to maintain the household. The court granted the divorce and divided the property.[60]

Notably, considering the different backgrounds of interethnic couples, spouses in divorce proceedings never raised ethnic or racial issues as causes for divorce. Furthermore, for all the charges of infidelity, violence, and abandonment, divorce litigants almost never mentioned the race or culture of their partners in a demeaning manner or as sources of tension. Only 2 of 103 divorce cases between 1873 and 1930 included culturally insensitive language, and neither divorce specifically focused on ethnic differences. In one case, Amelia Binning filed for divorce against Oscar Binning, citing failure to provide only as it pertained to the beating he gave her when she told him she could not obtain the ingredients to prepare him breakfast because he had canceled her store credit. He later struck his two stepchildren when they intervened to stop him from physically attacking their mother. All along, she stated, he kept calling her "a Mexican bastard, bitch and other names."[61]

In the other case, Rita Lee accused her estranged husband Alexander Mac-Minn of verbal and physical abuse. She declared that he called her a "d____ Mexican" and threatened to "cut all the Mexican blood out of" their young boy. The Tucson-born child embodied a particularly pluralistic ancestry: half Scottish due to his immigrant father, one-quarter Chinese, and one-quarter Mexican, since Rita had a Chinese father and a Mexican mother. The accusation, however, leaves the impression that MacMinn viewed his wife as entirely Mexican—an opinion that, as stated earlier in this chapter, probably facilitated their otherwise illegal marriage.[62] Both examples of ethnic epithets pointed to frustration with the relationship and gender inequality more than ethnic animosity. The men in these relationships sought to exert power over women they viewed and treated as their inferiors. By filing for divorce, the women demonstrated their unwillingness to play that role.

CONCLUSION

Divorce cases can indicate the type of fulfillment couples were seeking—and not receiving—and marital problems like theirs probably existed in marriages that remained intact, regardless of their longevity.[63] In all likelihood, many more men and women who never filed for divorce also experienced spousal abuse, economic hardship, infidelity issues, and temporary or permanent abandonment. These cases reveal, however, the conditions and situations that some spouses considered unacceptable and the proactive measures they took to secure a new start.

The story of Hiram and Petra Stevens illustrates how expectations could weigh heavily on the decisions of some people. At one point, Hiram must have realized that his reality no longer met his vision for the future. He shot his wife and committed suicide, but these actions do not overshadow the long marriage and local eminence the Stevenses enjoyed for more than thirty years and the good reputation Petra maintained after his death. On the contrary, the political, financial, and social achievements of the Stevens family still dominate their story as one of Tucson's most celebrated pioneer families. By far, most interethnic unions resemble the peaceful period of the Stevens marriage. After all, at every point between 1870 and 1930, more than 90 percent of Tucson's interethnic couples chose to remain married. Thus, the great majority of men and women involved in interethnic unions most likely met the expectations of their spouses or made compromises to reconcile the visions each partner had.

Some men and women, however, probably changed their visions for the future after they married, or perhaps they eventually realized that their goals proved too incompatible with those of their spouses. In either case, an incompatibility of expectations lay behind almost all the divorces of interethnic couples. An important aspect of the worldview of Mexican women certainly involved their close attachment to their families. One can thus understand why Mariana Brady acted bluntly and decisively when she informed her husband that she would rather live in a prison than in his house. She simply could not see herself leading the life that he envisioned for the marriage. She promptly returned to the comfort of her childhood home to live with her parents. Another component of the family attachments of Mexican women helps explain their unwillingness to give up their children. María Bonillas-Coppola, for instance, appeared in court only after her lawyer assured her that her husband could not take away her children, and she allowed him to see them only in the presence of a court official. Whatever the reason for the occasional judgments that granted custody of the children to husbands, Mexican women repeatedly responded to the possibility of losing their children by leaving the area, sometimes moving deep into Mexican territory.

One of the most striking revelations about these divorces is the frequency with which men and women abandoned their spouses. One might expect only men to use this recourse—due to the historiographical association between western migration and male mobility—but Mexican women frequently employed this method of ending their relationship, thanks largely to their local and regional networks. Desertion was in fact the most common route men and women took to end a marriage. It accounted for approximately half of all dissolutions of intermarriages. Many of those spouses probably escaped abusive situations, while others absconded with lovers or simply sought a fresh start. The extent of domestic violence thus remains elusive, especially among the couples that never resorted to divorce. These and other reasons for the departures of those who did desert reveal one of the characteristics of divorces in Tucson: men and women viewed the recourse of abandoning an unsatisfactory marriage as part of the expectations they had when they first married. By leaving, they expressed their dissatisfaction in a manner that underscored their worldview and determination.

Intermarriages, like endogamous unions, often experienced domestic discord, and white men who intermarried did not necessarily embrace all kinds of ethnic diversity or tolerance. Peter Brady, who married Mexican women on two occasions, had fought in the U.S.-Mexico War and violently removed Mexicans from mining towns.[64] William Oury, a southern Democrat from Virginia, fought against Mexico at the Battle of San Jacinto in 1836 and later belonged to the infamous Texas Rangers, who repeatedly persecuted people of Mexican ancestry along the border. Like his brother Granville, William belonged to the Confederate sympathizers who temporarily captured Tucson during the Civil War. He later led whites, Mexicans, and Indians during the Camp Grant Massacre against Apache Indians, in which zealous Republicans Hiram Stevens and Sam Hughes—both married to Mexican women—also participated.[65] Yet, no evidence suggests that these men viewed the race or culture of their wives as inferior. When divorces or violence did occur, those problems usually involved economic and domestic discord, not racial or cultural issues.

On the contrary, the hundreds of westering white men and the dozens of black and Chinese men who intermarried seemed to have openly embraced the Mexican domesticity of the women they married. After all, adapting to change characterized intermarrying partners. Mexican women, the heirs of centuries of racial blending in colonial and independent Mexico, had undoubtedly interacted with various groups along the Arizona and northern Mexico frontiers. The Tucson area they inhabited was but one of several settlements that held small populations and lay more than two hundred miles away from any major population center. Incoming settlers, like the long line of white frontiersmen in American history and the black and Chinese arrivals, soon became aware of the cultural uniqueness of the borderlands. Their immersion into Mexican culture simply followed their arrival into the larger cultural space of southern Arizona and the even larger American West. Many of these men learned Spanish and even received Spanish nicknames. Their daily lives included a plethora of Mexican cultural practices, especially food, traditions, and religion. Intermarriage brought hundreds of them into the kinship of compadrazgo with Mexicans and with other intermarried men, and most of them signaled their acceptance of Mexican culture by giving Spanish names to their children. Those first generations of children of mixed ancestry personified the blending of ethnic backgrounds and the dominance of their Mexican culture. Not surprisingly, they also entered into interethnic unions with great frequency.

EPILOGUE

CONTEMPORARY TUCSON maintains a strong connection to its nineteenth-century pioneers. Streets, schools, parks, businesses, and historical sites bear the names of renowned nineteenth-century figures. These landmarks illustrate the prominence of both Mexican and white residents, but an erasure has taken place over the last century, and it involves issues of race, class, and gender. Largely missing from the town's historical markers are references to blacks, Chinese, and working-class Mexicans and whites. Also generally absent are the names of the wives of famous Mexican and white Tucsonans. Patrilineal naming practices in both cultures—in passing down surnames and in naming businesses and landmarks—obscure the contributions of women. It seems as if those business owners and political players acted entirely on their own. For example, some landmarks hide the Mexican connections of the Sam Hughes Historical Neighborhood, Contzen and Meyer Avenues, Van Alstine Street, and Oury Park. They all bear the names of men who married Mexican women, but these women's names— Atanacia Santa Cruz, Margarita Ferrer, Encarnación Ramírez, Rita Campo, and María Inez García, respectively—fail to appear on these or any Tucson landmarks.

Those omissions notwithstanding, Mexican women and their cultural practices significantly influenced the family lives of Euro-American sheriffs, mayors, congressmen, and countless businessmen—and of prominent Mexican men as well. But even more significant was their influence on marriages with partners of various races from the working class, which accounted for a far greater number of interethnic unions. Marriage practices in Tucson reveal that Mexican women, who participated in both endogamous and exogamous relationships, stand out as pivotal actors in shaping family and social life between 1854 and 1930. Nearly all intermarriages before 1900 were between Mexican women and white men, and a large percentage of black and Chinese marriages until the 1920s were to Mexican women, facts that only begin to illustrate the importance of these women during the transformation of Tucson from a Mexican pueblo to an American town. They represent one of the principal reasons that the city has remained highly Mexicanized over the years.

One must keep in mind that all along, the prerogative to intermarry rested almost entirely with Mexican women. Tucson's Mexican population had always maintained relatively balanced sex ratios. Yet, the skewed sex ratios among whites, blacks, and Chinese resulted in a surplus of bachelors. Mexican women could then choose from a large pool of men. The hundreds of intermarriages that occurred in Pima County by 1910—before women from other ethnicities migrated in large numbers—indicate not only that men embraced interethnic relationships, but more important, that Mexican women did too. After all, Mexican women always had the option of marrying Mexican men in Tucson, in other southern Arizona towns, or in nearby Mexico. Yet, they consistently formed both endogamous and exogamous families.

Divorce cases illustrate the extent of agency Mexican women possessed. One of the most striking revelations about these separations is the frequency with which Mexican women abandoned their spouses. Whether the women were escaping an abusive situation or simply searching for a more fulfilling life, desertion emerged as the most recurrent complaint intermarried men cited in their divorce petitions. Once again, Mexican women aptly used their kinship networks to secure a place to stay when they decided to leave. At times, these relatives lived in Tucson, but women repeatedly traveled hundreds of miles into Mexican territory to start anew. American expansionists often spoke of their mission to incorporate northern Mexico and redeem its residents, of marrying Mexican women and allowing them the opportunity to live among a better people. If anything, it was Mexican women who seemed to have rescued white, black, and Chinese men from long or permanent bachelorhood in the West.

The presence of Mexican women thus proved particularly important for black and Chinese men. As skewed as sex ratios were for whites, they were far worse for black and Chinese residents. More important, white men could legally marry white women, who were numerous in other parts of Arizona and the West. These options were effectively closed for blacks and Chinese. Fortunately for them, Mexican women demonstrated an openness to enter into interethnic relationships, and civil and religious officials often ignored Arizona's miscegenation law to allow their marriages. In Tucson, the small number of black and Chinese residents lived in predominantly Mexican enclaves and interacted with Mexicans and poor whites in these working-class areas. Those who formed unions with Mexican women further benefited from those relationships because Mexican women belonged to kinship networks that allowed their nonwhite partners opportunities to form economic, social, and religious connections.

The history of Chinese-Mexican couples, for instance, proves the ability of men and women to make their own decisions during a highly intolerant period in both the United States and Mexico. The relatively successful experiences of Chinese men in Tucson were not unique, as historian Liping Zhu emphasizes in his studies on Chinese residents in Idaho and South Dakota at the turn of the twentieth century. As in Arizona, Chinese residents in those areas encountered legal discrimination as well as verbal and physical attacks, resulting, for instance, in twenty-five deaths in Idaho alone. But this mistreatment did not occur ubiquitously or uniformly. In the Boise Basin and in the Black Hills, Zhu explains, Chinese residents escaped the worst of attacks, participated in their local communities and in the legal system, and some even managed to prosper. Family life eluded them, however, because miscegenation laws and greatly imbalanced sex ratios inevitably precluded their marriages.[1] One can then appreciate the importance of Mexicans in Arizona for the Chinese men who managed to form families. Had Idaho and South Dakota contained sizeable enough Mexican populations to allow interaction between the groups, one can safely postulate that some Chinese men would have married Mexican women.

The influence of Mexican women coincidentally facilitated the legal marriages of their multiracial children. The ancestry clause of Arizona's miscegenation law stipulated that all marriages involving the descendants of black-Mexican and Chinese-Mexican couples were illegal, but there is no record that any of these couples faced disputes over the legality of the marriage. The cultural influence of Mexican mothers facilitated the de facto Mexicanization of these children of mixed ancestry. They grew up in Spanish-speaking, Catholic households, and most of them probably viewed themselves as Mexican.

Virtually all received Spanish names and married Mexicans. Perhaps only a few of them ever knew or learned that their marriages were in fact illegal. The law failed to prevent their marriages, but it could still prompt their dissolution, as the courts always upheld its constitutionality. Yet, the ancestry clause never arose in legal disputes in Tucson, and marriages of Mexicans with blacks or Chinese (or of the descendants of these couples) almost never ended in divorce, even though either spouse could have sought an annulment at any point.

The Old Pueblo, as Tucsonans refer to their town, experienced a major demographic transformation from its incorporation into the United States in 1854 to 1930. As in so many locales throughout the Southwest, its population shifted from an almost complete Mexican dominance to a very clear white majority. The year 1900 marked a watershed moment in that change. Mexicans accounted for slightly more than half the overall residents and households, but white couples now outnumbered their Mexican counterparts for the first time (453 to 394). Family stability and continuing migration by whites had started a switch in the population that coalesced by 1930. Interethnic unions as a share of all marriages for whites had dropped from the remarkable peaks of the 1860s and 1870s to about 23 percent by 1900 and slightly above 7 percent by 1930, and the number of single white women increased substantially after 1900. Based on those facts, the historiography of the Southwest has observed that (1) the intermarriage rate for whites decreased substantially by 1930; (2) the growing presence of white women caused the decline; and (3) intermarriage therefore became rare. None of the three conclusions, however, is correct. The data in this book demonstrate that white men who lived in Tucson while single consistently intermarried at high rates. Calculations generate a lower intermarriage rate only if one includes men who already had a spouse when they arrived in town, and thus did not have the option to marry locally. But that approach produces a *married*, not a marriage rate. Intermarriage was becoming not rare but more common, as the number of interethnic families in Tucson more than doubled by 1930. More important, files from Pima County, whose population resided primarily in the Tucson area, include records of people that the census might have missed because of their high mobility. They indicate that approximately 1,300 intermarriages took place between 1901 and 1930, almost three times as many as in the previous thirty years. Class, this book has argued, is the best explanation for the continuing and increasing practice. Mexicans, blacks, Chinese, and whites historically interacted in working-class neighborhoods, which tended to be ethnically diverse or largely Mexican. Race did matter, because whites rarely formed families with either blacks or Chinese. The racial ambiguity of Mexicans, on the other hand, facilitated their relationships with both whites and nonwhites. Such was the confluence of class and race in the Arizona borderlands.

NOTES

INTRODUCTION

1. Harry Lawson, *The History of African Americans in Tucson: An Afrocentric Perspective* (Tucson, AZ: Lawson's Psychological Services, 1996), 20–21; *The Howell Code, Adopted by the First Legislative Assembly of the Territory of Arizona* (Prescott: Office of the Arizona Miner, 1865), 230–31; marriage entry for Emet Wudly [*sic*] and Leonicia Terasas [*sic*], p. 93, St. Augustine Marriage Register, 1883–1899, Catholic Diocese of Tucson Archives, Arizona; for a record of the marriage license of Emet Wudley [*sic*] and Leonicia Ceraza [*sic*], see Floyd R. Negley and Marcia S. Lindley, *Arizona Territorial Marriages, Pima County, 1871–1912* (Tucson: Arizona State Genealogical Society, 1994), 83.

2. Certificate of death for Emmett Woodley, February 3, 1935, Phoenix, Maricopa County, Arizona Genealogy Birth and Death Certificates, Office of Vital Records, Arizona Department of Health Services, Phoenix, accessed April 4, 2012, http://genealogy.az.gov.

3. David J. Weber, *Foreigners in Their Native Land* (Albuquerque: University of New Mexico Press, 1973), 104, 225.

4. Reginald Horsman, *Race and Manifest Destiny: The Origins of American Racial Anglo-Saxonism* (Cambridge, MA: Harvard University Press, 1981), 300, 208, 210; Martha Menchaca, *Recovering History, Constructing Race: The Indian, Black, and White Roots of Mexican Americans* (Austin: University of Texas

Press, 2001), 215–28; Mario Barrera, *Race and Class in the Southwest: A Theory of Racial Inequality* (Notre Dame, IN: University of Notre Dame Press, 1979), 13, 213; Albert Camarillo, *Chicanos in a Changing Society: From Mexican Pueblos to American Barrios in Santa Barbara and Southern California, 1848–1930* (Cambridge, MA: Harvard University Press, 1996), 43, 100; David Montejano, *Anglos and Mexicans in the Making of Texas, 1836–1986* (Austin: University of Texas Press, 1987), 34–36; Rodolfo Acuña, *Occupied America: The Chicano's Struggle Toward Liberation* (New York: Harper and Row, 1972), 117; Ariela J. Gross, *What Blood Won't Tell: A History of Race on Trial in America* (Cambridge, MA: Harvard University Press, 2008), 5–8, 254–76; Thomas E. Sheridan, *Los Tucsonenses: The Mexican Community in Tucson, 1854–1941* (Tucson: University of Arizona Press, 1986), 118–19.

5. *Howell Code*, 172. Emphasis added.

6. Linda Gordon, *The Great Arizona Orphan Abduction* (Cambridge, MA: Harvard University Press, 1999), 3–12, 76–77, 96–97, 174–75, 180–81; Sheridan, *Los Tucsonenses*, 35, 89–91, 170–79.

7. Acuña, *Occupied America*, 31–33, 53, 83, 117; Tomás Almaguer, *Racial Fault Lines: The Historical Origins of White Supremacy in California* (Berkeley: University of California Press, 1994), 58–59; Camarillo, *Chicanos in a Changing Society*, 69–70; Manuel G. Gonzales, *Mexicanos: A History of Mexicans in the United States* (Bloomington: Indiana University Press, 2000), 90, 93, 101; Carey McWilliams, *North from Mexico: The Spanish-Speaking People of the United States* (New York: Praeger, 1990), 90; Sheridan, *Los Tucsonenses*, 145–48; María Raquél Casas, *Married to a Daughter of the Land: Spanish-Mexican Women and Interethnic Marriage in California, 1820–1880* (Reno: University of Nevada Press, 2007); Pablo Mitchell, "'You Just Don't Know Mrs. Baca': Intermarriage, Mixed Heritage, and Identity in New Mexico," *New Mexico Historical Review* 79, no. 4 (Fall 2004): 437–58; James E. Officer, "Historical Factors in Interethnic Relations in the Community of Tucson," *Arizoniana* 1, no. 1 (Spring 1960): 13–15; Richard Griswold del Castillo, *La Familia: Chicano Families in the Urban Southwest, 1848 to the Present* (Notre Dame, IN: University of Notre Dame Press, 1984), 67–69.

8. Officer, "Historical Factors," 13; Sheridan, *Los Tucsonenses*, 109–15, 146–49.

9. Officer, "Historical Factors," 12–16.

10. Ibid., 13–14; James E. Officer, *Hispanic Arizona, 1536–1856* (Tucson: University of Arizona Press, 1989), 311.

11. Sheridan, *Los Tucsonenses*, 150.

12. Thomas E. Sheridan, *Arizona: A History* (Tucson: University of Arizona Press, 1995), 123.

13. Deena J. González, *Refusing the Favor: The Spanish-Mexican Women of Santa Fe, 1820–1880* (New York: Oxford University Press, 2001), 113–14; Darlis Miller, "Cross-Cultural Marriages in the Southwest: The New Mexico Experience, 1846–1900," *New Mexico Historical Review* 57, no. 4 (October 1982): 335, 337, 340; Rebecca M. Craver, *The Impact of Intimacy: Mexican-Anglo Intermarriage in New Mexico, 1821–1846* (El Paso: Texas Western Press, 1982), 11; Jane Dysart, "Mexican Women in San Antonio, 1830–1860: The Assimilation Process," *Western Historical Quarterly* 7, no. 4 (Winter 1976): 370; Ana C. Downing de De Juana, "Intermarriage in Hidalgo County, 1860 to 1900" (master's thesis, University of Texas, Pan American, 1998), 94–96; Karen Isaksen Leonard, *Making Ethnic Choices: California's Punjabi Mexican Americans* (Philadelphia, PA: Temple University Press, 1992), 63–68, 186, 212; Katherine Benton, "Border Jews, Border Marriages, Border Lives: Mexican-Jewish Intermarriage in the Arizona Territory, 1850–1900" (master's thesis, University of Wisconsin, Madison, 1997); Pablo Mitchell, *Coyote Nation: Sexuality, Race, and Conquest in Modernizing New Mexico, 1880–1920* (Chicago, IL: University of Chicago Press, 2005); Pablo Mitchell, "You Just Don't Know Mrs. Baca," 437–58; Rudy P. Guevarra, *Becoming Mexipino: Multiethnic Identities and Communities in San Diego* (New Brunswick, NJ: Rutgers University Press, 2012), 130–39.

14. In the case of intermarriage, the best studies on the relationship between class and intermarriage are González's *Refusing the Favor*; Downing de De Juana's "Intermarriage in Hidalgo County"; Leonard's *Making Ethnic Choices*; Benton's "Border Jews, Border Marriages"; and Guevarra's *Becoming Mexipino*.

15. Deena Gonzalez's *Refusing the Favor*, although not entirely about intermarriage, does represent the exception.

16. For a discussion of Mexicans depicted as antagonists, see Richard Slotkin, *The Fatal Environment: The Myth of the Frontier in the Age of Industrialization, 1800–1890* (New York: Atheneum, 1985), 179–80, 191–92; for a discussion of the meaning of collectivity, see Alex Callinicos, *Making History: Agency, Structure and Change in Social Theory* (Cambridge: Polity Press, 1987), 134–35; for the use of manifest destiny to attempt to create a zeitgeist, see Mark Rifkin, *Manifesting America: The Imperial Construction of U.S. National Space* (New York: Oxford University Press, 2009), 7–8.

17. Ann Laura Stoler, *Carnal Knowledge and Imperial Power: Race and the Intimate in Colonial Rule* (Berkeley: University of California Press, 2002), 1–2.

18. Ibid., 6–7, 16, 29–30, 35–36, 42–47; Ann Laura Stoler, *Race and the Education of Desire: Foucault's* History of Sexuality *and the Colonial Order of Things* (Durham, NC: Duke University Press, 1995), 43–47, 105–7, 112–15.

19. Stoler, *Race and the Education of Desire*, 32.

20. Geraldo L. Cadava, *Standing on Common Ground: The Making of a Sunbelt Borderland* (Cambridge, MA: Harvard University Press, 2013); Grace Delgado, *Making the Chinese Mexican: Global Migration, Localism, and Exclusion in the U.S.-Mexico Borderlands* (Stanford, CA: Stanford University Press, 2012); Julia María Schiavone Camacho, *Chinese Mexicans: Transpacific Migration and the Search for a Homeland, 1910–1960* (Chapel Hill: University of North Carolina Press, 2012); Nicole M. Guidotti-Hernández, *Unspeakable Violence: Remapping U.S. and Mexican National Imaginaries* (Durham, NC: Duke University Press, 2011).

CHAPTER 1

1. *Arizona v. Frank Pass*, 59 Ariz. 16, 121 P.2d 882 (1942).

2. Ibid.

3. *Inland Steel Company v. Barcena*, 110 Ind. App. 551, 39 N.E.2d 800 (1942).

4. William Hand Browne, ed., *Archives of Maryland: Proceedings and Acts of the General Assembly of Maryland, January 1637/8–September 1664* (Baltimore: Maryland Historical Society, 1883), 533–34; Byron Curti Martyn, "Racism in the United States: A History of the Anti-Miscegenation Legislation and Litigation" (PhD diss., University of Southern California, 1979), 1, 22, 46, 50–51, 62–63, 120–21, 137–38, 140–41.

5. Peter Wallenstein, *Tell the Court I Love My Wife: Race, Marriage, and Law— An American History* (New York: Palgrave MacMillan, 2002), 3–5, and unpaginated maps following page 159. Martyn, "Racism in the United States," 1–8, 169–70.

6. Martyn, "Racism in the United States," 431–32, 453–56, 552–62, 877, 902, 911–12.

7. Ibid., 456–59, 546; *Laws of the Territory of New Mexico, Passed by the Legislative Assembly, 1855–56* (Santa Fe, NM: Santa Fe Weekly Gazette, 1856), 48–50.

8. Mark J. Stegmaier, "A Law that Would Make Caligula Blush?: New Mexico Territory's Unique Slave Code, 1859–1861," in *African American History in New Mexico: Portraits from Five Hundred Years*, ed. Bruce A. Glasrud (Albuquerque:

University of New Mexico Press, 2013), 56–84; Jay J. Wagoner, *Arizona Territory, 1863–1912: A Political History* (Tucson: University of Arizona Press, 1970), 3.

9. Roger D. Hardaway, "Unlawful Love: A History of Arizona's Miscegenation Law," *Journal of Arizona History* 27, no. 4 (1986): 377–78; Wagoner, *Arizona Territory*, 65.

10. John S. Goff, "William T. Howell and the Howell Code of Arizona," *American Journal of Legal History* 11 (1967): 221–28; *Howell Code*, xi–xii; Wagoner, *Arizona Territory*, 47.

11. Martyn points out that in 1706, New York passed legislation stipulating that children of interracial marriages would "follow the state and condition of the mother" regarding their slave status. Martyn, "Racism in the United States," 127, 221.

12. The reference to the use of the statutes of both New York and California comes from Goff, "William T. Howell," 229. I compared the wording of the California and Arizona laws. See *Howell Code*, 230–31. The California law appears in Martyn, "Racism in the United States," 453.

13. Hardaway, "Unlawful Love," 178.

14. U.S. Census Office, *Population of the United States in 1860; Compiled from the Original Returns of the Eighth Census* (Washington, DC: Government Printing Office, 1864), 567; U.S. Census Office, *Ninth Census—Volume I: The Statistics of the Population of the United States* (Washington, DC: Government Printing Office, 1872), xvii.

15. *The Revised Statutes of the Arizona Territory, Containing Also the Laws Passed by the Twenty-First Legislative Assembly, the Constitution of the United States, the Organic Law of Arizona and the Amendments of Congress Relating Thereto, 1901* (Columbia, MO: Press of E. W. Stephens, 1901), 809.

16. U.S. Census Office, *Population of the United States in 1860*, 567; U.S. Census Office, *Ninth Census—Volume I*, xvii.

17. Susan Lee Johnson, *Roaring Camp: The Social World of the California Gold Rush* (New York: Norton, 2000), 275–80.

18. Wagoner, *Arizona Territory*, 36, 45–47.

19. Ibid., 27–28.

20. Sarah H. Gordon, *Passage to Union: How the Railroads Transformed American Life, 1829–1929* (Chicago, IL: Ivan R. Dee, 1996), 122.

21. Wagoner, *Arizona Territory*, 34, 47–53, 67–70, 124.

22. Robert J. Chandler, "California's 1863 Loyalty Oaths: Another Look," *Arizona and the West* 21, no. 3 (1979): 215–43; Martha Menchaca, "The Anti-Miscegenation History of the America Southwest, 1837 to 1970: Transforming Racial Ideology into Law," *Cultural Dynamics* 20 (2008): 289–91.

23. Thomas Edwin Farish, *History of Arizona*, vol. 3 (Phoenix, AZ: Filmer Brothers, 1916), 27–30, 188; Patrick Lavin, *Arizona: An Illustrated History* (New York: Hippocrene Books, 2001), 188–90; Juan Gómez-Quiñones, *Roots of Chicano Politics, 1600–1940* (Albuquerque: University of New Mexico Press, 1994), 266–69. Of the five members present on the council, two were born in the South, and in the house, five of the ten were from the South. The seven southerners were a plurality because there were only six members from the North and two foreigners. *Journals of the Second Legislative Assembly of the Territory of Arizona* (Prescott: Office of the Arizona Miner, 1866), opening rosters, unpaginated.

24. *Journals of the Second Legislative Assembly*, 38–40, 104–5, 108–9, 122–23, 225. Nevada had banned marriages between whites and "Orientals" in 1861. Martyn, "Racism in the United States," 564.

25. Sheridan, *Arizona: A History*, 59–61, 77–78; Wagoner, *Arizona Territory*, 34, 47–53, 67–70, 124.

26. Emphasis added. The ancestry clause first appeared in 1887. The clause had not appeared in the statutes of 1877, and the legislature made no pertinent changes to the miscegenation law by 1887. John P. Hoyt, comp., *The Compiled Laws of the Territory of Arizona* (Detroit, MI: Richmond, Backus, 1877), 317; *The Revised Statutes of Arizona* (Prescott, AZ: Prescott Courier Print, 1887), 371.

27. As printed, the 1887 statutes neglected to include Indians in the list of groups ineligible to marry whites. The law had not changed, however, and Indians still could not marry whites. The next version of the statutes (1901) corrected the error, and Indians and their descendants reappeared. *Revised Statutes of the Arizona Territory*, 809.

28. Wallenstein, *Tell the Court*, 133–43.

29. Wagoner, *Arizona Territory*, 351.

30. The male-to-female ratios were as follows: in Arizona, 7–1 for Filipinos and 3–1 for "Hindus"; and in California, 15–1 for both groups. U.S. Census Office, *Fifteenth Census of the United States: 1930, Population*, 6 vols. (Washington, DC: Government Printing Office 1933), 3:143, 233.

31. Guevarra, *Becoming Mexipino*; Gross, *What Blood Won't Tell*, 219–21. My thanks to Katrina Jagodinsky for directing me to the latter source.

NOTES TO PAGES 30–33   171

32. Mae M. Ngai, *Impossible Subjects: Illegal Aliens and the Making of Modern America* (Princeton, NJ: Princeton University Press, 2004), 100–15; Leonard, *Making Ethnic Choices*, 174–75.

33. The states or territories that had banned white-Chinese marriages by 1910 were Arizona, California, Mississippi, Montana, Nevada, Oregon, and Utah. By 1950 the following states also had prohibited these marriages: Georgia, Idaho, Maryland, Missouri, Nebraska, Virginia, and Wyoming. Hrishi Karthikeyan and Gabriel J. Chin, "Preserving Racial Identity: Population Patterns and the Application of Anti-Miscegenation Statutes to Asian Americans, 1910–1950," *Asian Law Journal* 9 (2002): 1, 16–18; Gross, *What Blood Won't Tell*, 219.

34. *Arizona v. Frank Pass.*

35. *Journal of the House of Representatives, First Special Session, Fifteenth Legislature of the State of Arizona, 1942* (Phoenix, AZ: s.n., 1942), 117, 210; *Journal of the Senate, First Special Session, Fifteenth Legislature of the State of Arizona, 1942* (Phoenix, AZ: s.n., 1942), 147; Hardaway, "Unlawful Love," 383–86.

36. Alison R. Bernstein, *American Indians and World War II: Toward a New Era in Indian Affairs* (Norman: University of Oklahoma Press, 1991), 3–19, 64–67, 87–88, 89–97, 110–11, 156–66.

37. Vine Deloria, Jr., ed., *American Indian Policy in the Twentieth Century* (Norman: University of Oklahoma Press, 1992), 110–11.

38. Terry Goddard, "The Promise of *Brown v. Board of Education*," March 2005, accessed April 20, 2006, http://azmemory.azlibrary.gov/cdm/ref/collection/state pubs/id/21093.

39. Abraham L. Davis and Barbara Luck Graham, *The Supreme Court, Race, and Civil Rights* (Thousand Oaks, CA: Sage, 1995), 214–16.

40. Horsman, *Race and Manifest Destiny*, 300, 208, 210.

41. Article IX of the Treaty of Guadalupe Hidalgo, included in Richard Griswold del Castillo, *The Treaty of Guadalupe Hidalgo: A Legacy of Conflict* (Norman: University of Oklahoma Press, 1990), 190.

42. Weber, *Foreigners in Their Native Land*, 104, 225.

43. Acuña, *Occupied America*, 117.

44. Linda K. Kerber, *No Constitutional Right to Be Ladies: Women and the Obligations of Citizenship* (New York: Hill and Wang, 1998), 50–58, 71, 80.

45. Barrera, *Race and Class in the Southwest*, 13, 213; Camarillo, *Chicanos in a Changing Society*, 100; Montejano, *Anglos and Mexicans*, 34–36.

46. Menchaca, *Recovering History*, 215–28; Gross, *What Blood Won't Tell*, 5–8, 254–76.

47. *Howell Code*, 172 (emphasis added); Menchaca, *Recovering History*, 220.

48. *Howell Code*, 50, 264, 294. Only the law on the qualifications of juries offered a definition of black (one-quarter or more black ancestry) and Indian (one-half or more Indian ancestry). "Mongolians" and "Asiatics" could not be witnesses either. Nonwhites could not serve on juries because only electors qualified, and only whites had the right to vote.

49. One of the original three Mexican legislators resigned amid allegations that he was not an American citizen. Menchaca, "Anti-Miscegenation History," 391. The name Francisco S. León, of Tucson, appears on the list of council members for the second assembly, but he resigned. Only one of the nine Pima County members attended the second assembly. Wagoner, *Arizona Territory*, 505–9.

50. Griswold del Castillo, *Treaty of Guadalupe Hidalgo*, 66.

51. The California Supreme Court ruled that, based on the Treaty of Guadalupe Hidalgo, Mexicans were not subject to the foreign miners' tax. *People v. Naglee*, 1 Cal. 232 (1850).

52. Camarillo, *Chicanos in a Changing Society*, 43. De la Guerra had also been a delegate in the constitutional convention and a state senator. Menchaca, *Recovering History*, 221–22.

53. Sheridan, *Los Tucsonenses*, 118–19.

54. Ian F. Haney López, *White by Law: The Legal Construction of Race* (New York: New York University Press, 1996), 1–3, 5–9, 61, 203; Ian F. Haney López, "Race and Erasure: The Salience of Race in Latinos/as," in *The Latino/a Condition: A Critical Reader*, ed. Richard Delgado and Jean Stefancic (New York: New York University Press, 1998), 182; *In re Rodriguez*, 81 Fed. 337 (W.D. Texas 1897). For a discussion of the social and psychological advantages of being accepted as white, see David R. Roediger, *The Wages of Whiteness: Race and the Making of the American Working Class* (London: Verso, 2007).

55. Gordon, *Great Arizona Orphan Abduction*, 174–75, 180–81; Sheridan, *Tucsonenses*, 3–12, 76–77, 35, 89–91, 96–97, 170–79; Sheridan, *Arizona: A History*, 151.

56. Madison Grant, *The Passing of the Great Race, or The Racial Basis of European History* (New York: Scribner, 1917), 15.

57. Charles C. Alexander, "Prophet of American Racism: Madison Grant and the Nordic Myth," *Phylon* 23, no. 1 (1962): 73–90.

58. Quoted in Sarah Deutsch, *No Separate Refuge: Culture, Class, and Gender on an Anglo-Hispanic Frontier in the American Southwest, 1880–1940* (New York: Oxford University Press, 1987), 121–22.

NOTES TO PAGES 35–38   173

59. Lynne M. Getz, "Biological Determinism in the Making of Immigration Policy in the 1920s," *International Science Review* 70, nos. 1–2 (2001): 26–28.

60. Ngai, *Impossible Subjects*, xx, 158–70.

61. Mexicans also endured invasive examinations and chemical baths and delousing in the late 1910s, all under the pretext of a typhus epidemic. Alexandra Minna Stern, "Buildings, Boundaries, and Blood: Medicalization and Nation-Building on the U.S.-Mexico Border, 1910–1930," *Hispanic American Historical Review* 79, no. 1 (1999): 44–47, 52, 80–81; Alexandra Minna Stern, "Eugenics Beyond Borders: Science and Medicalization in Mexico and the U.S. West, 1900–1950" (PhD diss., University of Chicago, 1999), 25. For more on the 1930 census, see Ngai, *Impossible Subjects*, 29–32.

62. Peggy Pascoe, *What Comes Naturally: Miscegenation Law and the Making of Race in America* (New York: Oxford University Press, 2009), 20–24, 42, 137.

63. Peggy Pascoe, "Race, Gender, and the Privileges of Property: On the Significance of Miscegenation Law in the U.S. West," in *Over the Edge: Remapping the American West*, ed. Valerie J. Matsumoto and Blake Allmendinger (Berkeley: University of California Press, 1999), 217–18; Peggy Pascoe, "Miscegenation Law, Court Cases, and Ideologies of 'Race' in Twentieth-Century America," *Journal of American History* 83, no. 1 (June 1996): 49–50.

64. Pascoe, *What Comes Naturally*, 22–26.

65. Ibid., 101–2.

66. *In re Walker's Estate*, 5 Ariz. 70, 46 P. 67 (1896).

67. Marriage license for Joe Kirby and Maryella [*sic*] Conner, Floyd R. Negley and Marcia S. Lindley, *Arizona Marriages, Pima County, Marriage Books 5–10, February 1912 through December 1926* (Tucson: Arizona State Genealogical Society, 1997), 165; 1920 U.S. census, Pima County, Arizona, population schedules, city of Tucson, district 94, p. 1B, lines 68–71, microfilm T625, roll 50, U.S. Census Records, National Archives and Records Administration, Washington, DC (hereafter NARA); 1920 U.S. census, Pima County, Arizona, population schedules, city of Tucson, district 95, p. 1A, lines 19–24, microfilm T625, roll 50, NARA; 1930 U.S. census, Pima County, Arizona, population schedules, city of Tucson, district 43, p. 17B, lines 52–54, microfilm T626, roll 62, NARA.

68. See Pascoe, *What Comes Naturally*, for more on this interpretation.

69. Joe's mother stated that both of her grandfathers were Spanish and both of her grandmothers were Mexican.

70. *Kirby v. Kirby*, 24 Ariz. 9, 206 P. 405 (1922); Pascoe, *What Comes Naturally*, 109–11, 123.

71. *In re Monks' Estate*, 48 Cal. App. 2d 603, 120 Pac. 2d 167, 173 (1941); Pascoe, *What Comes Naturally*, 126–28.

72. Gross, *What Blood Won't Tell*, 1–10.

73. Ibid.

74. *In re Monks' Estate*; Pascoe, *What Comes Naturally*, 126–28.

75. "Jap Would Wed German Girl," *Tucson Daily Citizen*, May 12, 1909. Annie's surname might have been Brau or Braun. Certificate of birth for Merris Brau Togo, October 12, 1909, Prescott, Yavapai County; certificate of birth for still-born infant, December 29, 1912, Prescott, Yavapai County, Arizona Genealogy Birth and Death Certificates.

76. The story appeared in "An Illegal Marriage," *Prescott Evening Courier*, January 30, 1904. The article cited the original source as *Bisbee Review*, January 27, 1904. The law appears in *Revised Statutes of the Arizona Territory*, 809.

77. "American Girl Clings to Her Chink Hubby," *Prescott Journal Miner*, September 20, 1918. For the prevailing law, see Samuel L. Pattee, comp., *The Revised Statutes of Arizona, 1913, Civil Code* (Phoenix, AZ: McNeil, 1913), 1310. For more on the opposition to Chinese-white couples in Jerome, see Kathryn Reisdorfer, "Charley Hong, Racism, and the Power of the Press in Jerome, Arizona Territory, 1909," *Journal of Arizona History* 43, no. 2 (Summer 2002): 138–42.

78. Pascoe, "Miscegenation Law," 48–51; Patricia Hill Collins, "Gender, Black Feminism, and Black Political Economy," in *Mixed Race America and the Law*, ed. Kevin R. Johnson (New York: New York University Press, 2003), 235; Wallenstein, *Tell the Court*, 80–81, 162–63.

79. "Mixed Colors Are Involved: Strange Case of Chinaman and Mexican," *Tucson Daily Citizen*, September 4, 1909.

80. Pascoe, *What Comes Naturally*, 20–24, 42, 137.

CHAPTER 2

1. Sam Houston, *The Writings of Sam Houston, 1813–1863*, vol. 5, ed. Amelia W. Williams and Eugene C. Barker (Austin: University of Texas Press, 1941), 29–35; William F. Pinar, *The Gender of Racial Politics and Violence in America: Lynching, Prison Rape, and the Crisis of Masculinity* (New York: Peter Lang, 2001), 271–75; Giovanna Dell'Orto, *Giving Meanings to the World: The First U.S. Foreign Correspondents, 1838–1859* (Westport, CT: Greenwood Press, 2002). For a discussion of Anglo-Saxonism in relation to the Mexican war and the

use of the phrase "discourse of manifest destiny," see Horsman, *Race and Manifest Destiny*, 93, 208, 300

2. Houston, *Writings*, 34–36.

3. See the following articles in the *United States Magazine and Democratic Review*: "The Mexican War: Its Origin and Conduct," April 1847, 291–99; "The Mexican War: Its Origin, Its Justice, and Its Consequences," January 1848, 1–11; "The Mexican War: Its Origin, Its Justice, and Its Consequences," February 1848, 119; "Mexico and the Mexicans," June 1850, 547; "Mexico and the Monroe Doctrine," May 1853, 439, 447, 451; "The Fate of Mexico," May 1858, 344–45. See also, "The Agricultural Fair," *New York Times*, November 1, 1858; "Mexico and the United States," *Putnam's Magazine*, May 1869, 618–20; "Mexico," *Albion*, April 11, 1846, 179; "Mexican Argument for Annexation," *Littell's Living Age*, September 19, 1846, 573–74.

4. William Shaler, "Journal of a Voyage between China and the North-Western Coast of America Made in 1804," *American Register*, January 1, 1808, 151–53.

5. Cited in David J. Weber, "'Scarce More than Apes': Historical Roots of Anglo American Stereotypes of Mexicans in the Border Region," in *New Spain's Far Northern Frontier: Essays on Spain in the American West, 1540–1821*, ed. David J. Weber (Dallas, TX: Southern Methodist University Press, 1988), 297–302. Weber underscores that Texans deprecated Mexicans most of all social classes.

6. Joel Roberts Poinsett, *Notes on Mexico, Made in the Autumn of 1822* (London: John Miller, 1825), 36–37, 51, 88, 94, 107–8, 159–63, 266; Joel Roberts Poinsett, "The Mexican Character," in *The Mexico Reader: History, Culture, Politics*, ed. Gilbert Michael Joseph and Timothy J. Henderson (Durham, NC: Duke University Press, 2002), 11–13.

7. Timothy Flint, *Francis Berrian, or the Mexican Patriot*, vol. 2 (Boston, MA: Cummings, Hilliard, 1826), 92–93.

8. John T. Flanagan and Raymond L. Grismer, "Mexico in American Fiction Prior to 1850," *Hispania* 23, no. 4 (December 1940): 307–10.

9. Albert Pike, *Prose, Sketches, and Poems Written in the Western Country*, ed. David J. Weber (College Station: Texas A&M University Press, 1987), xv, 103, 106, 108–9, 115–16, 186–87, 247.

10. Flanagan and Grismer, "Mexico in American Fiction," 311–17.

11. Norman D. Smith, "Mexican Stereotypes on Fictional Battlefields: Or Dime Novel Romances of the Mexican War," *Journal of Popular Culture* 13, no. 3 (Spring 1980): 526–32.

12. John Quincy Adams, Andrew Jackson, and John Tyler attempted to purchase Mexican territory during their presidencies. See Ray Allen Billington and

Martin Ridge, *Westward Expansion: A History of the American Frontier*, 5th ed. (New York: MacMillan, 1982), 435, 505–10; Norman A. Graebner, "The Mexican War: A Study in Causation," *Pacific Historical Review* 49, no. 3 (August 1980): 405–26; Rockwell D. Hunt, "A Prize and a National Policy: The Contest for California," *Annual Publications of the Historical Society of Southern California* (1923): 128–39; Peter M. Jonas, "William Parrott, American Claims, and the Mexican War," *Journal of the Early Republic* 12, no. 2 (Summer 1992): 213–40; Gary May, *John Tyler* (New York: Times Books, 2008), 96–105.

13. John O'Sullivan, "The Mexican Question," *United States Magazine and Democratic Review*, May 1845, 419–28; James K. Polk, "Address to the Senate and House of Representatives, May 11, 1846," in *A Compilation of the Messages and Papers of the Presidents, 1789–1908*, vol. 6, ed. James D. Richardson (Washington, DC: Bureau of National Literature and Art, 1908), 438. For a longer discussion of the topic of the Mexican Question, see chapter 2 in John-Michael Rivera, *The Emergence of Mexican America: Recovering Stories of Mexican Peoplehood in U.S. Culture* (New York: New York University Press, 2006).

14. John O'Sullivan, "Annexation," *United States Magazine and Democratic Review*, July–August 1845, 5, 7, 9.

15. "Mexico," *United States Magazine and Democratic Review*, June 1846, 434–35; "Fate of Mexico," 337–45. See also the derisive response of the *Democratic Review* to a sympathetic depiction by the Englishman George Frederick Augustus Ruxton: "Review of *Mexico and the Rocky Mountains*," *United States Magazine and Democratic Review*, March 1848, 288; George Frederick Augustus Ruxton, *Adventures in Mexico and the Rocky Mountains* (New York: Harper and Brothers, 1848), 304–5.

16. "Mexico: Its Population, the Character of its People," *Pittsfield Sun*, September 4, 1845; "Mexico, Its Territory and Its People," *Anglo American*, October 3, 1846, 565–67; "The Inhabitants of the United States," *American Quarterly Register and Magazine*, May 1848, 203–7; "Mexican Races," *Christian Secretary*, March 19, 1847, 4; "Mexico," *Zion's Herald and Wesleyan Journal*, July 15, 1846, 147.

17. "Mexican Skulls," *American Phrenological Journal* 9 (1847): 155.

18. Robert Newton, "Original Communications," *New York Journal of Medicine and Collateral Sciences* (November 1848): 297, 300–303; "The Mexican Race," *Littell's Living Age*, July 17, 1847, 135–36.

19. J. J. von Tschudi, *Travels in Peru during the Years 1838–1842*, trans. by Thomasina Ross (New York: Wiley and Putnam, 1847). Tschudi's work also appeared as

Sketches of Travel in Peru. "Inhabitants of the United States," 206–7; Thomas Jefferson Farnham, *Life, Travels, and Adventures in California, and Scenes in the Pacific Ocean* (New York: W. H. Graham, 1847), 309, 363, 412–13.

20. Rufus B. Sage, *Rocky Mountain Life* (Boston: Wentworth, 1857), 211; Robert A. Wilson, *Mexico and Its Religion* (New York: Harper and Brothers, 1856), 262, 309–10; Benjamin Keen, *The Aztec Image in Western Thought* (New Brunswick, NJ: Rutgers University Press, 1971), 381–82; Samuel Kneeland, Jr., "The Hybrid Races of Animals and Men," *Debow's Review* 19, no. 5 (November 1855): 535–39. Kneeland, as did many scientific aficionados of the second half of the nineteenth century, most likely based his conclusions on Tschudi's *Travels in Peru.* Gregory Castle, ed., *Postcolonial Discourses: An Anthology* (Malden, MA: Blackwell, 2001), 86–88.

21. Jimmy L. Bryan, "The American Elsewhere: Adventurism and Manliness in the Age of Expansion, 1815–1848" (PhD diss., University of Texas, Arlington, 2006), 198, 204; Raymund A. Paredes, "The Mexican Image in American Literature, 1831–1869," *New Mexico Historical Review* 52, no. 1 (January 1977): 19–20.

22. Lansford W. Hastings, *The Emigrant's Guide to Oregon and California* (1845; repr., New York: Da Capo Press, 1969), 112–14; Cecil Robinson, *Mexico and the Hispanic Southwest in American Literature* (Tucson: University of Arizona Press, 1977), 71–73; Bryan, "American Elsewhere," 214, 217–19.

23. Josiah Clark Nott and George R. Gliddon, *Types of Mankind* (Philadelphia, PA: Lippincott, Grambo, 1855), 276–77, 454–55; John S. Haller, "The Species Problem: Nineteenth-Century Concepts of Racial Inferiority in the Origin of Man Controversy," *American Anthropologist* 72, no. 6 (December 1970): 1319–29.

24. "Texas and Naturalization," *Liberator*, March 14, 1845; "The Peace Treaty of Mexico, and the Elements which Compose the Mexican Nation," *Littell's Living Age*, August 28, 1847, 431–32.

25. Samuel E. Chamberlain, *My Confession*, with introduction and postscript by Roger Butterfield (New York: Harper and Brothers, 1956), 273.

26. For an excellent study of the debates over expansionism vis-à-vis racial anxieties, see Thomas R. Hietala, "Continentalism and the Color Line," in *The Impact of Race on U.S. Foreign Policy*, ed. Michael L. Krenn (New York: Garland, 1999), 48–89.

27. Reginald Horsman, "Scientific Racism and the American Indian in the Mid-Nineteenth Century," *American Quarterly* 27, no. 2 (May 1975): 166. For a

somewhat positive and rare perspective on the historical accomplishments of Mexicans and thus on the potential for American redemption, see "The Mexican Question," *Knickerbocker/New York Monthly Magazine*, March 1859, 2–10.

28. "Speech of Hon. Lewis Cass," *Nile's National Register*, March 20, 1847, 41–43; Cong. Globe, 29th Cong., 2nd Sess. (1847–1848), 109, 301, 516. For a similar but more aggressive proposition, see "From the *Washington Union*," *Daily Ohio Statesman*, October 22, 1847.

29. Corydon Donnavan, who had numerous accolades for Mexican women of all classes and complexions, described men as "ignorant, indolent, inefficient creatures, distinguished but by one trait of character—that trait is treachery." Corydon Donnavan, *Adventures in Mexico, Experienced during a Captivity of Seven Months* (Boston, MA: George R. Hollbrook, 1848), 24; Robinson, *Mexico and the Hispanic Southwest*, 35–40, 56, 77. Robinson bases his assessment on a study of numerous novels, travel accounts, newspaper reports, and short stories.

30. The author made a more sweeping remark when he described Mexico City: "Mexico is the head quarters of dirt. The streets are dirty, the houses are dirty, the men are dirty, and the women dirtier, and everything you eat and drink is dirty." George Frederick Augustus Ruxton, *Adventures in Mexico: From Veracruz to Chihuahua in the Days of the Mexican War*, ed. Horace Kephart (1848; repr., New York: Outing, 1915), 13, 74. Philip S. G. Cooke, *The Conquest of New Mexico and California* (New York: Putnam, 1878), 49–50; F. Adolphus Wislizenus, *Memoir of a Tour to Northern Mexico* (Washington, DC: Tippin and Streeper, 1848).

31. Thomas B. Thorpe, *Our Army at Monterey* (Philadelphia, PA: Carey and Hart, 1847), 121–23.

32. Donnavan, *Adventures in Mexico*, 23–24.

33. George Wilkins Kendall, *Narrative of the Texan Santa Fe Expedition*, vol. 1 (London: Wiley and Putnam, 1844), 321. A version of this description also appeared as a sketch in a periodical, as did so many book-length narratives. "Mexican Women," *New York Mirror*, October 8, 1842, 323; Beverly Trulio, "Anglo-American Attitudes toward New Mexican Women," *Journal of the West* 12, no. 2 (April 1973): 232–38. Susan Magoffin, who eventually developed an appreciation for Mexican culture, initially described New Mexico women as exhibitionists and noted that some of them were "not the prettiest or whitest." Susan Shelby Magoffin, *Down the Santa Fe Trail and into Mexico: The*

Diary of Susan Shelby Magoffin, 1846–1847, ed. Stella M. Drumm (1926; repr., Lincoln: University of Nebraska Press, 1982), 93–95; George Rutledge Gibson, *Journal of a Soldier under Kearny and Doniphan, 1846–1847*, ed. Ralph P. Bieber (Glendale, CA: Arthur H. Clark, 1935), 195.

34. Farnham, *Life, Travels, and Adventures*, 363; William A. McClintock, "Journal of a Trip through Texas and Northern Mexico in 1846–1847," *Southwestern Historical Quarterly* 34 (1930): 142–43; George Winston Smith and Charles Judah, eds., *Chronicles of the Gringos: The U.S. Army in the Mexican War, Accounts of Eyewitnesses and Combatants* (Albuquerque: University of New Mexico Press, 1968), 303–4; Ralph W. Kirkham, *The Mexican War Journal and Letters of Ralph W. Kirkham*, ed. Robert Ryal Miller (College Station: Texas A&M University, 1991), 20–21; Mark L. Gardner and Marc Simmons, eds., *The Mexican War Correspondence of Richard Smith Elliott* (Norman: University of Oklahoma Press, 1997), 174; Trulio, "Anglo-American Attitudes," 230–32.

35. Smith and Judah, *Chronicles of the Gringos*, 124. For an excellent account of a contemporaneous conflation of race, age, and gender, see Deena J. González's discussion of "La Tules" from Santa Fe. González, *Refusing the Favor*.

36. Lewis H. Garrard, *Wah-to-yah and the Taos Trail, or, Prairie Travel and Scalp Dances, with a Look at Los Rancheros from Muleback and the Rocky Mountain Campfire* (1850; repr., Norman: University of Oklahoma Press, 1973), 171.

37. "The Conquest of California, and the Case of Lieut. Col. Fremont," *Southern Quarterly Review* 15, no. 30 (July 1849): 420–21.

38. Bryan, "American Elsewhere," 221–28; L. N. Weed, "Narrative of a Journey to California," manuscript, Beinecke Rare Book Library, Yale University, cited in Howard R. Lamar, *Texas Crossings: The Lone Star State and the American Far West, 1836–1986* (Austin: University of Texas Press, 1991), 63.

39. Chamberlain, *My Confession*, 273; Donnavan, *Adventures in Mexico*, 62–63; Kendall, *Narrative*, 247; William W. Carpenter, *Travels and Adventures in Mexico* (New York: Harper and Brothers, 1851), 247–51.

40. Samuel E. Chamberlain, *My Confession: Recollections of a Rogue*, ed. William H. Goetzmann (Austin: Texas State Historical Association, 1996), 273. A milder version appears in the 1956 edition, 236–38.

41. James Ohio Pattie, *Personal Narrative of James O. Pattie: The True Wild West of New Mexico and California* (1833; repr., Santa Barbara, CA: Narrative Press, 2001), 65–69.

42. Thorpe, *Our Army*, 123.

43. "Conquest of California," 420–21.

44. Cited in Bryan, "American Elsewhere," 228; "Mexican Annexation," *Spirit of the Times*, January 1, 1847, 526; editorial, *Philadelphia Ledger*, December 11, 1847, cited in Amy S. Greenberg, *Manifest Manhood and the Antebellum American Empire* (New York: Cambridge University Press, 2005), 89–90. Early in the war, the *Philadelphia Ledger* predicted that Americans would eventually Anglo-Saxonize Mexico, but first, the editor explained, "Yankee young fellows and the pretty senoritas" should complete the annexation. "The Yankees and the Senoritas," *Spirit of the Times*, September 11, 1847, 337.

45. Both editorials appeared in "Civilizing Mexico," *Hartford Daily Courant*, July 31, 1849.

46. Donnavan, *Adventures in Mexico*, 82; Benjamin Huger to his wife, April 25, 1847, cited in Peggy M. Cashion, "Women and the Mexican War, 1846–1848" (PhD diss., University of Texas, Arlington, 1990), 140.

47. "Effects of Peace," *Baltimore Sun*, July 24, 1848. For other examples of relationships with Mexican women, see "Mexican Ladies," *Dwight's American Magazine*, July 17, 1847, 460; Randy W. Hackenburg, *Pennsylvania in the War with Mexico* (Shippensburg, PA: White Mane, 1992), 83; "The American Wife and the Mexican Sweetheart," *Spirit of the Times*, September 23, 1848, 365. See Chamberlain, *My Confession*; Chamberlain, *Recollections*. Immigration numbers appear in *Historical Statistics of the United States, Millennial Edition Online*, accessed July 23, 2008, http://hsus.cambridge.org. I used the census to verify twenty-eight cases of intermarriage in the states of Alabama, Illinois, Kentucky, Missouri, Ohio, and Pennsylvania. I chose these states because they sent large numbers of volunteers. These results are clearly an undercount. A newspaper from 1847 indicated that the return of just one Pennsylvania battalion included more than a dozen Mexican wives. "Effects of Peace"; *Main Cultivator and Hallowell Gazette*, July 3, 1847.

48. Steven Seidman, "The Power of Desire and the Dangers of Pleasure: Victorian Sexuality Reconsidered," *Journal of Social History* 24, no. 1 (Fall 1990): 49–50, 60–62.

49. Valerie Steele, *Fashion and Eroticism: Ideals of Feminine Beauty from the Victorian Era to the Jazz Age* (New York: Oxford University Press, 1985), 27, 42, 51–52; Gayle V. Fischer, *Pantaloons and Power: Nineteenth-Century Dress Reform in the United States* (Kent, OH: Kent University Press, 2001), 20, 30.

50. Trulio, "Anglo-American Attitudes," 229–31; Kendall, *Narrative*, 234.

51. Bryan, "American Elsewhere," 224

52. Steele, *Fashion and Eroticism*, 113–15; Fischer, *Pantaloons and Power*, 20–21; Kendall, *Narrative*, 383–85; Abraham Robinson Johnston, Marcellus Ball, and Philip Gooch Ferguson, *Marching with the Army of the West, 1846–1848*, ed. Ralph Paul Bieber (Glendale, CA: Arthur H. Clark, 1936), 342; E. M. Violette, "Review of *Marching with the Army of the West: 1846–1848*, by Abraham R. Johnston et al., Ralph P. Bieber, ed.," *Mississippi Valley Historical Review* 24, no. 1 (June 1937): 83–85.

53. "New Mexicans, Males and Females," *Nile's National Register*, April 10, 1847, 87–88.

54. Ibid.

55. Shaler, "Journal of a Voyage," 151–52.

56. Newton, "Original Communications," 297, 304.

57. Richard F. Pourade, ed., *The Sign of the Eagle: A View of Mexico, 1830 to 1855* (San Diego, CA: Union-Tribune Publishing, 1970), 29–30, 63.

58. Raphael Semmes, *The Campaign of General Scott in the Valley of Mexico* (Cincinnati, OH: Moore and Anderson, 1852), 77–81; Waddy Thompson, *Recollections of Mexico* (New York: Wiley and Putnam, 1847), 161–62.

59. Sage, *Rocky Mountain Life*, 211, 221–26.

60. These passages are cited in James M. McCaffrey, *Army of Manifest Destiny: The American Soldier in the Mexican War, 1846–1848* (New York: New York University Press, 1992), 78–79, 199–200.

61. Kirkham, *Journal and Letters*, 13–15.

62. Kendall, *Narrative*, 234; Donnavan, *Adventures in Mexico*, 22–23; Zo S. Cook, "Mexican War Reminiscences," *Alabama Historical Quarterly* 19 (1957): 457; Gibson, *Journal of a Soldier*, 216, 316.

63. Sandra L. Myres, "Mexican Americans and Westering Anglos: A Feminine Perspective," *New Mexico Historical Review* 57, no. 4 (1982): 317–33.

64. Magoffin, *Down the Santa Fe Trail*, xix, 130–31.

65. Martha Summerhayes, *Vanished Arizona: Recollections of the Army Life of a New England Woman* (Salem, MA: Salem Press, 1911), 44, 94, 156–58, 158, 234. For other examples of positive depictions from longtime residents, see Paredes, "Mexican Image," 7–8, 13–16; Trulio, "Anglo-American Attitudes," 229–39.

66. Andrea Boardman, "The U.S.-Mexican War and the Beginnings of American Tourism in Mexico," in *Holiday in Mexico: Critical Reflections on Tourism and Tourist Encounters*, ed. Dina Berger and Andrew Grant Wood (Durham, NC: Duke University Press, 2010), 21–53.

67. Magoffin, *Down the Santa Fe Trail*, 92–95, 131. For more on the friendships of Mexican and American women, see Myres, "Mexican Americans and Westering Anglos," 317–34. Donnavan, *Adventures in Mexico*, 23; Cook, "Mexican War Reminiscences," 460.

68. Pike, *Prose, Sketches, and Poems*, xvi. The references appear in the introduction by David J. Weber. See also José María Sánchez, "A Trip to Texas in 1828," trans. Carlos E. Castañeda, *Southwestern Historical Quarterly* 29, no. 4 (April 1926): 260–61, 271. Cecil Robinson captures the fictionalization of those attitudes in his *Mexico and the Hispanic Southwest*, especially in chapters 1–3.

69. Magoffin, *Down the Santa Fe Trail*, 131; Susanna Bryant Dakin, *A Scotch Paisano: Hugo Reid's Life in California, 1832–1852, Derived from His Correspondence* (Berkeley: University of California Press, 1939), 41–43, 153–55; Iris H. W. Engstrand and Mary F. Ward, "Rancho Guajome: An Architectural Legacy Preserved," *Journal of San Diego History* 41, no. 4 (Fall 1995): 1–6; Dydia DeLyser, *Ramona Memories: Tourism and the Shaping of Southern California* (Minneapolis: University of Minnesota Press, 2005), 88, 209.

70. Genaro Padilla, "'Yo Sola Aprendí': Personal Narratives from Nineteenth-Century California," in *Writing the Range: Race, Class, and Culture in the Women's West*, ed. Elizabeth Jameson and Susan Armitage (Norman: University of Oklahoma Press, 1997), 197; Guadalupe Vallejo, "Ranch and Mission Days in Alta California," *Century Magazine*, December 1890, 183, 190; Prudencia Higuera, "Californiana: Trading with the Americans," *Century Magazine*, December 1890, 193–94.

71. Myres, "Mexican Americans and Westering Anglos," 327.

72. Padilla, "Yo Sola Aprendí," 197–98.

73. Angustias Ord [née María de las Angustias de la Guerra], "Ocurrencias en California, Relatadas a Thomas Savage en Santa Bárbara, 1878," 140–41, 144, Manuscript Collection, Bancroft Library, Berkeley, California.

74. Ibid., 143. The mistranslation appears in Angustias Ord, *Occurrences in Hispanic California*, trans. and ed. Francis Price and William E. Ellison (Washington, DC: Academy of American Franciscan History, 1956), 59. The Spanish original reads, "La toma del país no nos gustó nada á [*sic*] los Californios, y menos á [*sic*] las mujeres." The authors interpreted the sentence as, "The conquest of California did not bother the Californians, least of all the women." The correct translation is, "We, Californios, least of all the women, did not like the occupation of the country at all." Many authors have cited the mistranslated passage, including Sandra L. Myres ("Mexican Americans and

Westering Anglos," 329). I learned about the error from Genaro Padilla ("Yo Sola Aprendí," 198), but I use my own translation of the original.

75. Valerie Wheeler, "Travelers' Tales: Observations on the Travel Book and Ethnography," *Anthropological Quarterly* 59, no. 2 (April 1986): 52–53.

76. That is, the otherness of the purported indolent lay in their class, not in their race. Marilyn McAdams Sibley, *Travelers in Texas, 1761–1860* (Austin: University of Texas Press, 1967), 91; Sánchez, "Trip to Texas," 260–61, 271.

77. See Sibley, *Travelers in Texas*, 3–21; Paredes, "Mexican Image," 5–29. For examples of the infusion of scientific language, see Wilson, *Mexico and Its Religion*, 262, 309–10; Keen, *Aztec Image*, 381–82.

78. "Arizona—West and South from Prescott," *Weekly Arizona Miner*, May 24, 1873.

79. Chamberlain, *Recollections*, 295–96. For more on the danger of total acculturation—going native, as writers often call it—see also Harvey Fergusson, *In those Days: An Impression of Change* (New York: Knopf, 1929), 43–44; Robert F. Gish, *Frontier's End: The Life and Literature of Harvey Fergusson* (Lincoln: University of Nebraska Press, 1988), 11, 43, 54–55, 193, 295.

80. "It Occurred in Tucson," *Overland Monthly and Out West Magazine*, June 1872, 518.

81. "From the Rome Southerner," *Georgia Telegraph*, September 25, 1849; "Another New Territory," *Pittsfield Sun*, November 4, 1856; "Letter from Tucson," *Arizona Weekly Miner*, November 4, 1871.

82. *Arizona Weekly Miner*, October 18, 1878.

83. J. Ross Browne, *Adventures in the Apache Country: A Tour through Arizona and Sonora, with Notes on the Silver Regions of Nevada* (New York: Harper and Brothers, 1869), 131–34, 169–72. As journalist and author Margaret Regan notes, "Browne's racial views are the most troubling part of his Arizona book. He could be a sharp-eyed reporter, but he often fell into stereotypes when he was describing minorities." Margaret Regan, "The City of Mud Boxes: Meet J. Ross Browne: Irish Native, World Traveler, Esteemed Writer and Unimpressed Tucson Visitor, 1864," *Tucson Weekly*, March 2010, accessed August 1, 2015, http://www.tucsonweekly.com/tucson/the-city-of-mud-boxes/Content?oid=1858027.

84. The Society of Arizona Pioneers later became the Arizona Pioneers Historical Society and eventually the Arizona Historical Society. Eleanor B. Sloan, "Seventy-Five Years of the Arizona Pioneers' Historical Society, 1884–1959," *Arizona and the West* 1, no. 1 (Spring 1959): 66–70.

85. For some examples of the use of the word "greaser" in the *Arizona Weekly Miner*, see the following dates: February 13, 1869; May 29, 1869; August 28, 1869; April 9, 1875; July 6, 1877; October 19, 1877.

86. "The Mexican Question," *Arizona Weekly Miner*, March 30, 1872; April 6, 1872; April 20, 1872; May 4, 1872.

87. Browne, *Adventures in the Apache Country*, 169–72; "Miscegenation," *Weekly Arizona Miner*, January 2, 1869; "An Exchange," *Weekly Arizona Miner*, February 6, 1869; "Inequality of Races," *Weekly Arizona Miner*, February 22, 1868; "Letter from Canandaigua," *Weekly Arizona Miner*, June 18, 1870.

88. See the anti-Chinese rhetoric of the following newspaper accounts: "The Argonaut on the Chinese Question," *Arizona Weekly Miner*, March 7, 1879; "Our Asiatic Friends," *Arizona Weekly Miner*, April 11, 1879; "The Chinese Question," *Arizona Weekly Star*, January 22, 1880; "Hon. Thomas Fitch," *Arizona Weekly Star*, April 20, 1882; "The Chinese Question," *Tombstone Epitaph Prospector*, February 5, 1886; "The Chinese Question," *Tombstone Epitaph Prospector*, February 9, 1886; "The Chinese Question," *Tombstone Epitaph Prospector*, February 20, 1886; "Unrestricted Immigration," *Republican Herald*, July 12, 1900; "The Chinese Curse," *Arizona Weekly Star*, August 7, 1879; "America for White Men," *Daily Tombstone Epitaph*, February 28, 1886.

89. "The Mexican Question," *Arizona Miner*, January 24, 1866.

90. "The Lower California Company," *Arizona Weekly Miner*, August 8, 1868.

91. "New Projects," *Arizona Weekly Miner*, December 24, 1870.

92. "The Mexican Annexation Scheme," *Arizona Weekly Miner*, December 30, 1871.

93. "Let Our Eagle Spread Its Wings," *Arizona Weekly Miner*, February 17, 1872; "The Mexican Question," *Arizona Weekly Miner*, November 16, 1872; "Mexican Spoliations," *Arizona Weekly Miner*, June 14, 1873; "Mexico," *Arizona Weekly Miner*, June 14, 1873; "Delenda Est Carthago," *Arizona Weekly Miner*, September 6, 1878. The *Miner* also called for annexation on October 23, 1874, and on March 26, 1875.

94. For the role of rhetoric about Mexicanization in a transnational context, see Gregory P. Downs, "The Mexicanization of American Politics: The United States' Transnational Path from Civil War to Stabilization," *American Historical Review* 117, no. 2 (April 2012): 387–409.

95. "Captain of Canines: A Dog that Would Seem to Be Entitled to Citizenship," *Tombstone Prospector*, June 26, 1891.

96. "Result of the Election," *Arizona Miner*, June 20, 1868.

97. For an explanation of the concerns of whites in Prescott, see Joseph F. Park, "The History of Mexican Labor in Arizona during the Territorial Period" (master's thesis, University of Arizona, 1961), 234–49.

98. Ibid., 238–39.

99. For an excellent account of the political motivations of various factions of whites in the 1850s through the 1870s, see ibid., 234–49.

100. "Telegraph," *Arizona Weekly Star*, December 27, 1877; "How Mexicans Do It," *Arizona Weekly Star*, September 4, 1879; "Border Bandits," *Arizona Weekly Star*, February 17, 1881.

101. *Weekly Arizonian* issues from 1859: March 3, April 28, May 5, June 2, and June 30, all as cited in Park, "History of Mexican Labor," 19, 31, 52, 80, 236.

102. "Telegraph," *Arizona Weekly Star*, December 13, 1877; "Ticklish State of the Mexican Question," *Arizona Weekly Star*, October 18, 1877; "Sensational Gossip," *Arizona Weekly Star*, January 8, 1880.

103. "Situation in Sonora," *Arizona Weekly Star*, August 24, 1882; "Mexico," *Arizona Weekly Star*, July 24, 1879.

104. Committee on the Territories, *Statehood for Arizona and New Mexico* (Washington, DC: Government Printing Office, 1906), 18, 24–32, 39–43, 103.

105. "American Railroads in Sonora," *Arizona Weekly Star*, February 5, 1880.

106. Park, "History of Mexican Labor," 24–28.

107. "[illegible] and Railroads," *Arizona Weekly Star*, June 16, 1881; *Tucson Citizen*, November 29, 1873.

108. "The Two Republics," *Arizona Weekly Star*, May 5, 1881; "Washington," *Arizona Weekly Star*, June 23, 1877.

109. Charles D. Poston, "Building a State in Apache Land," *Overland Monthly and Out West Magazine*, August 1894, 207–8.

110. William A. Duffen, ed., "Overland Via 'Jackass Mail' in 1858: The Diary of Phocion R. Way," pt. 1, *Arizona and the West* 2, no. 1 (Spring 1960): 35–36; pt. 2, *Arizona and the West* 2, no. 2 (Summer 1960): 159–61.

111. Poston, "Building a State in Apache Land," 207–8.

112. "The Local Look-Out," *Arizona Weekly Miner*, November 11, 1871; "Southern Arizona," *Arizona Weekly Miner*, January 2, 1874; "Vasquez History," *Arizona Weekly Miner*, May 29, 1874.

113. *Tucson Citizen* quoted in "Pima Items," *Arizona Weekly Miner*, May 12, 1876.

114. C. M. Goethe, "The Influx of Mexican Amerinds," *Eugenics* 2, no. 1 (January 1929): 6–9; Randall D. Bird and Garland Allen, "The J.H.B. Archive Report:

The Papers of Harry Hamilton Laughlin," *Journal of the History of Biology* 14, no. 2 (Fall 1981): 344–45.

CHAPTER 3

1. Sheridan, *Los Tucsonenses*, 126.

2. The 1890 census actually shows a 37 percent decrease in the size of Tucson's population, from 7,007 to 5,150. By 1900, the population had rebounded to 7,531, and more important for the purpose of this study, it now contained 453 white nuclear families versus only 394 Mexican. Mexicans did outnumber whites in single-headed households (346 to 228), which might indicate that Mexicans spouses resided nearby or in Mexico due to temporary labor-related separations. The overall number of households was fairly similar for whites (682) and Mexicans (740). U.S. Census Office, *Report on the Population of the United States at the Eleventh Census: 1890, Part I*, Washington, DC: Government Printing Office, 1895.

3. For more on the Mexican tone of social, cultural, and religious celebrations in Tucson, see Sheridan, *Arizona: A History*, 109–12.

4. All demographic information in this chapter comes from census schedules, in this case, from 1900 and 1910. It will become apparent in several instances that 1890 census schedules do not exist, since these records were destroyed in a 1921 fire. The 1900 census lists the wife as Katie, but she appears as Kittie on the marriage license. Negley and Lindley, *Arizona Territorial Marriages*, 9–10, 73; baptismal entries for Guillermo Carlos Brown and Catalina McKenna, St. Augustine Baptismal Register, 1888–1891, pp. 83, 233, Catholic Diocese of Tucson Archives, Arizona.

5. U.S. Census Office, *Ninth Census—Volume I*, 606–15; U.S. Census Office, *Statistics of the United States at the Tenth Census, June 1 1880* (Washington, DC: Government Printing Office, 1882), 543–45; U.S. Census Office, *Report on the Population*, 398–401, 486–88; U.S. Census Office, *Twelfth Census of the United States, Taken in the Year 1900: Population, Part I* (Washington, DC: U.S. Census Office, 1901), 490–92.

6. James H. McClintock, *Arizona, Prehistoric, Aboriginal, Pioneer, Modern: The Nation's Youngest Commonwealth within a Land of Ancient Culture* (Chicago, IL: S. J. Clarke, 1916), 597. Various works and websites frequently cite the accomplishment, along with other famous firsts attributed to William H. Kirk-

NOTES TO PAGES 76–80   187

land, like being the first white person to bring cattle into Arizona and the first to raise an American flag in Tucson.

7. The 1864 census, which took place after Arizona became a separate territory in 1863, reveals that the following families had children born in the 1850s who used their father's surname: William and Ignacia Oury, Frederick and Margarita Contzen, John and Concepción Clark, Solomon Warner and María Telles, Hill and María De Arnitt, John Ward and Jesusa Martínez, J. C. and Concepción Clark, and T. G. and Concepción Rusk. There were other interethnic families, not included here, where the children and the father had different surnames.

8. All census statistics come from a database I created based on the original census schedules. The numbers include only men and women over sixteen years of age but exclude nuns.

9. For a discussion of the difference between marriage and cohabitation in white-Mexican relationships, see Susan Lee Johnson, "Sharing Bed and Board: Cohabitation and Cultural Difference in Central Arizona Mining Towns, 1863–1873," in *The Women's West*, ed. Susan Armitage and Elizabeth Jameson (Norman: University of Oklahoma Press, 1987), 78, 82, 88.

10. The 1880 Tucson census schedules list only initials and last names for the Aínsas. I obtained the names by looking at the New York 1860 and the San Francisco 1900 censuses. The latter census lists the wife's name as Jeannie. The 1900 record lists Santiago's father as Filipino, not Mexican, which the 1880 census does. 1880 U.S. census, Pima County, Arizona Territory, population schedules, city of Tucson, district 39, p. 18, lines 25–27, microfilm T9, roll 36, NARA; 1860 U.S. census, Westchester County, New York, population schedules, town of West Farms, p. 545, line 3, microfilm M653, roll 878, NARA; 1900 U.S. census, San Francisco County, California, population schedules, city of San Francisco, district 297, p. 11A, lines 38–42, microfilm T623, roll 107, NARA; Sheridan, *Los Tucsonenses*, 146–47.

11. I checked language spoken, year of entry, surnames, and more important, birthplace of parents. For instance, the first two were born in New York of parents also born in New York, and the third was born in Missouri of a West Virginian father and a Missourian mother.

12. Sheridan, *Los Tucsonenses*, 90, 122–23.

13. Acuña, *Occupied America*, 83, 89, 92–96; Montejano, *Anglos and Mexicans*, 92; Sheridan, *Los Tucsonenses*, 150.

14. Gordon, *Passage to Union*, 3–9, 122, 165.

15. Sheridan, *Arizona: A History*, 165–70.

16. Wagoner, *Arizona Territory*, 57. The creation of Santa Cruz County most likely removed a high number of potential intermarriages from the Pima County totals because the area included towns where Mexicans outnumbered whites by large margins, a condition that consistently led to high rates of intermarriage.

17. González, *Refusing the Favor*, 113–14.

18. Unfortunately, the jobs of women were routinely unlisted in most census years, and when they did appear, they typically excluded occupations in the informal labor market. One must, therefore, rely heavily on the class status of men.

19. Sheridan, *Los Tucsonenses*, 35–38, 88, 106.

20. For the purpose of this study, any marriage involving a person of white-Mexican ancestry qualifies as intermarriage. After all, including only their marriages with either whites or Mexicans would imply that one knew for certain that the spouses in question identified racially with a specific ethnic group. In this regard, even assuming that the marriage of two people of white-Mexican ancestry is endogamous falls under such a presumption (these marriages accounted for only 6 percent of all intermarriages as late as 1930).

21. Anthropologist Thomas E. Sheridan avers that from 1900 to 1910, sixty-four intermarriages in Pima County involved Hispanic men and white women. Sheridan, *Los Tucsonenses*, 149.

22. Negley and Lindley, *Arizona Territorial Marriages*, 62; Negley and Lindley, *Arizona Marriages*, 166. Jordán is a Hispanic surname pronounced *hor-DAN*.

23. These figures are for Tucson only. The city consistently accounted for 50 to 60 percent of the population of Pima County. Therefore, it would be highly unlikely that the rest of the county contained dozens of Mexican man–white woman marriages, while Tucson never had more than twelve.

24. For a discussion on the limits of agency, see Judith Butler, *The Psychic Life of Power: Theories in Subjection* (Stanford, CA: Stanford University Press, 1997), 10–12; Judith Butler, *Undoing Gender* (New York: Routledge, 2004), 3–5.

25. Sheridan, *Los Tucsonenses*, 58–59.

26. The calculations are as follows for scenario 4, leaving only those foreign whites who probably (Cohort D) and almost certainly (Cohort E) met their spouses in Arizona: 1860, 100 percent; 1864, 100 percent; 1870, 100 percent; 1880, 89 percent; 1900, 92 percent; 1910, 78 percent; 1920, 67 percent; 1930, 55 percent.

CHAPTER 4

1. As is the case for most states and territories, the original manuscripts for the census of 1890 do not exist for Arizona. But in 1900, approximately twenty years after his immigration to the United States, Manuel Ahloy still worked as a common laborer. The schedule listed no occupation for Isabel, who was most likely a homemaker, since the couple had five young children at the time. 1900 U.S. Census, Pima County, Arizona Territory, population schedules, city of Tucson, district 48, p. 10B, lines 73–74, microfilm T623, roll 47, NARA. Calculations based on contemporary sources indicate that ten years earlier the train fare had been approximately twenty-two dollars per person each way. David F. Myrick, "Railroads of Arizona," in *The Westerners Brand Book XII*, ed. George Koenig (Los Angeles: Los Angeles Corral, Stephens Printing, 1966), 23; and Patrick Hamilton, comp., *The Resources of Arizona, Its Mineral, Farming, Grazing and Timber Lands; Its History, Climate, Productions, Civil and Military Government, Pre-History Ruins, Early Missionaries, Indian Tribes, Pioneer Days, Etc., Etc.*, 3rd ed. (San Francisco, CA: A. L. Bancroft, 1884), 123.

2. Marriage license for Manuel Ahloy and Isabel Escalante, August 29, 1891, Marriage Records, 1872–1899, Grant County, New Mexico, Clerk's Office, City of Silver City.

3. He most likely began using the name Manuel after his baptism in 1890. Manuel's godparents were Alfredo and Luisa Durazo, an indication that he maintained ties to the local Mexican community prior to his baptism and marriage. Baptismal entry for Manuel Ah Fo, March 2, 1890, p. 123, St. Augustine Baptismal Register, 1888–1891.

4. Nevada (1861), Idaho (1864), and Wyoming (1869) banned marriages of whites to blacks and Chinese in single laws, and in 1866, Oregon and Arizona added Chinese to laws that already forbade blacks from marrying whites since 1862 and 1865, respectively. Pascoe, *What Comes Naturally*, 10, 77–89, 91–93, 100, 120–22. Arizona legislators banned white-black marriages during the first territorial session in 1864. In 1865 they added Indians and "Mongolians" to the list of races that could not marry whites. The laws went into effect in 1865 and 1866. *Howell Code*, 230–31; *Journals of the Second Legislative Assembly*, 158.

5. Pascoe, *What Comes Naturally*, 109–14. Laura E. Gómez, *Manifest Destinies: The Making of the Mexican American Race* (New York: New York University

Press, 2007), 1–4, 43–45. For the loss of rights after the annexation, see Menchaca, *Recovering History*, 215–28.

6. Gómez, *Manifest Destinies*, 9–11, 114–15, 142; Mitchell, *Coyote Nation*, 102, 108, 120–21, 174–75; John M. Nieto-Phillips, *The Language of Blood: The Making of Spanish American Identity in New Mexico, 1880s–1930s* (Albuquerque: University of New Mexico Press, 2004); Pascoe, *What Comes Naturally*, 89–90, 152–54; Neil Foley, *The White Scourge: Mexicans, Blacks, and Poor Whites in Texas Cotton Culture* (Berkeley: University of California Press, 1997), 208; Guevarra, *Becoming Mexipino*, 130–39; Leonard, *Making Ethnic Choices*, 63–68.

7. His name variably appears as Manuel Ahloy, Manuel Ah Loy, Manuel Aloy, Fô Manuel Ah, and Fô Ah Loy. The Chinese *Ah* is an informal addition that friends and relatives use as a form of endearment, but it frequently made it to official records in the United States. 1900 U.S. census, Pima County, Arizona Territory, population schedules, city of Tucson, district 48, p. 10B, line 73, microfilm T623, roll 47, NARA; 1910 U.S. census, Pima County, Arizona Territory, population schedules, city of Tucson, district 107, p. 5A, line 10, microfilm T624, roll 41, NARA; 1930 U.S. census, Pima County, Arizona, population schedules, city of Tucson, district 56, p. 11B, line 55, microfilm T626, roll 62, NARA; 1900 U.S. census, Pima County, Arizona Territory, population schedules, city of Tucson, district 48, p. 10B, line 74, microfilm T623, roll 47, NARA; 1910 U.S. census, Pima County, Arizona Territory, population schedules, city of Tucson, district 107, p. 5A, line 10, microfilm T624, roll 41, NARA; 1920 U.S. census, Pima County, Arizona, population schedules, city of Tucson, district 101, p. 18A, line 24; microfilm T625, roll 50, NARA; certificate of death for Isabel Escalante Aloy [*sic*], August 28, 1932, Tucson, Pima County, Arizona Genealogy Birth and Death Certificates.

8. John W. Stephens, "A Quantitative History of Chinatown, San Francisco, 1870 and 1880," in *The Life, Influence and the Role of the Chinese in the United States, 1776–1960*, Proceedings of the National Conference at the University of San Francisco, July 10–12, 1975 (San Francisco, CA: Chinese Historical Society of America, 1976), 72–73, 77–78; Edward J. M. Rhoads, "The Chinese in Texas," *Southwestern Historical Quarterly* 81, no. 1 (July 1977): 3, 8, 14–15; Arnoldo De León, *Racial Frontiers: Africans, Chinese, and Mexicans in Western America, 1848–1890*, Histories of the American Frontier, ed. Ray Allen Billington (Albuquerque: University of New Mexico Press, 2002), 75–77, 82; Stanford M. Lyman, "Marriage and Family among Chinese Immigrants to America, 1850–1960," *Phylon* 29, no. 4 (Winter 1968): 322–28; S. Michael Opper and Lillie L.

Lew, "A History of the Chinese in Fresno, California," in *The Life, Influence and the Role of the Chinese*, 47–55; Deenesh Sohoni, "Unsuitable Suitors: Anti-Miscegenation Laws, Naturalization Laws, and the Construction of Asian Identity," *Law and Society Review* 41, no. 3 (September 2007): 588–89, 597–98; Edward C. Lydon, "The Anti-Chinese Movement in Santa Cruz County, California, 1859–1900," in *The Life, Influence and the Role of the Chinese*, 219–42; Jian Li, "A History of the Chinese in Charleston," *South Carolina Historical Magazine* 99, no. 1 (January 1998): 49; Liping Zhu, *A Chinaman's Chance: The Chinese on the Rocky Mountain Mining Frontier* (Niwot: University Press of Colorado, 1997), 59, 87, 119–20, 188; Liping Zhu, "Ethnic Oasis: Chinese Immigrants in the Frontier Black Hills," *South Dakota History* 33, no. 4 (Winter 2003): 295–96.

9. Not surprisingly, California legislation soon prohibited Chinese-white marriages in 1880. Nayan Shah, *Contagious Divides: Epidemics and Race in San Francisco's Chinatown* (Berkeley: University of California Press, 2001), 1–2, 25–26, 80–89, 94, 97–99, 107–9; Yong Chen, *Chinese San Francisco, 1850–1943: A Trans-Pacific Community* (Stanford, CA: Stanford University Press, 2000), 75–83; George Anthony Peffer, *If They Don't Bring Their Women Here: Chinese Female Immigration before Exclusion* (Urbana: University of Illinois Press, 1999), 1–13; Judy Yung, *Unbound Feet: A Social History of Chinese Women in San Francisco* (Berkeley: University of California Press, 1995), 26–34; Lydon, "Anti-Chinese Movement," 219–42; Stephens, "Quantitative History," 72–73, 77–78; John R. Wunder, "Anti-Chinese Violence in the American West, 1850–1910," in *Law for the Elephant, Law for the Beaver: Essays in the Legal History of the North American West*, ed. John McLaren, Hamar Foster, and Chet Orloff (Regina, SK: Canadian Plains Research Center, 1992), 212–18; Sucheng Chan, "Introduction: The Significance of Locke in Chinese American History," in *Bitter Melon: Inside America's Last Rural Chinese Town*, ed. Jeff Gillenkirk and James Motlow (Berkeley, CA: Heyday Books, 1997), 24–25; Shih-Shan Henry Tsai, *The Chinese Experience in America* (Bloomington: Indiana University Press, 1986), 68; Rhoads, "Chinese in Texas," 15–16, 24–25; Paul A. Frisch, "'Gibraltar of Unionism': Women, Blacks and the Anti-Chinese Movement in Butte, Montana, 1880–1900," *Southwest Economy and Society* 6, no. 3 (Spring 1984): 3–13.

10. De León, *Racial Frontiers*, 35–36; Frisch, "Gibraltar of Unionism," 3–13; William Loren Katz, *The Black West* (Garden City, NY: Doubleday, 1971), 54–59, 298; Eugene H. Berwanger, *The West and Reconstruction* (Urbana: University of

Illinois Press, 1981); Michael S. Coray, "'Democracy' on the Frontier: A Case Study of Nevada Editorial Attitudes on the Issue of Nonwhite Equality," *Nevada Historical Society Quarterly* 21, no. 3 (Fall 1978): 189–204; Roger D. Hardaway, "Prohibiting Interracial Marriage: Miscegenation Laws in Wyoming," *Annals of Wyoming* 52, no. 1 (Spring 1980): 55–60; William M. King, "Black Children, White Law: Black Efforts to Secure Public Education in Central City, Colorado, 1864–1869," *Essays and Monographs in Colorado History* 3 (1984): 56–79; Eric Margolis, "Western Coal Mining as a Way of Life: An Oral History of the Colorado Coal Miners to 1914," *Journal of the West* 24, no. 3 (July 1985): 33–42; Elmer R. Rusco, *"Good Time Coming?": Black Nevadans in the Nineteenth Century* (Westport, CT: Greenwood Press, 1975), 145–52; Robert A. Campbell, "Blacks and the Coal Mines of Western Washington, 1888–1896," *Pacific Northwest Quarterly* 73, no. 4 (October 1982): 146–55; Barbara Carol Behan, "Forgotten Heritage: African Americans in the Montana Territory, 1864–1889," in "The African American Experience in the Western States," special issue, *Journal of African American History* 91, no. 1 (Winter 2006): 23–40; Quintard Taylor, *In Search of the Racial Frontier: African Americans in the American West, 1528–1990* (New York: Norton, 1998), 103–14, 172–81; James N. Leiker, "Black Soldiers at Fort Hays, Kansas, 1867–69: A Study in Civilian and Military Violence," in *Buffalo Soldiers in the West: A Black Soldiers Anthology*, ed. Bruce A. Glasrud and Michael N. Searles (College Station: Texas A&M University Press, 2007), 157–75; Frank N. Schubert, "Black Soldiers on the White Frontier: Some Factors Influencing Race Relations," in Glasrud and Searles, *Buffalo Soldiers in the West*, 174–84; Susan Bragg, "'Anxious Foot Soldiers': Sacramento's Black Women and Education in Nineteenth-Century California," in *African American Women Confront the West: 1600–2000*, ed. Quintard Taylor and Shirley Ann Wilson Moore (Norman: University of Oklahoma Press, 2003), 97–116; Lynn M. Hudson, "Mining a Mythic Past: The History of Mary Ellen Pleasant," in Taylor and Moore, *African American Women Confront the West*, 56–70.

11. Rhoads, "Chinese in Texas," 1–36; Julian Lim, "*Chinos* and *Paisanos*: Chinese Mexican Relations in the Borderlands," *Pacific Historical Review* 79, no. 1 (February 2010): 50–85.

12. Evelyn Hu-DeHart, "Immigrants to a Developing Society: The Chinese in Northern Mexico, 1875–1932," *Journal of Arizona History* 21, no. 3 (Autumn 1980): 288–95; Delgado, *Making the Chinese Mexican*, 166–89; Schiavone Camacho, *Chinese Mexicans*, 81–90; Julia María Schiavone Camacho, "Crossing

Boundaries, Claiming a Homeland: The Mexican Chinese Transpacific Journey to Becoming Mexican, 1930s–1960s," *Pacific Historical Review* 78, no. 4 (November 2009): 545–77; Gerardo Rénique, "Race, Region, and Nation: Sonora's Anti-Chinese Racism and Mexico's Postrevolutionary Nationalism, 1920s–1930s," in *Race and Nation in Modern Latin America*, ed. Nancy P. Appelbaum, Anne S. Macpherson, and Karin Alejandra Rosemblatt (Chapel Hill: University of North Carolina Press, 2003), 227–30.

13. For examples of anti-Chinese sentiments that were pervasive more in small mining towns and in Phoenix than in Tucson, see Melissa Keane, A. E. Rogge, and Bradford Luckingham, *The Chinese in Arizona, 1870–1950: A Context for Historic Preservation Planning* (Phoenix: Arizona State Historic Preservation Office, 1992), 8–22; Rhonda Tintle, "A History of Chinese Immigration into Arizona Territory: A Frontier Culture in the American West" (master's thesis, Oklahoma State University, 2006), 39, 43, 49–52, 58–60, 64, 73–76.

14. John R. Wunder, "Law and the Chinese on the Southwest Frontier, 1850s–1902," *Western Legal History* 2 (Summer/Fall 1989): 140–42; Wunder, "Anti-Chinese Violence," 214, 220–22, 231; Andrea Pugsley, "'As I Kill This Chicken So May I Be Punished If I Tell an Untruth': Chinese Opposition to Legal Discrimination in Arizona Territory," *Journal of Arizona History* 44, no. 2 (Summer 2003): 170–90; Lawrence Michael Fong, "Sojourners and Settlers: The Chinese Experience in Arizona," *Journal of Arizona History* 21, no. 3 (Autumn 1980): 227–56; De León, *Racial Frontiers*, 48; Bradford Luckingham, *Minorities in Phoenix: A Profile of Mexican American, Chinese American, and African American Communities, 1860–1992* (Tucson: University of Arizona Press, 1994), 87–100; Floyd Doon Cheung, "'Kingdoms of Manly Style': Performing Chinese American Masculinity, 1865–1941" (PhD diss., Tulane University, 1999), 102–33; Paul Hietter, "A Surprising Amount of Justice: The Experience of Mexican and Racial Minority Defendants Charged with Serious Crimes in Arizona, 1865–1920," *Pacific Historical Review* 70, no. 2 (May 2001): 183–219. For negative depictions of Chinese in Arizona newspapers, see "The Argonaut on the Chinese Question," *Arizona Weekly Miner*, March 7, 1879; "Our Asiatic Friends," *Arizona Weekly Miner*, April 11, 1879; "The Chinese Question," *Arizona Weekly Star*, January 22, 1880; "Hon. Thomas Fitch," *Arizona Weekly Star*, April 20, 1882; "The Chinese Question," *Tombstone Epitaph Prospector*, February 5, 1886; "The Chinese Question," *Tombstone Epitaph Prospector*, February 9, 1886; "The Chinese Question," *Tombstone Epitaph Prospector*, February 20, 1886; "Unrestricted Immigration," *Republican Herald*, July 12,

1900; "The Chinese Curse," *Arizona Weekly Star*, August 7, 1879; "America for White Men," *Daily Tombstone Epitaph*, February 28, 1886.

15. Luckingham, *Minorities in Phoenix*, 87–100, 139–55, 161; Matthew C. Whitaker, "The Rise of Black Phoenix: African-American Migration, Settlement and Community Development in Maricopa County, Arizona 1868–1930," *Journal of Negro History* 85, no. 3 (Summer 2000): 197–209; Mary Melcher, "'This Is Not Right': Rural Arizona Women Challenge Segregation and Ethnic Division, 1925–1950," in "Motherhood and Maternalism," special issue, *Frontiers: A Journal of Women Studies* 20, no. 2 (1999): 190–214; Mary E. Gill and John S. Goff, "Joseph H. Kibbey and School Segregation in Arizona," *Journal of Arizona History* 21, no. 4 (Winter 1980): 411–22.

16. John S. Goff, "William T. Howell and the Howell Code of Arizona," *American Journal of Legal History* 11, no. 3 (July 1967): 221–28; Martyn, "Racism in the United States," 127, 221, 453; *Howell Code*, xi–xii, 230–31; Wagoner, *Arizona Territory*, 47; *Journals of the Second Legislative Assembly*, 38–40, 104–5, 108–9, 122–23, 225; Andrew D. Weinberger, "A Reappraisal of the Constitutionality of Miscegenation Statutes," *Journal of Negro Education* 26, no. 4 (Autumn 1957): 443n1.

17. *Revised Statutes of the Arizona Territory*, 809.

18. Sohoni, "Unsuitable Suitors," 588; Karthikeyan and Chin, "Preserving Racial Identity," 1–2.

19. U.S. Census Office, *Fifteenth Census*, 2:59.

20. U.S. Census Office, *Population of the United States in 1860*, 567; U.S. Census Office, *Ninth Census—Volume I*, xvii.

21. Emphasis added. *Revised Statutes of Arizona*, 371. The clause had not appeared in the statutes of 1877, Hoyt, *Compiled Laws*, 317.

22. Database I created based on the following reports: U.S. Census Office, *Statistics of the United States*, 544–45; U.S. Census Office, *Report on the Population*, 488; U.S. Census Office, *Twelfth Census*, 492; U.S. Census Office, *Thirteenth Census of the United States, Taken in the Year 1910: Volume I, Population, 1910, General Report and Analysis* (Washington, DC: Government Printing Office, 1913), 258, 273; U.S. Census Office, *Fourteenth Census of the United States, Taken in the Year 1920: Volume II, Population, 1920, General Report and Analytical Tables* (Washington, DC: Government Printing Office, 1922), 108, 110; U.S. Census Office, *Abstract of the Fifteenth Census of the United States* (Washington, DC: Government Printing Office, 1933), 91, 93.

23. Fong, "Sojourners and Settlers," 227–56.

24. Keane, Rogge, and Luckingham, *Chinese in Arizona*, 8–22; Luckingham, *Minorities in Phoenix*, 82–85; Fong, "Sojourners and Settlers," 228–35; Florence C. Lister and Robert H. Lister, *The Chinese of Early Tucson: Historic Archaeology from the Tucson Urban Renewal Project* (Tucson: University of Arizona Press, 1989), 1–15; Pugsley, "As I Kill This Chicken," 170–90; Cheung, "Kingdoms of Manly Style," 102–33. Louis C. Hughes—owner of the *Star*—traveled to the mining town of Tombstone to express his solidarity with an anti-Chinese gathering. "The Chinese Question," *Arizona Weekly Star*, January 22, 1880; *El Fronterizo* (Tucson), March 11, 1893. See also "Hon. Thomas Fitch," *Arizona Weekly Star*, April 20, 1882.

25. Andrea Juliette Lightbourne, "Shining Through the Clouds: An Historical Case Study of Dunbar, a Segregated School in Tucson, Arizona" (PhD diss., University of Arizona, 2004), 84–95, 277.

26. For examples of these accusations, see the following issues of *El Fronterizo*: July 20, 1889; September 5, 1891; December 3, 1892; February 16, 1893.

27. Delgado, *Making the Chinese Mexican*, 41–47. My mapping of the census schedules corroborates Delgado's conclusion and supports my statements in this paragraph.

28. For examples of the willingness and ability of Chinese business owners to learn local languages in Arizona, see Fong, "Sojourners and Settlers," 236; and Heather S. Hatch, "The Chinese in the Southwest," *Journal of Arizona History* 21, no. 3 (Autumn 1980): 264.

29. John Martin, "Biographical Sketch of Judge Rush Elmore," *Transactions of the Kansas State Historical Society* (1903–1904): 435–36; Mike Speelman, "Samuel Bostick: African-American Pioneer," *Downtown Tucsonan* 80 (2009): 21.

30. In 1900 Bostick gave his date of birth as December 1833. 1900 U.S. census, Pinal County, Arizona Territory, population schedules, unincorporated township, district 56, p. 26A, line 48, microfilm T623, roll 47, NARA.

31. *Weekly Arizonan*, October 8, 1870, 3; *Tucson Citizen*, November 19, 1870, 3.

32. Albina's surname also appears as Barraga and Barras. Only three children were definitely born in the Tucson area, since they received their baptism at Saint Augustine's: María Francisca Sara (b. 1870), Samuel Nepomuceno (b. 1872), and Santiago (b. 1874). Six other children were most likely born in Florence, Arizona: Miguel (b. 1875), Charles (b. 1878), Alexander (b. 1882), Claudia (b. 1884), Luisa (b. 1887), and Richard (b. 1890). St. Augustine Baptismal Register, pp. 129, 178, 269, Catholic Diocese of Tucson Archives, accessed April 13, 2013, http://azmemory.lib.az.us/cdm4/ browse.php?CISOROOT=/rcdhilites.

1900 U.S. census, Pinal County, Arizona Territory, population schedules, Florence Township, district 55, p. 1A, lines 39–44, microfilm T623, roll 47, NARA.

33. Mike Speelman, "A Barber of African Persuasion: Samuel Bostick in Tucson, Arizona Territory, 1868–1874," Ephemera Files, Arizona Historical Society, 3–9.

34. Ibid., 1, 8. Sam died in Florence in 1903, and the *Tucson Daily Citizen* reported the event on September 1, 1903, an indication that he probably retained ties to the city.

35. Martyn, "Racism in the United States," 458–59, 602.

36. According to James Walter Yancy, in the 1890s, a man named Joe Mitchell lived with a Mexican woman whom his friends identified as his wife. James Walter Yancy, "The Negro of Tucson, Past and Present" (master's thesis, University of Arizona, 1933), 18–19; Bernard Wilson, "The Black Residents of Tucson and Their Achievements, 1860–1900: A Reference Guide," 50–51, Special Collections, University of Arizona Libraries, Tucson; 1860 U.S. census, Arizona County, New Mexico Territory, population schedules, city of Tucson, p. 3, lines 25–26, microfilm M653, roll 712, NARA; 1900 U.S. census, Pima County, Arizona Territory, population schedules, city of Tucson, district 48, p. 12B, lines 93–99, microfilm T623, roll 47, NARA; 1900 U.S. census, Pima County, Arizona Territory, population schedules, city of Tucson, district 48, p. 10B, lines 73–79, microfilm T623, roll 47, NARA.

37. A newspaper reported that Francisca was a "Papago Indian" (now Tohono O'odham), but this self-identification might have been a strategy to evade the miscegenation law. The report might also have erred. The clerk made no annotation that Francisca Valdez was American Indian, and her death certificate listed her as Mexican. "Peculiar Marriage Alliance: Arizona Chinaman and Papago Indian Wed," *Tombstone Epitaph*, April 17, 1910; certificate of death for Lupa [*sic*, Lupe is short for Guadalupe] Ransom, October 16, 1929, Tucson, Pima County, Arizona Genealogy Birth and Death Certificates; Negley and Lindley, *Arizona Territorial Marriages*, 34, 41, 75, 83; Negley and Lindley, *Arizona Marriages*, 262, 355. 1880 U.S. census, Pima County, Arizona Territory, population schedules, city of Tucson, district 39, p. 16, lines 10–11, microfilm T9, roll 36, NARA; Yancy, "Negro of Tucson," 17–18.

38. Pima County Book of Miscellaneous Records, book 1, p. 93, cited in Speelman, "Barber of African Persuasion," 3.

39. Marriage entry for Samuel Bostick and Albina Barraza, p. 64, and marriage entry for Emmett Woodley and Leonicia Terrazas, p. 93, St. Augustine Marriage Register, 1883–1899, Catholic Diocese of Tucson Archives.

NOTES TO PAGES 114–116   197

40. Census records indicate that their first child was born in May 1896. Note that the other child listed was not Esperanza's, for the schedule states that she had given birth only once by 1900. 1900 U.S. census, Santa Cruz County, Arizona Territory, population schedules, unincorporated area, district 60, p. 2A, lines 6–9, microfilm T623, roll 47, NARA. Marriage license for You Cang and Esperanza Frijo [Fraijó], July 18, 1896, Grant County Marriage Records, 1872–1899. The record is housed in Grant County, but their marriage took place in Lordsburg, before the southern half of Grant County became Hidalgo County in 1919. Marriage entry for You Cong [Cang] and Esperanza Fraijó, July 20, 1896, p. 202, St. Augustine Marriage Register, 1883–1899, Catholic Diocese of Tucson Archives, Arizona.

41. *Mercedes [Chávez] Kow v. Lee Kow*, SCC 7280, September 15, 1920, Clerk's Office, Pima County Superior Court, Tucson, Arizona.

42. Wong's name first appears as Tsue Chung Wing and Pascuala's as Pasquala Nova and later as Pasenala Nava. *Spokane Daily Chronicle*, October 7, 1916; *Spokesman-Review*, October 10, 1916; *Spokane Daily Chronicle*, October 11, 1916. For the Washington law, see Martyn, "Racism in the United States," 456–57, 547–48, 605. The Helena-to-Spokane trip took between ten and twelve hours. *The Official Railway Guide: North American Freight Service* (Philadelphia, PA: National Railway, 1896), 504–5.

43. For the miscegenation laws of Idaho, Montana, and Wyoming, see Martyn, "Racism in the United States," 561, 832, 898–99, 1053–54, 1049, 1211–13. Idaho allowed Chinese-white marriages between 1887 and 1921. Wong and Pascuala might have unsuccessfully tried to marry there.

44. As discussed above, the Arizona legislature added an ancestry clause to the territorial law in 1887. Therefore, even if the judge had accepted the claim that these Mexican women had "Moorish and Indian" ancestry, a strict interpretation of the law would have allowed the marriages only if he determined that the women had no white ancestry whatsoever. The original story appeared in the *Tucson Daily Citizen* on August 28, 1891, and other Arizona newspapers cited it days later, including the weekend summary of the *Citizen*, the *Arizona Weekly Citizen*, on September 5, 1891; *Prescott Evening Courier*, September 2, 1891; *Mohave County Miner*, September 5, 1891; and *St. Johns Herald*, September 10, 1891.

45. "A Cosmopolitan Wedding," *Los Angeles Times*, April 29, 1895, 5. The *Times* used the phrase "Moorish and Indian ancestry" and indicated that the case took place in recent years. The variance on the expression "love laughs at locksmiths" appears in both *LA Times* and *Tucson Citizen*, leaving little doubt that

they discuss the same couples. No other Chinese-Mexican couples from Tucson married in New Mexico between 1891 and 1895.

46. "Cupid Loses Bout with Eth Nology [*sic*]," *Arizona Journal-Miner*, May 3, 1912. For information on the ancestry of Teresa's family, see 1910 U.S. census, Maricopa County, Arizona Territory, population schedules, city of Phoenix, district 73, p. 37A, lines 31–38, microfilm T624, roll 40, NARA. Census and vital records indicate that the couple resided in Phoenix, except when they made the wedding trip to New Mexico. 1920 U.S. census, Maricopa County, Arizona, population schedules, city of Phoenix, district 134, p. 2B, lines 82–85, microfilm T625, roll 49, NARA; 1930 U.S. census, Maricopa County, Arizona, population schedules, city of Phoenix, district 7–42, p. 10B, lines 66–73, microfilm T626, roll 58, NARA; certificate of birth for Adele Morellos [*sic*] Fong Ling, March 27, 1916, Phoenix, Maricopa County, Arizona Genealogy Birth and Death Certificates; certificate of birth for Amapol Ling, June 10, 1923, Phoenix, Maricopa County, Arizona Genealogy Birth and Death Certificates. The marriage license lists Teresa as Juanita, a name she also used on one of her children's birth certificate. Marriage license for Fong Ling and Juanita Moralez [Morales], July 4, 1915, p. 1611, book 6, Marriage Records, Hidalgo County, New Mexico, Clerk's Office, City of Lordsburg.

47. The marriage license lists her as Mary Lee, but her given name was María. Baptismal entry for María Lee, p. 121, St. Augustine Baptismal Register, 1893–1896, Catholic Diocese of Tucson Archives, Arizona; marriage license for Manuel Samaniego and Mary Lee, March 13, 1920, p. 8, book 1, Hidalgo County Marriage Records; marriage license for Harry Williams Nelson and Yaura [Isaura] Lee Yee, March 20, 1921, p. 114, book 1, Hidalgo County Marriage Records; certificate of death for Yee Tong [Tong Yee], March 15, 1919, Tucson, Pima County, Arizona Genealogy Birth and Death Certificates; *Acts, Resolutions, and Memorials of the Regular Session Third Legislature of the State of Arizona* (Phoenix, AZ: McNeil, 1917), 75.

48. "A Cosmopolitan Wedding." The marriage might have involved the aforementioned Joe Mitchell and an unidentified Mexican woman.

49. Marriage license for Forest Gaskins, born in Virginia, and Nicanoda (Nicanora) Zuniga (Zúñiga) Campos, born in Mexico, married on February 15, 1929, p. 684, book 3, Hidalgo County Marriage Records; marriage license for Walter A. Walker, born in Alabama, and Concepción Peltan (Beltrán?), born in Mexico, married on December 27, 1929, p. 420, book 4, Hidalgo County Marriage Records. For the racial classifications of Forest and Nicanora Gaskins and Walter and Concepción Walker, see 1930 U.S. census, Santa Cruz

County, Arizona, population schedules, city of Nogales, district 3, p. 4A, lines 27–28, microfilm T626, roll 62, NARA; 1930 U.S. census, Santa Cruz County, Arizona, population schedules, city of Nogales, district 2, p. 5A, lines 16–17, microfilm T626, roll 62, NARA.

50. Marriage license for Manuel Ahloy and Isabel Escalante, August 29, 1891, and marriage license for Jim Lee and Concepción Moreno, August 29, 1891, Grant County Marriage Records, 1872–1899.

51. This Charles Lee is not the same as the one who married Mercedes Gálvez in 1888. No record exists of Lee and Chávez in either New Mexico or Arizona, but Wo and Moreno resided in Tucson and Benson, Arizona, where they had children before and after their wedding year. Their friendship suggests that Lee and Chávez most likely lived nearby. Wo also appears as Woo. Although the latter spelling occurs more frequently in the records, Wo was actually used on the tombstone of the couple. Marriage license for Charles Lee and Concepción Chabes [Chávez], March 13, 1898, Grant County Marriage Records, 1872–1899; marriage license for Hi Woo and E. [Emeteria] Morano [Moreno], July 14, 1898, Grant County Marriage Records, 1872–1899; certificate of birth for José Ong Wo, November 15, 1891, Benson, Cochise County, Arizona Genealogy Birth and Death Certificates; certificate of birth for unnamed female child [Isabel] of Hi Wo and [Emeteria] Morano [Moreno], April 2, 1906, Benson, Cochise County, Arizona Genealogy Birth and Death Certificates. Loreto Moreno was Emetería's sister and Hi Wo's first wife. It is very likely that Hi legally married Loreto in Arizona. A person named H. W. Ben (they lived in Benson, Arizona) married a Loreto Moreno in 1893 in Tucson. Negley and Lindley, *Arizona Territorial Marriages*, 7.

52. For other couples whose census or vital records place them in Arizona at around the time they claimed residence in New Mexico, see marriage license for Sing Sang and Amelia [Emilia] Lee, December 23, 1912, p. 971, book 4, Grant County Marriage Records; 1910 Census, Santa Cruz County, Arizona Territory, population schedules, city of Nogales, district 114, p 13A, line 30, microfilm T624, roll 41, NARA; marriage license for Fong Ling and Juanita Moralez [Morales], July 4, 1915, p. 1611, book 6, Grant County Marriage Records; certificate of birth for Adele Fong Ling, April 27, 1916, Phoenix, Maricopa County, Arizona Genealogy Birth and Death Certificates; marriage license for Yee Get and Eliza Nais, April 16, 1917, p. 2110, book 7, Grant County Marriage Records; certificate of birth for Virginia Yee Get, September 22, 1918, Phoenix, Maricopa County, Arizona Genealogy Birth and Death Certificates.

53. All information for Chinese-Mexican and black-Mexican couples derives from a database I created based on census and vital records and on marriage records at Grant and Hidalgo counties in New Mexico cited throughout this study. The most common of these marriages were (groom listed first): Chinese-Mexican (fifteen), Japanese-Mexican (four), black-Mexican (five), and Chinese-white (five). The two other men were the aforementioned white and Mexican men who married women of Chinese-Mexican ancestry. In addition to the five white women, the brides were as follows: twenty-four Mexican, two Chinese-Mexican, one Spaniard, and one Puerto Rican.

54. The newspaper did not identify the Mexican eloper. "Chinatown Belle Elopes; Marries Mexican; Father of Beautiful Oriental Very Angry," *Bisbee Daily Review*, September 29, 1920; 1910 U.S. census, Pima County, Arizona Territory, population schedules, city of Tucson, district 102, pp. 8B-9A, lines 50, 1–3, microfilm T624, roll 41, NARA; 1920 U.S. census, Pima County, Arizona, population schedules, city of Tucson, district 92, p. 3A, lines 14–21, microfilm T625, roll 50, NARA. According to historian Grace Delgado, two Chinese-American women married Mexican men in the Tucson area. She states that Lily Liu was a second-generation Chinese-American woman who traveled to Lordsburg to obtain a legal marriage to Frank Valenzuela, a Mexican man. Delgado maintains that the marriage of Lily's sister, Amelia, to a Mexican man was therefore also an intermarriage. Yet her source (an oral interview from 1984) as well as census and vital records demonstrate that Lily and Amelia were not in fact Chinese. Lily was born Elidia Olivares, and several of her comments also indicate that she was Mexican. In a revealing exchange, for example, the interviewer asks, "I find it unusual for a Mexican woman to be divorced in those days. Were you unusual? Were there many Mexican women who were divorced?" Lily responds that there were many divorced Mexican women. By then she had already divorced Frank Valenzuela. Her trip to New Mexico, therefore, was not to marry Frank but to marry her second husband, Raymond Liu. Raymond was Chinese, and he and Lily could not marry in Arizona—as she also states in her interview. Delgado, *Making the Chinese Mexican*, 140, 252n42. For Lily's interview, see oral history interview with Lily Olivaras [*sic*] Valenzuela Liu, July 5, 1984, Tucson Railroaders Oral History Project, AV 0001 15, Arizona Historical Society, Tucson. The following documents indicate that both sisters were Mexican, with the maiden name of Olivares: 1920 U.S. census, Pima County, Arizona, population schedules, city of Tucson, district 104, p. 5A, lines 18–21, microfilm T625, roll 50, NARA;

1930 U.S. census, Pima County, Arizona, population schedules, city of Tucson, district 10–29, p. 10B, lines 97–100, microfilm T626, roll 61, NARA; 1940 U.S. census, Pima County, Arizona, population schedules, city of Tucson, district 10–28, p. 10A, lines 29–39, microfilm T627, roll 111, NARA. Certificate of death for María Elvida [*sic*, Elvira?] Valenzuela, December 25, 1936; certificate of birth for Sylvia Valenzuela, December 4, 1937; certificate of birth for Amelia Oliveres [*sic*] Mendez, January 16, 1937, Tucson, Pima County, Arizona Genealogy Birth and Death Certificates. "Funeral Notices," *Tucson Citizen*, March 18, 2000, accessed April 6, 2013, http://tucsoncitizen.com/morgue2/tag/death/page/230.

55. 1920 U.S. census, Maricopa County, Arizona, population schedules, city of Phoenix, district 68, p. 10A, lines 42–43, microfilm T625, roll 49, NARA; 1930 U.S. census, Maricopa County, Arizona, population schedules, city of Phoenix, district 7–7, p. 9A, lines 13–15, microfilm T626, roll 57, NARA.

56. As explained in chapter 1, Joe Kirby, the son of a white man and a Mexican woman, married Mayellen Conner, a black woman from Kansas, in Tucson in the early 1900s. He successfully sued for an annulment based on Arizona's miscegenation law.

57. Certificate of death for Charles Embers, November 27, 1935, Tucson, Pima County, Arizona Genealogy Birth and Death Certificates.

58. Yancy, "Negro of Tucson," 15–17. Census schedules listed Embers's birthplace as Utah, Maryland, and California (see next note), but in his interview for the slave narratives of the 1930s, he said he was born in California. George P. Rawick, ed., *The American Slave: A Composite Autobiography*, suppl., series 2, vol. 1 (Westport, CT: Greenwood Press, 1979), 17.

59. The research by Yancy relied on personal interviews during the 1930s. He talked to Embers and even took a photograph of the eighty-three-year-old. Most likely, Embers himself told Yancy that he and Dolores had a child who lived in California in 1933. Yancy, "Negro of Tucson," 17; 1870 U.S. census, Pima County, Arizona Territory, population schedules, township of Maricopa Wells, p. 1, line 30, microfilm M593, roll 46, NARA; 1900 U.S. census, Pima County, Arizona Territory, population schedules, city of Tucson, district 49, p. 28A, lines 3–4, microfilm T623, roll 47, NARA; 1920 U.S. census, Pima County, Arizona, population schedules, city of Tucson, district 94, p. 3A, lines 11–12, microfilm T625, roll 50, NARA.

60. Certificate of death for Dolores Salcido de Embers, November 6, 1925, Tucson, Pima County, Arizona Genealogy Birth and Death Certificates. Hispanic

legal and cultural conventions prescribe that a woman maintain her maiden name after marriage. In some cases, a woman adds her husband's surname with the possessive preposition *de* (of) before it.

61. For instance, Antonio Van Alstine—his father was from New York, and his mother from Mexico—was classified as Mexican on his daughter's birth certificate. His sister, however, was classified as white. Both siblings had Mexican spouses. Certificate of birth for María Dolores Van Alstine, April 10, 1884; certificate of birth for Albert Jimenez, March 8, 1908, Tucson, Pima County, Arizona Genealogy Birth and Death Certificates. Francisco Clark, of white-Mexican ancestry, was classified as Latino-Saxon on his daughter's birth certificate. Certificate of birth for unnamed child of Francisco Clark and Librada Campillo, February 14, 1910, Tucson, Pima County, Arizona Genealogy Birth and Death Certificates.

62. The 1930 instructions read: "[I]t has been decided that all persons born in Mexico, or having parents born in Mexico, who are not definitely white, Negro, Indian, Chinese, or Japanese, should be returned as Mexican ('Mex')." *Twenty Censuses: Population and Housing Questions, 1790–1980* (Washington, DC: U.S. Department of Commerce, Bureau of the Census, 1979), 52. For more on the racial classifications in the census, see Jennifer L. Hochschild and Brenna Marea Powell, "Racial Reorganization and the United States Census 1850–1930: Mulattoes, Half-Breeds, Mixed Parentage, Hindoos, and the Mexican Race," *Studies in American Political Development* 22, no. 1 (March 2008): 59–96.

63. *Twenty Censuses*, 32–33.

64. Leonicia Terrazas also appears as Dionicia. Based on census instructions, Frank should have appeared as mulatto in 1910 and 1920 and as black in 1930. See all sources for the classification of the Woodley children in note 67 below. See *Twenty Censuses*, 42, 50; Gary A. Greenfield and Don B. Kates, Jr., "Mexican Americans, Racial Discrimination, and the Civil Rights Act of 1866," *California Law Review* 63, no. 3 (May 1975): 699, 700n197.

65. 1900 U.S. census, Pima County, Arizona Territory, population schedules, city of Tucson, district 48, p. 6A, line 6, microfilm T623, roll 47, NARA; 1920 U.S. census, Pima County, Arizona, population schedules, city of Tucson, district 102, p. 15A, line 42, microfilm T625, roll 50, NARA; 1930 U.S. census, Pima County, Arizona, population schedules, city of Tucson, district 44, p. 36B, line 96, microfilm T626, roll 62, NARA.

NOTES TO PAGES 127–128 203

66. Brian Gratton and Myron P. Gutmann, "Hispanics in the United States, 1850–1990: Estimates of Population Size and National Origin," *Historical Methods: A Journal of Quantitative and Interdisciplinary History* 33, no. 3 (2000): 149–50.

67. Frank Woodley was living alone in 1920. See 1920 U.S. census, Maricopa County, Arizona, population schedules, city of Buckeye, district 49, p. 6B, line 97, microfilm T625, roll 50, NARA; 1930 U.S. census, Maricopa County, Arizona, population schedules, city of Buckeye, district 7–48, p. 7A, lines 18–23, microfilm T626, roll 58, NARA; 1930 U.S. census, Fresno County, California, population schedules, city of Riverdale, district 10–7, p. 61A, lines 12–20, microfilm T627, roll 200, NARA. For Frank Woodley classified as "Negro + Mexican," see certificate of birth for unnamed child, December 11, 1909, Tucson, Pima County, Arizona Genealogy Birth and Death Certificates. For Frank listed as living in Mexican Town, see certificate of birth for Domingo Woodley, October 30, 1921, Buckeye, Maricopa County, Arizona Genealogy Birth and Death Certificates. For Frank or children classified as Mexican, see certificate of death for Amelia Woodley, April 20, 1909, Tucson, Pima County; certificate of birth for Mary Woodley, February 17, 1927, Buckeye, Maricopa County; certificate of birth for Frank Woodley, August 24, 1929, Phoenix, Maricopa County; and certificate of birth for Augustine Woodley, May 28, 1934, Liberty, Maricopa County, Arizona Genealogy Birth and Death Certificates. For Frank classified as white, see certificate of birth for Robert Woodley, September 12, 1936, Buckeye, Maricopa County, Arizona Genealogy Birth and Death Certificates. For Frank's daughter classified as Spanish, see certificate of death for Mary Woodley, August 11, 1931, Buckeye, Maricopa County, Arizona Genealogy Birth and Death Certificates.

68. Certificate of death for Henry Ransom, January 20, 1955, Tucson, Pima County, Arizona Genealogy Birth and Death Certificates; crossing registry for Enrique Ransom, June 19, 1917, Manifests of Alien Arrivals at Naco, Arizona, 1908–1952, microfilm A3372, roll 4, RG 85, Records of the Immigration and Naturalization Service, NARA.

69. Simon and Carmen [née Palomino] West and their children were listed as black. 1900 U.S. census, Pima County, Arizona Territory, population schedules, city of Florence, district 55, p. 8B, lines 71–74, microfilm T623, roll 47, NARA. Carmen's parents were Abundio Palomino and Simona Morales, both born in northern Mexico. Certificate of death for Carmen West, November 24, 1920, Tucson, Pima County, Arizona Genealogy Birth and Death

Certificates. For a record of their marriage, see marriage license for Simon West and Carmen Palomeno [*sic*], May 6, 1896, Marriage Records, Pinal County, Arizona, vol. 1A, p. 120, Western States Marriage Records, Special Collections and Family History, BYU-Idaho, Rexburg, accessed March 29, 2015, http://abish.byui.edu/specialCollections/westernStates/westernStatesRecord Detail.cfm?recordID=32920.

70. 1900 U.S. census, Pinal County, Arizona Territory, population schedules, Florence Township, district 55, p. 1A, lines 39–44, microfilm T623, roll 47, NARA; 1910 Census of the Population, Phoenix, Maricopa County, Arizona, district 63, page 11A, microfilm T624, roll 40, NARA; 1910 Census of the Population, Pinal County, Arizona, district 111, page 4B and 5B, microfilm T624, roll 42, NARA; 1920 Census of the Population, Phoenix, Maricopa County, Arizona, district 68, page 10A and 14A, microfilm T625, roll 49, NARA; 1930 Census of the Population, Pirtleville, Cochise County, Arizona, district 3, page 2A, microfilm T626, roll 55, NARA; 1930 Census of the Population, Phoenix, Maricopa County, Arizona, district 2, page 9A, microfilm T626, roll 57, NARA; 1930 Census of the Population, San Bernardino, San Bernardino County, California, district 12, page 19B, microfilm T626, roll 187, NARA.

71. Certificate of death for María Ahloy, May 29, 1910, Tucson, Pima County; certificate of death for unnamed child of Dong Yet and Rosario Ramírez, May 19, 1924, Tucson, Pima County; certificate of death for María Dolores Lee, March 15, 1953, Tucson, Pima County; certificate of birth for José Vicente Lee, December 14, 1901, Tucson, Pima County, Arizona Genealogy Birth and Death Certificates; certificate of birth for José Ong Wo, November 15, 1891, Benson, Cochise County, Arizona Genealogy Birth and Death Certificates; certificate of birth for Julia Wo, June 27, 1913, Benson, Cochise County, Arizona Genealogy Birth and Death Certificates; certificate of birth for Gilbert Comadurand, September 10, 1913, Benson, Cochise County, Arizona Genealogy Birth and Death Certificates; certificate of birth for Julia Wo, July 7, 1917, Benson, Cochise County, Arizona Genealogy Birth and Death Certificates; certificate of birth for Arnoldo Wo, February 27, 1924, Benson, Cochise County, Arizona Genealogy Birth and Death Certificates.

72. In 1900 seven children, from two families, were classified as white (only two of Juana's children are Charley's): 1900 U.S. census, Pima County, Arizona Territory, population schedules, city of Tucson, district 48, p. 5A, lines 12–16, microfilm T623, roll 47, NARA; 1900 U.S. census, Pima County, Arizona Territory, population schedules, city of Tucson, district 48, p. 12B, lines 93–99,

microfilm T623, roll 47, NARA. Also in 1900, four children, from two families, were classified as Chinese: 1900 U.S. census, Pima County, Arizona Territory, population schedules, city of Tucson, district 49, p. 4B, lines 90–92, microfilm T623, roll 47, NARA; 1900 U.S. census, Pima County, Arizona Territory, population schedules, city of Tucson, district 49, pp. 21A-21B, lines 49–52, microfilm T623, roll 47, NARA. In 1910 eight children, from one family, were classified as white: 1910 U.S. census, Pima County, Arizona Territory, population schedules, city of Tucson, district 107, p. 5A, lines 10–19, microfilm T624, roll 41, NARA. Three, from one family, were classified as Chinese: 1910 U.S. census, Pima County, Arizona Territory, population schedules, city of Tucson, district 102, p. 8B, lines 95–99, microfilm T624, roll 41, NARA. In 1920 all twelve children, from three families, were classified as white: 1920 U.S. census, Pima County, Arizona, population schedules, city of Tucson, district 101, p. 3A, lines 23–27, microfilm T625, roll 50, NARA; 1920 U.S. census, Pima County, Arizona, population schedules, city of Tucson, district 101, p. 18A, lines 24–29, microfilm T625, roll 50, NARA; 1920 U.S. census, Pima County, Arizona, population schedules, city of Tucson, district 101, p. 4A, lines 36–42, microfilm T625, roll 50, NARA.

73. The census dictated that the children of nonwhite men were to follow the race of the father, regardless of the race of the mother. Rosa and Berta Llango, their two married sisters—María Garcia and Refugio Medel—and the widow Rita Back were all listed as Mexican. 1930 U.S. census, Pima County, Arizona, population schedules, city of Tucson, district 44, p. 10A, lines 38, 40–41, 43, microfilm T626, roll 61, NARA; 1930 U.S. census, Pima County, Arizona, population schedules, city of Tucson, district 66, p. 12B, line 54, microfilm T626, roll 61, NARA. María Teresa, George and Ludovina Lem, and María Dolores and José Vicente Lee appeared as Chinese. 1930 U.S. census, Pima County, Arizona, population schedules, city of Tucson, district 44, p. 15B, lines 65–67, microfilm T626, roll 61, NARA; 1930 U.S. census, Pima County, Arizona, population schedules, city of Tucson, district 43, p. 12B, lines 74–75, microfilm T626, roll 6, NARA.

CHAPTER 5

1. Hiram Stevens unquestionably intended to kill his wife, Petra. He shot her in the head at point-blank range, but she overcame the pain and was able to

fight him off, suffering the wound to the hand in the process. A third shot went into their bed. "H. S. Stevens Dead," *Arizona Daily Star*, March 22, 1893.

2. Ibid.; "How the Stevens Tragedy Occurred," *Arizona Daily Star*, March 23, 1893; "He Has Passed Away," *Tucson Daily Citizen*, March 22, 1893; "Laid to Rest," *Tucson Daily Citizen*, March 23, 1893; "A Dreadful Deed," *Arizona Weekly Journal*, March 29, 1893.

3. Benton, "Border Jews, Border Marriages," 20, 40–42.

4. See letters of March 14, 1871; October 18, 1871; February 23, 1875; October 9, 1876; October 25, 1883, in Jean Baptiste Salpointe, Correspondence, 1867–1884, Special Collections, University of Arizona Libraries, Tucson.

5. For the reference to concerns over the establishment of public schools, see Wagoner, *Arizona Territory*, 70; Mamie Bernard de Aguirre, "Spanish Trader's Bride," *Westport Historical Quarterly* 4, no. 3 (December 1968): 22.

6. Jean Baptiste Salpointe, Constitutions of the Vicariate Apostolic of Tucson, June 20, 1870, trans., p. 10, Special Collections, University of Arizona Libraries, Tucson.

7. According to Benton, all Jewish-Mexican marriages in the 1870s and 1880s involved foreign-born men, who were more likely to favor fraternal associations over religious ties. They acquiesced to the Catholic traditions of their Mexican wives. Benton, "Border Jews, Border Marriages," 20, 40–43, 46, 57–61.

8. Compadrazgo is the kinship tie between parents and godparents, who become compadres (etymologically, coparents) to each other upon the baptism ceremony.

9. For the pivotal networking roles of wives and mothers, see Micaela di Leonardo, "The Female World of Cards and Holidays: Women, Families, and the Work of Kinship," *Signs: Journal of Women in Culture and Society* 12, no. 3 (1987): 440–53.

10. St. Augustine Baptismal Register, p. 257, Catholic Diocese of Tucson Archives, accessed April 13, 2013, http://azmemory.lib.az.us/cdm4/browse.php ?CISOROOT=/rcdhilites.

11. Ibid., p. 363.

12. For the emphasis on a Chinese upbringing, see "Brief News Items of the Town," *Arizona Daily Star*, evening edition, February 18, 1901; Fong, "Sojourners and Settlers," 227–33. Only one union involved a black-Mexican woman and a Mexican man. In 1895 Manuela Woodley, daughter of Emmett Woodley and Leonicia Terrazas, legally married Manuel Amparano in Tucson. See

NOTES TO PAGES 138–141   207

the marriage entry for Manuel Amposano [Amparano] and Manuela Woodley in Negley and Lindley, *Arizona Territorial Marriages*, 3.

13. Rita Lee was the daughter of Santiago Lee (born in China) and Concepción Moreno. A margin note on her baptismal record (1893) indicates that she married Alexander McMinndie in Tucson in 1914. Alexander's surname appears as MacMinn on the county marriage license and in the newspaper article cited here. Baptismal entry for Rita Lee, July 4, 1893, p. 217, St. Augustine Baptismal Register, 1893–1896, Catholic Diocese of Tucson Archives, Arizona; Negley and Lindley, *Arizona Marriages*, 186.

14. *Washington Times*, March 24, 1919, 10; April 14, 1919, 2:12. *Washington DC Evening Star*, March 23, 1919, 3:1; January 24, 1920, 8. *Washington Herald*, March 24, 1919, 5; March 30, 1919, 6; April 14, 1919, 5. *New York Sun*, February 9, 1919, 4:22; March 25, 1919, 11. *Oregon Gazette Times*, April 10, 1919, 4. The quotation appeared in the *New York Sun* on February 9.

15. *Tucson Citizen*, May 23, 1921; May 5, 1921.

16. *Los Angeles Times*, February 22, 1922.

17. The jury ruled for Coppola by a vote of nine to three, which barely sufficed in a civil suit. I document direct quotations separately. The rest of the story from the trials derives from these sources: *María Coppola v. Giuseppe Coppola*, SCC 7767, September 15, 1921, Clerk's Office, Pima County Superior Court, Tucson, Arizona; *Tucson Citizen*, May 4, 1921; May 5, 1921; May 16, 1921; May 23, 1921; June 12, 1921; September 15, 1921; September 16, 1921; February 2, 1922; February 10, 1922; February 13, 1922; February 15, 1922; February 16, 1922; February 17, 1922; February 18, 1922; February 19, 1922; February 20, 1922; February 21, 1922; March 8, 1922; March 5, 1922; March 6, 1922; March 7, 1922; March 8, 1922; *Bisbee (AZ) Daily Review*, May 6, 1921; *Arizona Republican* (Phoenix), September 16, 1921; *Los Angeles Times*, February 20, 1922; February 22, 1922.

18. *Tucson Citizen*, February 20, 1922; February 21, 1922.

19. *Tucson Citizen*, March 8, 1922.

20. *Tucson Citizen*, March 5, 1922; March 6, 1922; March 7, 1922; March 8, 1922.

21. *Tucson Citizen*, September 16, 1921; March 7, 1922; March 8, 1922.

22. *Arizona Republican* (Phoenix), September 16, 1921; *Tucson Citizen*, March 7, 1922.

23. *Washington DC Evening Star*, March 23, 1919, 3:1; *Washington Herald*, March 24, 1919, 5; *New York Sun*, March 25, 1919, 11.

24. *Tucson Citizen*, February 16, 1922.

25. *Tucson Citizen*, May 5, 1921.

208 NOTES TO PAGES 141–149

26. *Tucson Citizen*, September 15, 1921.

27. 1930 U.S. census, Pima County, Arizona, population schedules, city of Tucson, district 67, p. 2B, lines 81–85, microfilm T626, roll 61, NARA; 1940 U.S. census, Pima County, Arizona, population schedules, city of Tucson, district 10–36, p. 12B, lines 58–62, microfilm T627, roll 111, NARA.

28. Myra K. Saunders, "California Legal History: A Review of Spanish and Mexican Legal Institutions," *Law Library Journal* 87 (Summer 1995): 487–89, 495–502.

29. *The Estate of Mahlon E. Moore*, Probate Superior Court, October 4, 1868, reel 1R, Territorial Miscellaneous Records, beginning 1864, Pima County Clerk, City of Tucson, Arizona.

30. McClintock, *Arizona, Prehistoric*, 578–79, 602, 606–7; C. L. Sonnichsen, *Tucson: The Life and Times of an American City* (Norman: University of Oklahoma Press, 1987), 50–51, 87, 92, 225.

31. *The Estate of Hugh Kennedy*, Probate Superior Court, June–December, 1870, Reel 1R, Territorial Miscellaneous Records, beginning 1864, Pima County, City of Tucson, Arizona.

32. U.S. Bureau of the Census, *Marriage and Divorce, 1867–1906, Part I* (Washington, DC: Government Printing Office, 1909), 10–16. Historian Glenda Riley argues that regional economic opportunities for women also contributed to a higher divorce rate in the West. Glenda Riley, *Building and Breaking Families in the American West* (Albuquerque: University of New Mexico Press, 1996), 113–19, 134–42.

33. U.S. Bureau of the Census, *Marriage and Divorce*, 10–16.

34. Elaine Tyler May, *Great Expectations: Marriage and Divorce in Post-Victorian America* (Chicago, IL: University of Chicago Press, 1980), 2–7. Later studies also corroborate these data. See Riley, *Building and Breaking Families*, 113–19; Glenda Riley, *Divorce: An American Tradition* (New York: Oxford University Press, 1991), 85–107.

35. Alvah L. Stinson, *Woman under the Law* (Boston, MA: Hudson, 1914), 194. An 1887 Arizona law converted all common-law unions into formal marriages, but all divorce cases discussed in this chapter mention a precise date and place for the marriage.

36. May, *Great Expectations*, 10.

37. *María Jaime Gay v. Mervin G. Gay*, SCC 196, August 29, 1873, Clerk's Office, Pima County Superior Court, Tucson, Arizona.

38. *Joaquina V. Franklin v. Charles Franklin*, SCC 198, October 4, 1873, Clerk's Office, Pima County Superior Court, Tucson, Arizona. In a similar case, William

Haynes accused his wife of infecting him with a venereal disease after returning from a trip to see her relatives. *William Haynes v. Eulalia Haynes*, SCC 2578, October 5, 1896, Clerk's Office, Pima County Superior Court, Tucson, Arizona.

39. *Manuela Fairbanks v. Benjamin D. Fairbanks*, SCC 222, September 25, 1874, Clerk's Office, Pima County Superior Court.

40. *Jacob Youstcy v. Dominga S. Youstcy*, SCC 202, October 31, 1873, Clerk's Office, Pima County Superior Court, Tucson, Arizona. Jacob found it difficult to remain married. He wed Mexican women on two more occasions, and those unions also ended in divorce after the women abandoned him. *Jacob Youstcy v. Mariana Youstcy*, SCC 1731, January 21, 1889, Clerk's Office, Pima County Superior Court, Tucson, Arizona; *Jacob Youstcy v. Julia Youstcy*, SCC 1894, April 1, 1891, Clerk's Office, Pima County Superior Court, Tucson, Arizona.

41. *Thomas Potts v. Angela R. de Potts*, SCC 3897, August 8, 1905, Clerk's Office, Pima County Superior Court, Tucson, Arizona.

42. These results are highly similar to what Robert L. Griswold observed for white endogamous couples in San Mateo and Santa Clara Counties in California between 1850 and 1890, where 64 percent of men's divorce petitions cited desertion as the main cause. Robert L. Griswold, *Family and Divorce in California, 1850–1890: Victorian Illusions and Everyday Realities* (Albany: State University of New York Press, 1982), 26–28, 78–80. Similarly, historian Glenda Riley notes that the incidence of desertion was higher in the West, and that women often deserted their husbands. She explains that husbands in the West cited desertion in their divorce petitions 23.1 percent (1867–1886) and 29.5 percent (1887–1906) of the time. Riley, *Divorce*, 85–88.

43. *Erasmus Wood v. Palmira [Roca] Wood*, SCC 862, January 4, 1883, Clerk's Office, Pima County Superior Court, Tucson, Arizona. Palmira's father was born in Chile according to the 1870 census.

44. *William Haynes v. Eulalia Haynes*.

45. *Jacob Youstcy v. Mariana Youstcy*, SCC 1731. In a similar case, Barney Smith won the dissolution of his marriage after his wife Concepción left him and moved to Mexico. *Barney Smith v. Concepción Smith*, SCC 7607, June 1, 1921, Clerk's Office, Pima County Superior Court, Tucson, Arizona. In another case, Andrew Roos divorced his wife, Justina, after she left him and purportedly married another man. *Andrew Roos v. Justina Roos*, SCC 7072, February 11, 1920, Clerk's Office, Pima County Superior Court, Tucson, Arizona.

46. For an excellent study of the porosity of the Mexico-U.S. border and the lack of emphasis on preventing Mexican immigration, see Patrick Ettinger,

Imaginary Lines: Border Enforcement and the Origins of Undocumented Immigration, 1882–1930 (Austin: University of Texas Press, 2009).

47. *James Brady v. Mariana Brady*, SCC 2107, July 3, 1892, Clerk's Office, Pima County Superior Court, Tucson, Arizona.

48. *Halim Karam v. Enriqueta Díaz-Karam*, SCC 6440, July 22, 1918, Clerk's Office, Pima County Superior Court, Tucson, Arizona. I determined Halim's Syrian nationality because he soon married another Mexican woman—Delfina Rodríguez—and the birth certificate of their first daughter identified him as Syrian. The birth certificate of his daughter with Enriqueta had used the more general nationality of "Arabian." Certificate of birth of nameless child, parents Halim Karam and Delphina [*sic*] Rodríguez, February 18, 1920, Tucson; certificate of birth of Leonor Caram y Diaz, parents Halim Caram and Enriqueta Diaz, January 13, 1918, Tucson, Arizona Genealogy Birth and Death Certificates.

49. *Sarah McDermott de Gil v. Francisco Gil*, SCC 9399, February 7, 1925, Clerk's Office, Pima County Superior Court, Tucson, Arizona; *Francisco Gil v. Sarah McDermott de Gil*, SCC 9872, February 12, 1927, Clerk's Office, Pima County Superior Court, Tucson, Arizona.

50. *Luz Houston v. Ezra B. Houston*, SCC 2684, July 21, 1897, Clerk's Office, Pima County Superior Court, Tucson, Arizona. Although uncommon, white men could also leave their wives and resettle in Mexico of all places. In 1928 Waldo Baldridge abandoned his wife, Inez, and moved to Mexico. She filed for divorce soon after. *Inez Baldridge v. Waldo Baldridge*, SCC 11606, November 3, 1928, Clerk's Office, Pima County Superior Court, Tucson, Arizona.

51. *Faustina Gilliland v. James Gilliland*, SCC 2772, March 12, 1898, Clerk's Office, Pima County Superior Court, Tucson, Arizona.

52. For general references to physical and verbal abuse, see, for instance, the succinct description in Josefa Gleason's divorce petition. *Josepha Gleason v. William R. Gleason*, SCC 1198, August 15, 1885, Clerk's Office, Pima County Superior Court, Tucson, Arizona. She spoke in general terms of "cruelty" and "nervous mental and bodily sufferings." Her testimony, however, sufficed to secure the divorce and alimony payments of fifty dollars per month, even though her husband denied the charges of abuse.

53. *Inez Tabor v. Walter C. Tabor*, SCC 7228, July 27, 1920, Clerk's Office, Pima County Superior Court, Tucson, Arizona.

54. *Joaquina Fisher v. Robert J. Fisher*, SCC 5953, October 26, 1916, Clerk's Office, Pima County Superior Court, Tucson, Arizona. See also the case of Matilda

NOTES TO PAGES 154–158   211

(Matilde) E. Carroll, whose brief marriage to Robert Carroll included episodes of jealousy, accusations of adultery, physical and mental abuse, and death threats. *Matilda E. Carroll v. Robert Carroll*, SCC 9342, December 29, 1924, Clerk's Office, Pima County Superior Court, Tucson, Arizona.

55. *Juanita Montgomery v. Donald F. Montgomery*, SCC 8664, September 15, 1923, Clerk's Office, Pima County Superior Court, Tucson, Arizona.

56. *María U. Van Alstine v. Pedro C. Van Alstine*, SCC 4765, August 18, 1910, Clerk's Office, Pima County Superior Court, Tucson, Arizona. Pedro's mother was Mexican, and his father was from New York. See also *Ysidra [Flores] Barrett v. Harry Barrett*, SCC 4136, March 14, 1907; and *Rita Leyva Bentley v. Victor Bentley*, SCC 11706, January 10, 1929, Clerk's Office, Pima County Superior Court, Tucson, Arizona.

57. See, for example, the general terms D. J. Burrow used to describe the abuse he claimed to suffer at the hands of his wife, Eufemia. He briefly spoke of "frequent excesses" and "cruel and outrageous treatment." He obtained the divorce in only three days. *D. J. Burrow v. Eufemia Burrow*, SCC 2838, September 17, 1898, Clerk's Office, Pima County Superior Court, Tucson, Arizona.

58. *Robert Fanchette v. Salsa Fanchette*, SCC 5138, October 28, 1912, Clerk's Office, Pima County Superior Court, Tucson, Arizona; *Frank M. Clarke v. Librada Clarke*, SCC 5211, December 11, 1912, Clerk's Office, Pima County Superior Court, Tucson, Arizona; *W. J. McKenzie v. Juanita McKenzie*, SCC 13082, October 5, 1930, Clerk's Office, Pima County Superior Court, Tucson, Arizona.

59. *Charles B. Harris v. Diega P. Harris*, SCC 6235, September 14, 1917, Clerk's Office, Pima County Superior Court, Tucson, Arizona.

60. *Thomas Johns v. Erminia Johns*, SCC 4966, January 13, 1912, Clerk's Office, Pima County Superior Court, Tucson, Arizona; "Accuses Wife of Poisoning," *Los Angeles Times*, January 13, 1912.

61. *Amelia Binning v. Oscar Binning*, SCC 7659, July 5, 1921, Clerk's Office, Pima County Superior Court, Tucson, Arizona.

62. "Alexander MacMinn Sued for Divorce by Mexican Wife," *Tucson Daily Citizen*, May 13, 1918.

63. May, *Great Expectations*, 155–63.

64. Francis P. Brady, "Portrait of a Pioneer: Peter R. Brady, 1825–1902," *Journal of Arizona History* 16, no. 2 (Summer 1975): 174–84.

65. The Camp Grant Massacre occurred in 1871 and resulted in the deaths of 144 Apache Indians. Wagoner, *Arizona Territory*, 7, 37, 77, 128–31; Sheridan, *Arizona: A History*, 79–82. For a topical treatment of the groups involved in

the massacre (whites, Mexicans, Tohono O'odham Indians, and Apaches), see Karl Jacoby, *Shadows at Dawn: A Borderlands Massacre and the Violence of History* (New York: Penguin, 2008); Chip Colwell-Chanthaphonh, *Massacre at Camp Grant: Forgetting and Remembering Apache History* (Tucson: University of Arizona Press, 2007).

EPILOGUE

1. Zhu, *Chinaman's Chance*, 1–4, 87, 114–20, 132–46, 159–66, 171–79, 183–89; Zhu, "Ethnic Oasis," 289–329.

BIBLIOGRAPHY

ARCHIVAL RECORDS

Arizona Genealogy Birth and Death Certificates. Office of Vital Records. Arizona Department of Health Services, Phoenix. http://genealogy.az.gov.

The Estate of Hugh Kennedy. Probate Superior Court, June-December, 1870. Territorial Miscellaneous Records, beginning 1864. Clerk's Office, Pima County Superior Court, Tucson, Arizona.

The Estate of Mahlon E. Moore. Probate Superior Court, October 4, 1868. Territorial Miscellaneous Records, beginning 1864. Clerk's Office, Pima County Superior Court, Tucson, Arizona.

Grant County Marriage Records. Clerk's Office, Silver City, New Mexico.

Hidalgo County Marriage Records. Clerk's Office, Lordsburg, New Mexico.

Liu, Lily Olivaras [Olivares] Valenzuela. Oral history interview, July 5, 1984. Tucson Railroaders Oral History Project. Arizona Historical Society, Tucson.

Manifests of Alien Arrivals at Naco, Arizona, 1908–1952. Records of the Immigration and Naturalization Service. National Archives and Records Administration, Washington, DC.

Ord, Angustias. "Ocurrencias en California, Relatadas a Thomas Savage en Santa Bárbara, 1878." Manuscript Collection. Bancroft Library, Berkeley, California.

Pima County Marriage Licenses, 1927–1930. SG 8 Superior Court, History and Archives Division. Arizona State Library, Archives and Public Records, Phoenix.

Salpointe, Jean Baptiste. Constitutions of the Vicariate Apostolic of Tucson, June 20, 1870. Special Collections. University of Arizona Libraries, Tucson.

———. Correspondence, 1867–1884. Special Collections. University of Arizona Libraries, Tucson.

Speelman, Mike. "A Barber of African Persuasion: Samuel Bostick in Tucson, Arizona Territory, 1868–1874." Ephemera Files, Arizona Historical Society, Tucson.

St. Augustine Baptismal Register, 1888–1891. Catholic Diocese of Tucson Archives, Arizona.

St. Augustine Baptismal Register. Catholic Diocese of Tucson Archives, Arizona. http://azmemory.lib.az.us/cdm4/browse.php?CISOROOT=/rcdhilites.

St. Augustine Marriage Register, 1883–1899. Catholic Diocese of Tucson Archives, Arizona.

Tucson Railroaders Oral History Project. Arizona Historical Society, Tucson.

United States Census, population schedules, 1850-1940, microfilm M653, rolls 712, 878; microfilm M593, roll 46; microfilm T9, roll 36; microfilm T623, rolls 47, 107; microfilm T624, rolls 40-41; microfilm T625, rolls 49-51; microfilm T626, rolls 57-8, 61-2; microfilm T627, rolls 111, 200, National Archives and Records Administration, Washington, DC.

Western States Marriage Records. Special Collections and Family History. BYU-Idaho, Rexburg.

Wilson, Bernard. "The Black Residents of Tucson and their Achievements, 1860–1900: A Reference Guide." Special Collections. University of Arizona Libraries, Tucson.

BOOKS, ARTICLES, REPORTS

Acts, Resolutions, and Memorials of the Regular Session Third Legislature of the State of Arizona. Phoenix, AZ: McNeil, 1917.

Acuña, Rodolfo. *Occupied America: The Chicano's Struggle Toward Liberation.* New York: Harper and Row, 1972.

Alexander, Charles C. "Prophet of American Racism: Madison Grant and the Nordic Myth." *Phylon* 23, no. 1 (1962): 73–90.

Almaguer, Tomás. *Racial Fault Lines: The Historical Origins of White Supremacy in California.* Berkeley: University of California Press, 1994.

Barrera, Mario. *Race and Class in the Southwest: A Theory of Racial Inequality.* Notre Dame, IN: University of Notre Dame Press, 1979.

Behan, Barbara Carol. "Forgotten Heritage: African Americans in the Montana Territory, 1864–1889." In "The African American Experience in the Western States," special issue, *Journal of African American History* 91, no. 1 (Winter 2006): 23–40.

Benton, Katherine. "Border Jews, Border Marriages, Border Lives: Mexican-Jewish Intermarriage in the Arizona Territory, 1850–1900." Master's thesis, University of Wisconsin, Madison, 1997.

Bernard de Aguirre, Mamie. "Spanish Trader's Bride." *Westport Historical Quarterly* 4, no. 3 (1968): 5–23.

Bernstein, Alison R. *American Indians and World War II: Toward a New Era in Indian Affairs.* Norman: University of Oklahoma Press, 1991.

Berwanger, Eugene H. *The West and Reconstruction.* Urbana: University of Illinois Press, 1981.

Billington, Ray Allen, and Martin Ridge. *Westward Expansion: A History of the American Frontier.* 5th ed. New York: MacMillan, 1982.

Bird, Randall D., and Garland Allen. "The J.H.B. Archive Report: The Papers of Harry Hamilton Laughlin." *Journal of the History of Biology* 14, no. 2 (Fall 1981): 339–53.

Boardman, Andrea. "The U.S.-Mexican War and the Beginnings of American Tourism in Mexico." In *Holiday in Mexico: Critical Reflections on Tourism and Tourist Encounters,* edited by Dina Berger and Andrew Grant Wood, 21–53. Durham, NC: Duke University Press, 2010.

Brady, Francis P. "Portrait of a Pioneer: Peter R. Brady, 1825–1902." *Journal of Arizona History* 16, no. 2 (Summer 1975): 174–84.

Bragg, Susan. "'Anxious Foot Soldiers': Sacramento's Black Women and Education in Nineteenth-Century California." In *African American Women Confront the West: 1600–2000,* edited by Quintard Taylor and Shirley Ann Wilson Moore, 97–116. Norman: University of Oklahoma Press, 2003.

Browne, J. Ross. *Adventures in the Apache Country: A Tour through Arizona and Sonora, with Notes on the Silver Regions of Nevada.* New York: Harper and Brothers, 1869.

Browne, William Hand, ed. *Archives of Maryland: Proceedings and Acts of the General Assembly of Maryland, January 1637/8–September 1664.* Baltimore: Maryland Historical Society, 1883.

Bryan, Jimmy L. "The American Elsewhere: Adventurism and Manliness in the Age of Expansion, 1815–1848." PhD diss., University of Texas, Arlington, 2006.

Butler, Judith. *The Psychic Life of Power: Theories in Subjection*. Stanford, CA: Stanford University Press, 1997.

———. *Undoing Gender*. New York: Routledge, 2004.

Cadava, Geraldo L. *Standing on Common Ground: The Making of a Sunbelt Borderland*. Cambridge, MA: Harvard University Press, 2013.

Callinicos, Alex. *Making History: Agency, Structure and Change in Social Theory*. Cambridge: Polity Press, 1987.

Camarillo, Albert. *Chicanos in a Changing Society: From Mexican Pueblos to American Barrios in Santa Barbara and Southern California, 1848–1930*. Cambridge, MA: Harvard University Press, 1996.

Campbell, Robert A. "Blacks and the Coal Mines of Western Washington, 1888–1896." *Pacific Northwest Quarterly* 73, no. 4 (October 1982): 146–55.

Carpenter, William W. *Travels and Adventures in Mexico*. New York: Harper and Brothers, 1851.

Casas, María Raquél. *Married to a Daughter of the Land: Spanish-Mexican Women and Interethnic Marriage in California, 1820–1880*. Reno: University of Nevada Press, 2007.

Cashion, Peggy M. "Women and the Mexican War, 1846–1848." PhD diss., University of Texas, Arlington, 1990.

Castle, Gregory, ed. *Postcolonial Discourses: An Anthology*. Malden, MA: Blackwell Publishing, 2001.

Chamberlain, Samuel E. *My Confession*. With introduction and postscript by Roger Butterfield. New York: Harper and Brothers, 1956.

———. *My Confession: Recollections of a Rogue*. Edited by William H. Goetzmann. Austin: Texas State Historical Association, 1996.

Chandler, Robert J. "California's 1863 Loyalty Oaths: Another Look." *Arizona and the West* 21, no. 3 (1979): 215–43.

Chan, Sucheng. "Introduction: The Significance of Locke in Chinese American History." In *Bitter Melon: Inside America's Last Rural Chinese Town*, edited by Jeff Gillenkirk and James Motlow, 18–25. Berkeley, CA: Heyday Books, 1997.

Chen, Yong. *Chinese San Francisco, 1850–1943: A Trans-Pacific Community*. Stanford, CA: Stanford University Press, 2000.

Cheung, Floyd. "'Kingdoms of Manly Style': Performing Chinese American Masculinity, 1865–1941." PhD diss., Tulane University, 1999.

Colwell-Chanthaphonh, Chip. *Massacre at Camp Grant: Forgetting and Remembering Apache History*. Tucson: University of Arizona Press, 2007.

Committee on the Territories. *Statehood for Arizona and New Mexico.* Washington, DC: Government Printing Office, 1906.

"The Conquest of California and the Case of Lieut. Col. Fremont." *Southern Quarterly Review* 15, no. 30 (July 1849): 410–44.

Cooke, Philip S. G. *The Conquest of New Mexico and California.* New York: Putnam, 1878.

Cook, Zo S. "Mexican War Reminiscences." *Alabama Historical Quarterly* 19 (1957): 435–60.

Coray, Michael S. "'Democracy' on the Frontier: A Case Study of Nevada Editorial Attitudes on the Issue of Nonwhite Equality." *Nevada Historical Society Quarterly* 21, no. 3 (Fall 1978): 189–204.

Craver, Rebecca M. *The Impact of Intimacy: Mexican-Anglo Intermarriage in New Mexico, 1821–1846.* El Paso: Texas Western Press, 1982.

Dakin, Susanna Bryant. *A Scotch Paisano: Hugo Reid's Life in California, 1832–1852, Derived from His Correspondence.* Berkeley: University of California Press, 1939.

Davis, Abraham L., and Barbara Luck Graham. *The Supreme Court, Race, and Civil Rights.* Thousand Oaks, CA: Sage, 1995.

De León, Arnoldo. *Racial Frontiers: Africans, Chinese, and Mexicans in Western America, 1848–1890.* Histories of the American Frontier, edited by Ray Allen Billington. Albuquerque: University of New Mexico Press, 2002.

Delgado, Grace. *Making the Chinese Mexican: Global Migration, Localism, and Exclusion in the U.S.-Mexico Borderlands.* Stanford, CA: Stanford University Press, 2012.

Dell'Orto, Giovanna. *Giving Meanings to the World: The First U.S. Foreign Correspondents, 1838–1859.* Westport, CT: Greenwood Press, 2002.

Deloria, Vine, Jr., ed. *American Indian Policy in the Twentieth Century.* Norman: University of Oklahoma Press, 1992.

DeLyser, Dydia. *Ramona Memories: Tourism and the Shaping of Southern California.* Minneapolis: University of Minnesota Press, 2005.

Deutsch, Sarah. *No Separate Refuge: Culture, Class, and Gender on an Anglo-Hispanic Frontier in the American Southwest, 1880–1940.* New York: Oxford University Press, 1987.

di Leonardo, Micaela. "The Female World of Cards and Holidays: Women, Families, and the Work of Kinship." *Signs: Journal of Women in Culture and Society* 12, no. 3 (1987): 440–53.

Donnavan, Corydon. *Adventures in Mexico, Experienced during a Captivity of Seven Months.* Boston, MA: George R. Hollbrook, 1848.

Downing de De Juana, Ana C. "Intermarriage in Hidalgo County, 1860 to 1900." Master's thesis, University of Texas, Pan American, 1998.

Downs, Gregory P. "The Mexicanization of American Politics: The United States' Transnational Path from Civil War to Stabilization." *American Historical Review* 117, no. 2 (April 2012): 387–409.

Duffen, William A., ed. "Overland Via 'Jackass Mail' in 1858: The Diary of Phocion R. Way." Pts. 1 and 2. *Arizona and the West* 2, no. 1 (Spring 1960): 35–54; *Arizona and the West* 2, no. 2 (Summer 1960): 159–61.

Dysart, Jane. "Mexican Women in San Antonio, 1830–1860: The Assimilation Process." *Western Historical Quarterly* 7, no. 4 (1976): 365–75.

Engstrand, Iris H. W., and Mary F. Ward. "Rancho Guajome: An Architectural Legacy Preserved." *Journal of San Diego History* 41, no. 4 (Fall 1995): 1–14.

Ettinger, Patrick. *Imaginary Lines: Border Enforcement and the Origins of Undocumented Immigration, 1882–1930.* Austin: University of Texas Press, 2009.

Farish, Thomas Edwin. *History of Arizona.* Volume 3. Phoenix, AZ: Filmer Brothers, 1916.

Farnham, Thomas Jefferson. *Life, Travels, and Adventures in California, and Scenes in the Pacific Ocean.* New York: W. H. Graham, 1847.

"The Fate of Mexico." *United States Magazine and Democratic Review*, May 1858, 337–45.

Fergusson, Harvey. *In those Days: An Impression of Change.* New York: Knopf, 1929.

Fischer, Gayle V. *Pantaloons and Power: Nineteenth-Century Dress Reform in the United States.* Kent, OH: Kent University Press, 2001.

Flanagan, John T., and Raymond L. Grismer. "Mexico in American Fiction Prior to 1850." *Hispania* 23, no. 4 (December 1940): 307–18.

Flint, Timothy. *Francis Berrian, or the Mexican Patriot.* Vol. 2. Boston, MA: Cummings, Hilliard, 1826.

Foley, Neil. *The White Scourge: Mexicans, Blacks, and Poor Whites in Texas Cotton Culture.* Berkeley: University of California Press, 1997.

Fong, Lawrence Michael. "Sojourners and Settlers: The Chinese Experience in Arizona." *The Journal of Arizona History* 21, no. 3 (Autumn 1980): 227–56.

Frisch, Paul A. "'Gibraltar of Unionism': Women, Blacks and the Anti-Chinese Movement in Butte, Montana, 1880–1900." *Southwest Economy and Society* 6, no. 3 (Spring 1984): 3–13.

Gardner, Mark L., and Marc Simmons, eds. *The Mexican War Correspondence of Richard Smith Elliott.* Norman: University of Oklahoma Press, 1997.

Garrard, Lewis H. *Wah-to-yah and the Taos Trail, or, Prairie Travel and Scalp Dances, with a Look at Los Rancheros from Muleback and the Rocky Mountain Campfire.* 1850. Reprint, Norman: University of Oklahoma Press, 1973.

Getz, Lynne M. "Biological Determinism in the Making of Immigration Policy in the 1920s." *International Science Review* 70, nos. 1–2 (2001): 26–35.

Gibson, George Rutledge. *Journal of a Soldier Under Kearny and Doniphan, 1846–1847.* Edited by Ralph P. Bieber. Glendale, CA: Arthur H. Clark, 1935.

Gill, Mary E., and John S. Goff. "Joseph H. Kibbey and School Segregation in Arizona." *Journal of Arizona History* 21, no. 4 (Winter 1980): 411–22.

Gish, Robert F. *Frontier's End: The Life and Literature of Harvey Fergusson.* Lincoln: University of Nebraska Press, 1988.

Goddard, Terry. "The Promise of *Brown v. Board of Education.*" March 2005. http://azmemory.azlibrary.gov/cdm/ref/collection/statepubs/id/21093. Accessed April 20, 2006.

Goethe, C. M. "The Influx of Mexican Amerinds." *Eugenics* 2, no. 1 (January 1929): 6–9.

Goff, John S. "William T. Howell and the Howell Code of Arizona." *American Journal of Legal History* 11, no. 3 (July 1967): 221–33.

Gómez, Laura E. *Manifest Destinies: The Making of the Mexican American Race.* New York: New York University Press, 2007.

Gómez-Quiñones, Juan. *Roots of Chicano Politics, 1600–1940.* Albuquerque: University of New Mexico Press, 1994.

González, Deena J. *Refusing the Favor: The Spanish-Mexican Women of Santa Fe, 1820–1880.* New York: Oxford University Press, 2001.

Gonzales, Manuel G. *Mexicanos: A History of Mexicans in the United States.* Bloomington: Indiana University Press, 2000.

Gordon, Linda. *The Great Arizona Orphan Abduction.* Cambridge, MA: Harvard University Press, 1999.

Gordon, Sarah H. *Passage to Union: How the Railroads Transformed American Life, 1829–1929.* Chicago, IL: Ivan R. Dee, 1996.

Graebner, Norman A. "The Mexican War: A Study in Causation." *Pacific Historical Review* 49, no. 3 (August 1980): 405–26.

Grant, Madison. *The Passing of the Great Race, or The Racial Basis of European History.* New York: Scribner, 1917.

Gratton, Brian, and Myron P. Gutmann, "Hispanics in the United States, 1850–1990: Estimates of Population Size and National Origin." *Historical Methods: A Journal of Quantitative and Interdisciplinary History* 33, no. 3 (2000): 137–53.

Greenberg, Amy S. *Manifest Manhood and the Antebellum American Empire*. New York: Cambridge University Press, 2005.

Greenfield, Gary A., and Don B. Kates, Jr. "Mexican Americans, Racial Discrimination, and the Civil Rights Act of 1866." *California Law Review* 63, no. 3 (May 1975): 662–731.

Griswold del Castillo, Richard. *La Familia: Chicano Families in the Urban Southwest, 1848 to the Present*. Notre Dame, IN: University of Notre Dame Press, 1984.

———. *The Treaty of Guadalupe Hidalgo: A Legacy of Conflict*. Norman: University of Oklahoma Press, 1990.

Griswold, Robert L. *Family and Divorce in California, 1850–1890: Victorian Illusions and Everyday Realities*. Albany: State University of New York Press, 1982.

Gross, Ariela J. *What Blood Won't Tell: A History of Race on Trial in America*. Cambridge, MA: Harvard University Press, 2008.

Guevarra, Rudy P. *Becoming Mexipino: Multiethnic Identities and Communities in San Diego*. New Brunswick, NJ: Rutgers University Press, 2012.

Guidotti-Hernández, Nicole M. *Unspeakable Violence: Remapping U.S. and Mexican National Imaginaries*. Durham, NC: Duke University Press, 2011.

Hackenburg, Randy W. *Pennsylvania in the War with Mexico*. Shippensburg, PA: White Mane, 1992.

Haller, John S. "The Species Problem: Nineteenth-Century Concepts of Racial Inferiority in the Origin of Man Controversy." *American Anthropologist* 72, no. 6 (December 1970): 1319–29.

Hamilton, Patrick, comp. *The Resources of Arizona, Its Mineral, Farming, Grazing and Timber Lands; Its History, Climate, Productions, Civil and Military Government, Pre-History Ruins, Early Missionaries, Indian Tribes, Pioneer Days, Etc., Etc.* 3rd ed. San Francisco, CA: A. L. Bancroft, 1884.

Haney López, Ian F. "Race and Erasure: The Salience of Race in Latinos/as." In *The Latino/a Condition: A Critical Reader*, edited by Richard Delgado and Jean Stefancic, 180–95. New York: New York University Press, 1998.

———. *White by Law: The Legal Construction of Race*. New York: New York University Press, 1996.

Hardaway, Roger D. "Prohibiting Interracial Marriage: Miscegenation Laws in Wyoming." *Annals of Wyoming* 52, no. 1 (Spring 1980): 55–60.

———. "Unlawful Love: A History of Arizona's Miscegenation Law." *Journal of Arizona History* 27, no. 4 (1986): 377–90.

Hastings, Lansford W. *The Emigrant's Guide to Oregon and California*. 1845. Reprint, New York: Da Capo Press, 1969.

Hatch, Heather S. "The Chinese in the Southwest." *Journal of Arizona History* 21, no. 3 (Autumn 1980): 257–74.

Hietala, Thomas R. "Continentalism and the Color Line." In *The Impact of Race on U.S. Foreign Policy*, edited by Michael L. Krenn, 48–89. New York: Garland, 1999.

Hietter, Paul. "A Surprising Amount of Justice: The Experience of Mexican and Racial Minority Defendants Charged with Serious Crimes in Arizona, 1865–1920." *Pacific Historical Review* 70, no. 2 (May 2001): 183–219.

Higuera, Prudencia. "Californiana: Trading with the Americans." *Century Magazine*, December 1890, 193–94.

Hill Collins, Patricia. "Gender, Black Feminism, and Black Political Economy." In *Mixed Race America and the Law*, edited by Kevin R. Johnson, 235–36. New York: New York University Press, 2003.

Historical Statistics of the United States, Millennial Edition Online. http://hsus .cambridge.org. Accessed July 23, 2008.

Hochschild, Jennifer L., and Brenna Marea Powell. "Racial Reorganization and the United States Census 1850–1930: Mulattoes, Half-Breeds, Mixed Parentage, Hindoos, and the Mexican Race." *Studies in American Political Development* 22, no. 1 (March 2008): 59–96.

Horsman, Reginald. *Race and Manifest Destiny: The Origins of American Racial Anglo-Saxonism.* Cambridge, MA: Harvard University Press, 1981.

———. "Scientific Racism and the American Indian in the Mid-Nineteenth Century." *American Quarterly* 27, no. 2 (May 1975): 152–68.

Houston, Sam. *The Writings of Sam Houston, 1813–1863.* Vol. 5. Edited by Amelia W. Williams and Eugene C. Barker. Austin: University of Texas Press, 1941.

The Howell Code, Adopted by the First Legislative Assembly of the Territory of Arizona. Prescott: Office of the Arizona Miner, 1865.

Hoyt, John P., comp. *The Compiled Laws of the Territory of Arizona.* Detroit, MI: Richmond, Backus, 1877.

Hu-DeHart, Evelyn. "Immigrants to a Developing Society: The Chinese in Northern Mexico, 1875–1932." *Journal of Arizona History* 21, no. 3 (Autumn 1980): 275–312.

Hudson, Lynn M. "Mining a Mythic Past: The History of Mary Ellen Pleasant." In *African American Women Confront the West: 1600–2000*, edited by Quintard Taylor and Shirley Ann Wilson Moore, 56–70. Norman: University of Oklahoma Press, 2003.

Hunt, Rockwell D. "A Prize and a National Policy: The Contest for California." *Annual Publications of the Historical Society of Southern California* (1923): 128–39.

"The Inhabitants of the United States." *American Quarterly Register and Magazine*, May 1848, 203–7.

"It Occurred in Tucson." *Overland Monthly and Out West Magazine*, June 1872, 518.

Jacoby, Karl. *Shadows at Dawn: A Borderlands Massacre and the Violence of History*. New York: Penguin, 2008.

Johnson, Susan Lee. *Roaring Camp: The Social World of the California Gold Rush*. New York: Norton, 2000.

———. "Sharing Bed and Board: Cohabitation and Cultural Difference in Central Arizona Mining Towns, 1863–1873." In *The Women's West*, edited by Susan Armitage and Elizabeth Jameson, 99–128. Norman: University of Oklahoma Press, 1987.

Johnston, Abraham Robinson, Marcellus Ball, and Philip Gooch Ferguson. *Marching with the Army of the West, 1846–1848*. Edited by Ralph Paul Bieber. Glendale, CA: Arthur H. Clark, 1936.

Jonas, Peter M. "William Parrott, American Claims, and the Mexican War." *Journal of the Early Republic* 12, no. 2 (Summer 1992): 213–40.

Journal of the House of Representatives, First Special Session, Fifteenth Legislature of the State of Arizona, 1942. Phoenix, AZ: s.n., 1942.

Journal of the Senate, First Special Session, Fifteenth Legislature of the State of Arizona, 1942. Phoenix, AZ: s.n., 1942.

Journals of the Second Legislative Assembly of the Territory of Arizona. Prescott: Office of the Arizona Miner, 1866.

Karthikeyan, Hrishi, and Gabriel J. Chin. "Preserving Racial Identity: Population Patterns and the Application of Anti-Miscegenation Statutes to Asian Americans, 1910–1950." *Asian Law Journal* 9 (2002): 1–40.

Katz, William Loren. *The Black West*. Garden City, NY: Doubleday, 1971.

Keane, Melissa, A. E. Rogge, and Bradford Luckingham. *The Chinese in Arizona, 1870–1950: A Context for Historic Preservation Planning*. Phoenix: Arizona State Historic Preservation Office, 1992.

Keen, Benjamin. *The Aztec Image in Western Thought*. New Brunswick, NJ: Rutgers University Press, 1971.

Kendall, George Wilkins. *Narrative of the Texan Santa Fe Expedition*. Vol. 1. London: Wiley and Putnam, 1844.

Kerber, Linda K. *No Constitutional Right to Be Ladies: Women and the Obligations of Citizenship*. New York: Hill and Wang, 1998.

King, William M. "Black Children, White Law: Black Efforts to Secure Public Education in Central City, Colorado, 1864–1869." *Essays and Monographs in Colorado History* 3 (1984): 56–79.

Kirkham, Ralph W. *The Mexican War Journal and Letters of Ralph W. Kirkham*. Edited by Robert Ryal Miller. College Station: Texas A&M University, 1991.

Kneeland, Samuel, Jr. "The Hybrid Races of Animals and Men." *Debow's Review* 19, no. 5 (November 1855): 535–39.

Lamar, Howard R. *Texas Crossings: The Lone Star State and the American Far West, 1836–1986*. Austin: University of Texas Press, 1991.

Lavin, Patrick. *Arizona: An Illustrated History*. New York: Hippocrene Books, 2001.

Laws of the Territory of New Mexico, Passed by the Legislative Assembly, 1855–56. Santa Fe, NM: Santa Fe Weekly Gazette, 1856.

Lawson, Harry. *The History of African Americans in Tucson: An Afrocentric Perspective*. Tucson, AZ: Lawson's Psychological Services, 1996.

Leiker, James N. "Black Soldiers at Fort Hays, Kansas, 1867–69: A Study in Civilian and Military Violence." In *Buffalo Soldiers in the West: A Black Soldiers Anthology*, edited by Bruce A. Glasrud and Michael N. Searles, 157–75. College Station: Texas A&M University Press, 2007.

Leonard, Karen Isaksen. *Making Ethnic Choices: California's Punjabi Mexican Americans*. Philadelphia, PA: Temple University Press, 1992.

Lightbourne, Andrea Juliette. "Shining Through the Clouds: An Historical Case Study of Dunbar, a Segregated School in Tucson, Arizona." PhD diss., University of Arizona, 2004.

Li, Jian. "A History of the Chinese in Charleston." *South Carolina Historical Magazine* 99, no. 1 (January 1998): 34–65.

Lim, Julian. "*Chinos* and *Paisanos*: Chinese Mexican Relations in the Borderlands." *Pacific Historical Review* 79, no. 1 (February 2010): 50–85.

Lister, Florence C., and Robert H. Lister. *The Chinese of Early Tucson: Historic Archaeology from the Tucson Urban Renewal Project*. Tucson: University of Arizona Press, 1989.

Luckingham, Bradford. *Minorities in Phoenix: A Profile of Mexican American, Chinese American, and African American Communities, 1860–1992*. Tucson: University of Arizona Press, 1994.

Lydon, Edward C. "The Anti-Chinese Movement in Santa Cruz County, California, 1859–1900." In *The Life, Influence and the Role of the Chinese in the United States, 1776–1960*, Proceedings of the National Conference at the University of San Francisco, July 10–12, 1975, 219–43. San Francisco: Chinese Historical Society of America, 1976.

Lyman, Stanford M. "Marriage and Family among Chinese Immigrants to America, 1850–1960." *Phylon* 29, no. 4 (Winter 1968): 322–28.

Magoffin, Susan Shelby. *Down the Santa Fe Trail and into Mexico: The Diary of Susan Shelby Magoffin, 1846–1847*. Edited by Stella M. Drumm. 1926. Reprint, Lincoln: University of Nebraska Press, 1982.

Margolis, Eric. "Western Coal Mining as a Way of Life: An Oral History of the Colorado Coal Miners to 1914." *Journal of the West* 24, no. 3 (July 1985): 3–115.

Martin, John. "Biographical Sketch of Judge Rush Elmore." *Transactions of the Kansas State Historical Society* (1903–1904): 435–36.

Martyn, Byron Curti. "Racism in the United States: A History of the Anti-Miscegenation Legislation and Litigation." PhD diss., University of Southern California, 1979.

Maverick, Mary Adams. *Memoirs of Mary A. Maverick*. Edited by Rena Maverick Green. San Antonio, TX: Alamo, 1921.

May, Elaine Tyler. *Great Expectations: Marriage and Divorce in Post-Victorian America*. Chicago, IL: University of Chicago Press, 1980.

May, Gary. *John Tyler*. New York: Times Books, 2008.

McCaffrey, James M. *Army of Manifest Destiny: The American Soldier in the Mexican War, 1846–1848*. New York: New York University Press, 1992.

McClintock, James H. *Arizona, Prehistoric, Aboriginal, Pioneer, Modern: The Nation's Youngest Commonwealth within a Land of Ancient Culture*. Chicago, IL: S. J. Clarke, 1916.

McClintock, William A. "Journal of a Trip through Texas and Northern Mexico in 1846–1847." *Southwestern Historical Quarterly* 34 (1930): 141–58.

McWilliams, Carey. *North from Mexico: The Spanish-Speaking People of the United States*. New York: Praeger, 1990.

Melcher, Mary. "'This Is Not Right': Rural Arizona Women Challenge Segregation and Ethnic Division, 1925–1950." In "Motherhood and Maternalism," special issue, *Frontiers: A Journal of Women Studies* 20, no. 2 (1999): 190–214.

Menchaca, Martha. "The Anti-Miscegenation History of the America Southwest, 1837 to 1970: Transforming Racial Ideology into Law." *Cultural Dynamics* 20 (2008): 279–318.

———. *Recovering History, Constructing Race: The Indian, Black, and White Roots of Mexican Americans*. Austin: University of Texas Press, 2001.

"Mexican Argument for Annexation." *Littell's Living Age*, September 19, 1846, 573–74.

"Mexican Ladies." *Dwight's American Magazine*, July 17, 1847, 460.

"The Mexican Question." *Knickerbocker/New York Monthly Magazine*, March 1859, 2–10.

"The Mexican Race." *Littell's Living Age*, July 17, 1847, 135–36.

"Mexican Skulls." *American Phrenological Journal* 9 (1847): 155.

"The Mexican War: Its Origin and Conduct." *United States Magazine and Democratic Review*, April 1847, 291–99.

"The Mexican War: Its Origin, Its Justice, and Its Consequences." *United States Magazine and Democratic Review*, January 1848, 1–11.

"The Mexican War: Its Origin, Its Justice, and Its Consequences." *United States Magazine and Democratic Review*, February 1848, 119.

"Mexico." *Albion*, April 11, 1846, 179.

"Mexico." *United States Magazine and Democratic Review*, June 1846, 434–35.

"Mexico and the Mexicans." *United States Magazine and Democratic Review*, June 1850, 547.

"Mexico and the Monroe Doctrine." *United States Magazine and Democratic Review*, May 1853, 439, 447, 451.

"Mexico and the United States." *Putnam's Magazine*, May 1869, 618–20.

Miller, Darlis. "Cross-Cultural Marriages in the Southwest: The New Mexico Experience, 1846–1900." *New Mexico Historical Review* 57, no. 4 (1982): 335–60.

Mitchell, Pablo. *Coyote Nation: Sexuality, Race, and Conquest in Modernizing New Mexico, 1880–1920*. Chicago, IL: University of Chicago Press, 2005.

———. "'You Just Don't Know Mrs. Baca': Intermarriage, Mixed Heritage, and Identity in New Mexico." *New Mexico Historical Review* 79, no. 4 (Fall 2004): 437–58.

Montejano, David. *Anglos and Mexicans in the Making of Texas, 1836–1986*. Austin: University of Texas Press, 1987.

Myres, Sandra L. "Mexican Americans and Westering Anglos: A Feminine Perspective." *New Mexico Historical Review* 57, no. 4 (1982): 317–34.

Myrick, David F. "Railroads of Arizona." In *The Westerners Brand Book XII*, edited by George Koenig, 18–35. Los Angeles: Los Angeles Corral, Stephens Printing, 1966.

Negley Floyd R., and Marcia S. Lindley. *Arizona Marriages, Pima County, Marriage Books 5–10, February 1912 through December 1926*. Tucson: Arizona State Genealogical Society, 1997.

———. *Arizona Territorial Marriages, Pima County, 1871–1912*. Tucson: Arizona State Genealogical Society, 1994.

Newton, Robert. "Original Communications." *New York Journal of Medicine and Collateral Sciences* (November 1848): 295–306.

Ngai, Mae M. *Impossible Subjects: Illegal Aliens and the Making of Modern America*. Princeton, NJ: Princeton University Press, 2004.

Nieto-Phillips, John M. *The Language of Blood: The Making of Spanish American Identity in New Mexico, 1880s–1930s*. Albuquerque: University of New Mexico Press, 2004.

Nott, Josiah Clark, and George R. Gliddon. *Types of Mankind*. Philadelphia, PA: Lippincott, Grambo, 1855.

Officer, James E. *Hispanic Arizona, 1536–1856*. Tucson: University of Arizona Press, 1989.

———. "Historical Factors in Interethnic Relations in the Community of Tucson." *Arizoniana* 1, no. 1 (Fall 1960): 12–16.

The Official Railway Guide: North American Freight Service. Philadelphia, PA: National Railway, 1896.

Opper, S. Michael, and Lillie L. Lew. "A History of the Chinese in Fresno, California." In *The Life, Influence and the Role of the Chinese in the United States, 1776–1960*, Proceedings of the National Conference at the University of San Francisco, July 10–12, 1975, 47–55. San Francisco: Chinese Historical Society of America, 1976.

Ord, Angustias. *Occurrences in Hispanic California*. Translated and edited by Francis Price and William E. Ellison. Washington, DC: Academy of American Franciscan History, 1956.

O'Sullivan, John. "Annexation." *United States Magazine and Democratic Review*, July–August 1845, 5, 7, 9.

———. "The Mexican Question." *United States Magazine and Democratic Review*, May 1845, 419–28.

Padilla, Genaro. "'Yo Sola Aprendí': Personal Narratives from Nineteenth-Century California." In *Writing the Range: Race, Class, and Culture in the Women's West*, edited by Elizabeth Jameson and Susan Armitage, 188–202. Norman: University of Oklahoma Press, 1997.

Paredes, Raymund A. "The Mexican Image in American Literature, 1831–1869." *New Mexico Historical Review* 52, no. 1 (January 1977): 5–29.

Park, Joseph F. "The History of Mexican Labor in Arizona during the Territorial Period." Master's thesis, University of Arizona, 1961.

Pascoe, Peggy. "Miscegenation Law, Court Cases, and Ideologies of 'Race' in Twentieth-Century America." *Journal of American History* 83, no. 1 (June 1996): 44–69.

———. "Race, Gender, and the Privileges of Property: On the Significance of Miscegenation Law in the U.S. West." In *Over the Edge: Remapping the American*

West, edited by Valerie J. Matsumoto and Blake Allmendinger, 215–30. Berkeley: University of California Press, 1999.

———. *What Comes Naturally: Miscegenation Law and the Making of Race in America*. New York: Oxford University Press, 2009.

Pattee, Samuel L., comp. *The Revised Statutes of Arizona, 1913, Civil Code*. Phoenix: McNeil, 1913.

Pattie, James Ohio. *Personal Narrative of James O. Pattie: The True Wild West of New Mexico and California*. 1833. Reprint, Santa Barbara, CA: Narrative Press, 2001.

"The Peace Treaty of Mexico, and the Elements which Compose the Mexican Nation." *Littell's Living Age*, August 28, 1847, 431–32.

Peffer, George Anthony. *If They Don't Bring Their Women Here: Chinese Female Immigration Before Exclusion*. Urbana: University of Illinois Press, 1999.

Pike, Albert. *Prose, Sketches, and Poems Written in the Western Country*. Edited by David J. Weber. College Station: Texas A&M University Press, 1987.

Pinar, William F. *The Gender of Racial Politics and Violence in America: Lynching, Prison Rape, and the Crisis of Masculinity*. New York: Peter Lang, 2001.

Poinsett, Joel Roberts. "The Mexican Character." In *The Mexico Reader: History, Culture, Politics*, edited by Gilbert Michael Joseph and Timothy J. Henderson, 11–14. Durham, NC: Duke University Press, 2002.

———. *Notes on Mexico, Made in the Autumn of 1822*. London: John Miller, 1825.

Polk, James K. "Address to the Senate and House of Representatives, May 11, 1846." In *A Compilation of the Messages and Papers of the Presidents, 1789–1908*, vol. 6, edited by James D. Richardson, 437–43. Washington, DC: Bureau of National Literature and Art, 1908.

Poston, Charles D. "Building a State in Apache Land." *Overland Monthly and Out West Magazine*, August 1894, 203–13.

Pourade, Richard F., ed. *The Sign of the Eagle: A View of Mexico, 1830 to 1855*. San Diego, CA: Union-Tribune Publishing, 1970.

Pugsley, Andrea. "'As I Kill This Chicken So May I Be Punished If I Tell an Untruth': Chinese Opposition to Legal Discrimination in Arizona Territory." *Journal of Arizona History* 44, no. 2 (Summer 2003): 171–90.

Rawick, George P., ed. *The American Slave: A Composite Autobiography*. Suppl., series 2, vol. 1. Westport, CT: Greenwood Press, 1979.

Reisdorfer, Kathryn. "Charley Hong, Racism, and the Power of the Press in Jerome, Arizona Territory, 1909." *Journal of Arizona History* 43, no. 2 (Summer 2002): 133–46.

Rénique, Gerardo. "Race, Region, and Nation: Sonora's Anti-Chinese Racism and Mexico's Postrevolutionary Nationalism, 1920's–1930s." In *Race and Nation in Modern Latin America*, edited by Nancy P. Appelbaum, Anne S. Macpherson, and Karin Alejandra Rosemblatt, 211–36. Chapel Hill: University of North Carolina Press, 2003.

"Review of *Mexico and the Rocky Mountains*." *United States Magazine and Democratic Review*, March 1848, 288.

The Revised Statutes of Arizona. Prescott, AZ: Prescott Courier Print, 1887.

The Revised Statutes of the Arizona Territory, Containing Also the Laws Passed by the Twenty-First Legislative Assembly, the Constitution of the United States, the Organic Law of Arizona and the Amendments of Congress Relating Thereto, 1901. Columbia, MO: Press of E. W. Stephens, 1901.

Rhoads, Edward J. M. "The Chinese in Texas." *Southwestern Historical Quarterly* 81, no. 1 (July 1977): 1–36.

Rifkin, Mark. *Manifesting America: The Imperial Construction of U.S. National Space*. New York: Oxford University Press, 2009.

Riley, Glenda. *Building and Breaking Families in the American West*. Albuquerque: University of New Mexico Press, 1996.

———. *Divorce: An American Tradition*. New York: Oxford University Press, 1991.

Rivera, John-Michael. *The Emergence of Mexican America: Recovering Stories of Mexican Peoplehood in U.S. Culture*. New York: New York University Press, 2006.

Robinson, Cecil. *Mexico and the Hispanic Southwest in American Literature*. Tucson: University of Arizona Press, 1977.

Roediger, David R. *The Wages of Whiteness: Race and the Making of the American Working Class*. London: Verso, 2007.

Rusco, Elmer R. *"Good Time Coming?": Black Nevadans in the Nineteenth Century*. Westport, CT: Greenwood Press, 1975.

Ruxton, George Frederick Augustus. *Adventures in Mexico and the Rocky Mountains*. New York: Harper and Brothers, 1848.

———. *Adventures in Mexico: From Veracruz to Chihuahua in the Days of the Mexican War*. Edited by Horace Kephart. 1848. Reprint, New York: Outing, 1915.

Sage, Rufus B. *Rocky Mountain Life*. Boston: Wentworth, 1857.

Sánchez, José María. "A Trip to Texas in 1828." Translated by Carlos E. Castañeda. *Southwestern Historical Quarterly* 29, no. 4 (April 1926): 249–88.

Saunders, Myra K. "California Legal History: A Review of Spanish and Mexican Legal Institutions." *Law Library Journal* 87 (Summer 1995): 487–514.

Schiavone Camacho, Julia María. *Chinese Mexicans: Transpacific Migration and the Search for a Homeland, 1910–1960*. Chapel Hill: University of North Carolina Press, 2012.

———. "Crossing Boundaries, Claiming a Homeland: The Mexican Chinese Transpacific Journey to Becoming Mexican, 1930s–1960s." *Pacific Historical Review* 78, no. 4 (2009): 545–77.

Schubert, Frank N. "Black Soldiers on the White Frontier: Some Factors Influencing Race Relations." In *Buffalo Soldiers in the West: A Black Soldiers Anthology*, edited by Bruce A. Glasrud and Michael N. Searles, 176–84. College Station: Texas A&M University Press, 2007.

Seidman, Steven. "The Power of Desire and the Dangers of Pleasure: Victorian Sexuality Reconsidered." *Journal of Social History* 24, no. 1 (Fall 1990): 47–67.

Semmes, Raphael. *The Campaign of General Scott in the Valley of Mexico*. Cincinnati, OH: Moore and Anderson, 1852.

Shah, Nayan. *Contagious Divides: Epidemics and Race in San Francisco's Chinatown*. Berkeley: University of California Press, 2001.

Shaler, William. "Journal of a Voyage between China and the North-Western Coast of America Made in 1804." *American Register*, January 1, 1808, 137–77.

Sheridan, Thomas E. *Arizona: A History*. Tucson: University of Arizona Press, 1995.

———. *Los Tucsonenses: The Mexican Community in Tucson, 1854–1941*. Tucson: University of Arizona Press, 1986.

Sibley, Marilyn McAdams. *Travelers in Texas, 1761–1860*. Austin: University of Texas Press, 1967.

Sloan, Eleanor B. "Seventy-Five Years of the Arizona Pioneers' Historical Society, 1884–1959." *Arizona and the West* 1, no. 1 (Spring 1959): 66–70.

Slotkin, Richard. *The Fatal Environment: The Myth of the Frontier in the Age of Industrialization, 1800–1890*. New York: Atheneum, 1985.

Smith, George Winston, and Charles Judah, eds. *Chronicles of the Gringos: The U.S. Army in the Mexican War, Accounts of Eyewitnesses and Combatants*. Albuquerque: University of New Mexico Press, 1968.

Smith, Norman D. "Mexican Stereotypes on Fictional Battlefields: Or Dime Novel Romances of the Mexican War." *Journal of Popular Culture* 13, no. 3 (Spring 1980): 526–40.

Sohoni, Deenesh. "Unsuitable Suitors: Anti-Miscegenation Laws, Naturalization Laws, and the Construction of Asian Identity." *Law and Society Review* 41, no. 3 (September 2007): 587–618.

Sonnichsen, C. L. *Tucson: The Life and Times of an American City.* Norman: University of Oklahoma Press, 1987.

Speelman, Mike. "Samuel Bostick: African-American Pioneer." *Downtown Tucsonan* 80 (2009): 21.

Steele, Valerie. *Fashion and Eroticism: Ideals of Feminine Beauty from the Victorian Era to the Jazz Age.* New York: Oxford University Press, 1985.

Stegmaier, Mark J. "A Law that Would Make Caligula Blush?: New Mexico Territory's Unique Slave Code, 1859–1861." In *African American History in New Mexico: Portraits from Five Hundred Years,* edited by Bruce A. Glasrud, 56–84. Albuquerque: University of New Mexico Press, 2013.

Stephens, John W. "A Quantitative History of Chinatown, San Francisco, 1870 and 1880." In *The Life, Influence and the Role of the Chinese in the United States, 1776–1960,* Proceedings of the National Conference at the University of San Francisco, July 10–12, 1975, 71–88. San Francisco, CA: Chinese Historical Society of America, 1976.

Stern, Alexandra Minna. "Buildings, Boundaries, and Blood: Medicalization and Nation-Building on the U.S.-Mexico Border, 1910–1930." *Hispanic American Historical Review* 79, no. 1 (1999): 41–82.

———. "Eugenics Beyond Borders: Science and Medicalization in Mexico and the U.S. West, 1900–1950." PhD diss., University of Chicago, 1999.

Stinson, Alvah L. *Woman under the Law.* Boston, MA: Hudson, 1914.

Stoler, Ann Laura. *Carnal Knowledge and Imperial Power: Race and the Intimate in Colonial Rule.* Berkeley: University of California Press, 2002.

———. *Race and the Education of Desire: Foucault's* History of Sexuality *and the Colonial Order of Things.* Durham, NC: Duke University Press, 1995.

Stuart Wortley, Lady Emmeline. *Travels in the United States, Etc. during 1848 and 1850.* New York: Harper and Brothers, 1851.

Summerhayes, Martha. *Vanished Arizona: Recollections of the Army Life of a New England Woman.* Salem, MA: Salem Press, 1911.

Taylor, Quintard. *In Search of the Racial Frontier: African Americans in the American West, 1528–1990.* New York: Norton, 1998.

Thompson, Waddy. *Recollections of Mexico.* New York: Wiley and Putnam, 1847.

Thorpe, Thomas B. *Our Army at Monterey.* Philadelphia, PA: Carey and Hart, 1847.

Tintle, Rhonda. "A History of Chinese Immigration into Arizona Territory: A Frontier Culture in the American West." Master's thesis, Oklahoma State University, 2006.

Trulio, Beverly. "Anglo-American Attitudes toward New Mexican Women." *Journal of the West* 12, no. 2 (April 1973): 229–39.

Tsai, Shih-Shan Henry. *The Chinese Experience in America*. Bloomington: Indiana University Press, 1986.

Tschudi, J. J. von. *Travels in Peru during the Years 1838–1842*. Translated by Thomasina Ross. New York: Wiley and Putnam, 1847.

U.S. Bureau of the Census. *Marriage and Divorce, 1867–1906, Part I*. Washington, DC: Government Printing Office, 1909.

———. *Twenty Censuses: Population and Housing Questions, 1790–1980*. Washington, DC: U.S. Department of Commerce, Bureau of the Census, 1979.

U.S. Census Office. *Abstract of the Fifteenth Census of the United States*. Washington, DC: Government Printing Office, 1933.

———. *Fifteenth Census of the United States: 1930, Population*. 6 vols. Washington, DC: Government Printing Office 1933.

———. *Fourteenth Census of the United States, Taken in the Year 1920: Volume II, Population, 1920, General Report and Analytical Tables*. Washington, DC: Government Printing Office, 1922.

———. *Ninth Census—Volume I: The Statistics of the Population of the United States*. Washington, DC: Government Printing Office, 1872.

———. *Population of the United States in 1860; Compiled from the Original Returns of the Eighth Census*. Washington, DC: Government Printing Office, 1864.

———. *Report on the Population of the United States at the Eleventh Census: 1890, Part I*. Washington, DC: Government Printing Office, 1895.

———. *Statistics of the United States at the Tenth Census, June 1, 1880*. Washington, DC: Government Printing Office, 1882.

———. *Thirteenth Census of the United States, Taken in the Year 1910: Volume I, Population, 1910, General Report and Analysis*. Washington, DC: Government Printing Office, 1913.

———. *Twelfth Census of the United States, Taken in the Year 1900: Population, Part I*. Washington, DC: United States Census Office, 1901.

Vallejo, Guadalupe. "Ranch and Mission Days in Alta California." *Century Magazine*, December 1890, 183–92.

Violette, E. M. "Review of *Marching with the Army of the West: 1846–1848*, by Abraham R. Johnston et al., Ralph P. Bieber, ed." *Mississippi Valley Historical Review* 24, no. 1 (June 1937): 83–85.

Wagoner, Jay J. *Arizona Territory, 1863–1912: A Political History*. Tucson: University of Arizona Press, 1970.

Wallenstein, Peter. *Tell the Court I Love My Wife: Race, Marriage, and Law—An American History*. New York: Palgrave MacMillan, 2002.

Weber, David J. *Foreigners in Their Native Land*. Albuquerque: University of New Mexico Press, 1973.

———. "'Scarce More than Apes': Historical Roots of Anglo American Stereotypes of Mexicans in the Border Region." In *New Spain's Far Northern Frontier: Essays on Spain in the American West, 1540–1821*, edited by David J. Weber, 293–307. Dallas, TX: Southern Methodist University Press, 1988.

Weinberger, Andrew D. "A Reappraisal of the Constitutionality of Miscegenation Statutes." *Journal of Negro Education* 26, no. 4 (Autumn 1957): 435–46.

Wheeler, Valerie. "Travelers' Tales: Observations on the Travel Book and Ethnography." *Anthropological Quarterly* 59, no. 2 (April 1986): 52–63.

Whitaker, Matthew C. "The Rise of Black Phoenix: African-American Migration, Settlement and Community Development in Maricopa County, Arizona 1868–1930." *Journal of Negro History* 85, no. 3 (Summer 2000): 197–209.

Wilson, Robert A. *Mexico and Its Religion*. New York: Harper and Brothers, 1856.

Wislizenus, F. Adolphus. *Memoir of a Tour to Northern Mexico*. Washington, DC: Tippin and Streeper, 1848.

Wunder, John R. "Anti-Chinese Violence in the American West, 1850–1910." In *Law for the Elephant, Law for the Beaver: Essays in the Legal History of the North American West*, edited by John McLaren, Hamar Foster, and Chet Orloff, 212–36. Regina, SK: Canadian Plains Research Center, 1992.

———. "Law and the Chinese on the Southwest Frontier, 1850s–1902." *Western Legal History* 2 (Summer/Fall 1989): 139–58.

Yancy, James Walter. "The Negro of Tucson, Past and Present." Master's thesis, University of Arizona, 1933.

Yung, Judy. *Unbound Feet: A Social History of Chinese Women in San Francisco*. Berkeley: University of California Press, 1995.

Zhu, Liping. *A Chinaman's Chance: The Chinese on the Rocky Mountain Mining Frontier*. Niwot: University Press of Colorado, 1997.

———. "Ethnic Oasis: Chinese Immigrants in the Frontier Black Hills." *South Dakota History* 33, no. 4 (Winter 2003): 289–329.

LEGAL CASES

Amelia Binning v. Oscar Binning. SCC 7659, July 5, 1921.

Andrew Roos v. Justina Roos. SCC 7072, February 11, 1920.

Arizona v. Frank Pass. 59 Ariz. 16, 121 P.2d 882 (1942).

Barney Smith v. Concepción Smith. SCC 7607, June 1, 1921.

Charles B. Harris v. Diega P. Harris. SCC 6235, September 14, 1917.

Erasmus Wood v. Palmira [Roca] Wood. SCC 862, January 4, 1883.

Faustina Gilliland v. James Gilliland. SCC 2772, March 12, 1898.

Francisco Gil v. Sarah McDermott de Gil. SCC 9872, February 12, 1927.

Frank M. Clarke v. Librada Clarke. SCC 5211, December 11, 1912.

Halim Karam v. Enriqueta Díaz-Karam. SCC 6440, July 22, 1918.

In re Monks' Estate. 48 Cal. App. 2d 603, 120 Pac. 2d 167, 173 (1941).

In re Rodriguez, 81 Fed. 337 (W.D. Texas 1897).

In re Walker's Estate. 5 Ariz. 70, 46 P. 67 (1896).

Inez Baldridge v. Waldo Baldridge. SCC 11606, November 3, 1928.

Inez Tabor v. Walter C. Tabor. SCC 7228, July 27, 1920.

Inland Steel Company v. Barcena. 110 Ind. App. 551, 39 N.E.2d 800 (1942).

Jacob Youstcy v. Dominga S. Youstcy. SCC 202, October 31, 1873.

Jacob Youstcy v. Julia Youstcy. SCC 1894, April 1, 1891.

Jacob Youstcy v. Mariana Youstcy. SCC 1731, January 21, 1889.

James Brady v. Mariana Brady. SCC 2107, July 3, 1892.

Joaquina Fisher v. Robert J. Fisher. SCC 5953, October 26, 1916.

Joaquina V. Franklin v. Charles Franklin. SCC 198, October 4, 1873.

Josepha Gleason v. William R. Gleason. SCC 1198, August 15, 1885.

Juanita Montgomery v. Donald F. Montgomery. SCC 8664, September 15, 1923.

Kirby v. Kirby. 24 Ariz. 9, 206 P. 405 (1922).

Luz Houston v. Ezra B. Houston. SCC 2684, July 21, 1897.

Manuela Fairbanks v. Benjamin D. Fairbanks. SCC 222, September 25, 1874.

María Coppola v. Giuseppe Coppola. SCC 7767, September 15, 1921.

María Jaime Gay v. Mervin G. Gay. SCC 196, August 29, 1873.

María U. Van Alstine v. Pedro C. Van Alstine. SCC 4765, August 18, 1910.

Matilda E. Carroll v. Robert Carroll. SCC 9342, December 29, 1924.

Mercedes [Chávez] Kow v. Lee Kow. SCC 7280, September 15, 1920.

People v. Naglee. 1 Cal 232 (1850).

Rita Leyva Bentley v. Victor Bentley. SCC 11706, January 10, 1929.

Robert Fanchette v. Salsa Fanchette. SCC 5138, October 28, 1912.

Sarah McDermott de Gil v. Francisco Gil. SCC 9399, February 7, 1925.

Thomas Johns v. Erminia Johns. SCC 4966, January 13, 1912.

Thomas Potts v. Angela R. de Potts. SCC 3897, August 8, 1905.

W. J. McKenzie v. Juanita McKenzie. SCC 13082, October 5, 1930.

William Haynes v. Eulalia Haynes. SCC 2578, October 5, 1896.

Ysidra [Flores] Barrett v. Harry Barrett. SCC 4136, March 14, 1907.

INDEX

Page numbers in **boldface** refer to photographs.

abandonment, as cause of divorce, 148–57, 160

adultery, as cause of divorce, 148–50, 154–56

Ahloy, Manuel, 101–3, 112, 116, 118, 128, 136

Aínsa, Santiago, 78

Alabama, 29, 110–11

alienation, in divorce case, 138–41

annexation, of Tucson, 17, 88, 132

annulment, in application of miscegenation law, 30, 36–43, 162

Apache Indians, 7, 158

Arizona Miner, 61–66

Arizona miscegenation law: adoption and amendments, 25–32; and Asian Indians, 18, 23, 30, 32; and blacks, 26; and Chinese, 26–27; circumvented, 41, 101–3, 113–25, 129; in court cases, 22, 30–32, 37–43; and Filipinos, 30; and Native Americans, 26–27, 30–31; and people of mixed ancestry, 28–31

Arizona statehood, 33–34, 66–67

Arizona Supreme Court, 22–23, 30–33, 37–41

Arizona v. Frank Pass, 22–24, 30–31

Arizona Weekly Star, 67–68

Arkansas, 57, 113, 126

Asian Indians, in miscegenation law, 18, 23, 30, 32

Baffert, Luisa, **72**

Baffert, Pierre "Pedro," 72

baptism, 134–35

Barraza, Albina, 111–12, 122, 127–28, 135–36

Bernal, Inés, 76, 112

black men: and Mexican women, 3–5; obstacles in forming families, 102–6, 108–9

blacks, discrimination against, 102–5

black women, 37–43, 106, 110, 122, 128

Boise, Idaho, 161

Bonillas, María, 138–43, 153, 157

Bostick, Miguel, 122, 127–28, 136

Bostick, Samuel, 108–13, 122, 127–28, 135–36

Bowie, Arizona, 41

Brady, James, 151, 157

Brady, Mariana, 151, 157

Brady, Peter, 158
Brown, Guillermo/William, 71–73, 86
Browne, J. Ross, 64
Buckeye, Arizona, 126

Cadava, Geraldo L., 20–21
California court cases, 32–33, 38–41
California miscegenation law, 25–33
Campo, Rita, 159
Cang, You, 113–14, 197n40
Catholicism, role of, 134–36, 140–41
Catholic priests, 3–4, 21, 48, 56, 113–14, 134
Census Bureau, 35, 126
census data, 71–88, 95–99, 104–7, 112–16, 147, 162
census enumerators, 4, 112, 120, 126–29
Chamberlain, Samuel E., 63
Chávez, Concepción, 118
Chávez, Mercedes, 114
Chicago, 153
Chinese, discrimination against, 102–4; placed in miscegenation law, 26–27; in South Dakota, 161; massacre in Coahuila, Mexico, 103
Chinese men: and Mexican women, 101–3, 112–36, 156–63; in northern Mexico, 103–4; obstacles in forming families, 103–10
Chinese women, 105–6, 106, 110, 122
Clifton, Arizona, 104
Coahuila, Mexico, massacre of Chinese, 103
Colorado, 6, 75
compadrazgo, as kinship and network, 64, 135, 158, 206n8
Conner, Mayellen, 37–43, 122
Contreras, Ruby, 22–24, 30–31
Contzen, Frederick, 10, 159
Cooper, 76, 112
Copeman, Ruth Mary, 10–11
Coppola, Giuseppe, 138–43, 153, 157
custody, in divorce cases, 139, 150–52, 157

Dalton, Guadalupe "Lupe," 10–11, **11**, **72**
Dalton, Henry (father of Winnal Dalton), 10–11
Dalton, Henry (son of Winnal Dalton), **11**
Dalton, Hortense, **11**, **72**
Dalton, Natalie, **11**
Dalton, Winnall, 10–11, **11**
de la Guerra, María, 60
de la Guerra, Pablo, 33
Delaware, 112
Delgado, Grace, 20–21, 200n54
Democratic Party, 44, 111
Democratic Review, 46–49, 64–65
discourse, of manifest destiny, 13–16, 18, 44–70, 121, 174–75n1; defined, 46
discrimination, against Mexicans, 4–7, 16, 23, 30, 32–35
divorce, among interethnic couples, 13, 20, 36–38, 43, 114, 117, 131, 133, 138–62; data for Pima County, 147, 149
Dooner, Pierton W., 111
Douglas, Arizona, 121

Ellwood, Lucille, 41–42
Elmore, Rush, 109–11
Embers, Charles, 124–25
Escalante, Isabel Ahloy, 101–3, 112, 116, 118, 128, 136
expansionist rhetoric, 13–16, 43–51, 59–65, 70

failure to support, as cause for divorce, 147–49, 152–55
Fairbanks, Benjamin D., 149
Fairbanks, Manuela, 149
Fee, Ah, 41–42
Ferrer, Margarita, 10, 159
Filipinos, 8, 18, 23, 30, 32, 170n30, 187n10; placed in miscegenation law, 30
Fish, Edward, 144
Flagstaff, Arizona, 104
Flint, Timothy, 47

INDEX 237

Florence, Arizona, 111, 127–28, 196n34
Fraijó, Esperanza, 113–14, 197n40
Francis Berrian, 47
Franklin, Charles, 148–49
Franklin, Joaquina, 148–49

García, María Inez, 159
Georgia, 25, 29–30, 72, 76, 171n33
Gil, Francisco, 152
Giraudo-Monks, Antoinette, 38–41
Goodwin, Adelina "Lily," **72**
Goodwin, Charles, 72
Goodwin, John N., 26, 28
Grant, Madison, 34–35
greaser, as racist epithet, 32, 63–64, 68, 184n85
Guidotti-Hernández, Nicole M., 20–21

Healy, Thomas, 72
Hermosillo, Mexico, 152
Houston, Ezra B., 152
Houston, Sam, 44–46
Howell Code, 26, 33
Howell, William T., 26
Hughes, Samuel, 8, **9**, 10, 124, 132, 158–59

Idaho, 96, 115, 161; miscegenation law, 25, 103
Illinois, 55, 94, 96, 180n47
illiteracy, in divorce cases, 144–45
Indiana, 24, 96
interfaith marriage, 3–4, 134–35, 146
Ireland, 38, 71, 84, 94, 96, 134
Italy, 134, 138–43, 153, 157

Jácome, Anita, 11
Jerome, Arizona, 41–42, 174n77

Kansas, 37, 96, 110
Kansas City, Missouri, 122, 153
Kennedy, Hugh, 144–45
Kennedy, Manuela, 144–45
Kentucky, 38, 80, 81, 180n47

Kirby, Joe, 37–43, 122
Kow, Lee, 114
Ku Klux Klan, 116, 118

Lee, Jim, 116, 118
Lee, Rita, 136, 138, 156, 207n13
Legarra, J. A., 80
legitimacy, of children, 41, 43, 121; of mixed marriages, 18, 26, 41–43, 78
Leon-Aldrich, Faustina, 152–53
Levin, Alexander, **68**, 72
Levin, Sofía, **72**
Lincoln, Abraham, 27
Ling, Fong, 116–17, 198n46, 199n52
Lippincott, Aubrey, 72
Lordsburg, New Mexico, as location to circumvent Arizona's miscegenation law, 41, 113–14, 117–18
Los Angeles, 122, 146
Los Angeles Times, 116, 155
Louisiana, 67, 76, 96
Low, John, 122–23
Low, Yoke Shem, 122–23

MacMinn, Alexander, 136, 138, 156, 207n13
Maine miscegenation law, 25
marital status, statistics on, 77–78, 86–92, 103–8
marriageable, versus married as categories, 92–98
marriage licenses, in Arizona, 3–5, 16–17, 35–36, 39, 41, 83, 85, 102, 112–17, 121–22, 123, 124–25, 129, 138, 203–4n69; in New Mexico, 41, 101–3 113–19
Maryland, 24–25, 30, 171n33
Massachusetts, 94
McCaffry, J. E., 111
McCormick, Richard, 66
McDermott, Sarah, 152
McKenna, Catalina/Katie, 71–73, 86
mendacious, as racist epithet, 47, 51
mestizo, 29–33, 49–50, 56, 105

Meyers, Charles H., 144, 159

Michigan, 11, 80, 96

Midwest, as place of origin of Tucson residents, 85–86, 92, 96–98

migration entrepôts, 94–97

mining towns, discrimination in, 28, 34, 41–42, 62–63, 68, 103–4, 108–9, 158, 193n13, 195n24

Minnesota, 72, 96

Mississippi, 171n33

Missouri, 80, 94, 96, 171n33, 180n47, 187n11

Molina, Zenona, **68**, 72

Mongolian, as category in miscegenation law, 26–28, 31, 105; to refer to Chinese, 116, 172n42

mongrel, as a racist epithet, 35, 50–51, 57, 63–64, 66

Monks, Allan, 38–41

Montana, 25, 114–15, 171n33, 197n43

Monterey, California, 11

Montoya, Frecia, **72**

Moore, Dolores, 144

Moore, Mahlon E., 144

Morales, Teresa, 116–17, 198n46, 199n52

Moreno, Concepción, 116, 118

Moreno, Emeteria, **119**, 128, 199n51

Moreno, Loreto, 119, 128, 199n51

Moreno, Petra, 72

mulatto, as racial category, 32, 49–50, 76, 121, 126–28; term used in miscegenation laws, 25–26, 33, 104

Native Americans, 5–7, 43, 45, 47, 49, 52, 64, 71, 102–4, 133, 158; in Arizona miscegenation law, 22–27, 30–31

Nava, Pascuala, 114–16, 197n43

negro, as racial category, 126–27; as racist epithet, 57; term used in miscegenation laws, 26, 31, 39, 104

Nevada, 75; miscegenation law, 25, 171n33, 189n4

New Mexico miscegenation law, 23, 25–27. *See also* Lordsburg; Silver City

New York, 26, 35, 44, 71–72, 78, 80, 94, 96, 138

Nogales, 117, 121, 132, 150

Officer, James, 7–8

Ohio, 94, 96

Oklahoma, miscegenation law in, 29

Oregon, 48, 96, 103; miscegenation law in, 25, 171n33, 189n4

O'Sullivan, John, 13, 48–49, 64–65

Osuna-Houston, Luz, 152

Oury, William, 158–59, 187n7

Oyama v. O'Neill, 32

Paiute Indians, 22

Pantano, Arizona, 151

Pascoe, Peggy, 20

Pass, Frank, 22–24, 30–31

Pennsylvania, 53–54, 180n47

Perez v. Lippold, 32

Phoenix, 2, 22, 66, 116–18, 127; discrimination in, 62–63, 104, 109, 193n13

Pierce, Franklin, 109–10

Pike, Albert, 47–48

Pima County, intermarriage data for, 80, 83, 147, 160, 162

Poinsett, Joel Roberts, 47

Prescott, Arizona, 41–42, 61–62, 66–67, 104, 109

Prescott Journal Miner, 42

Protestant, 3, 92, 134, 140–41

Providence, role of, 44, 46, 49, 53

Punjabi, marriages with Mexicans, 8

Qui, Wong, 114–16, 197n43

racial admixture: and the law, 4–6, 18, 22–24, 28–32, 38–42, 105; as concern for whites, 15, 18, 35, 45–52, 57, 60, 63–66

racial ambiguity: and Mexicans, 5, 13–14, 19, 23, 62, 101–2, 115–18, 125–26, 131; in racial classifications, 29, 49, 125–29

racist epithets, used against Mexicans, 32, 35, 47, 50–52, 57, 63–64, 66, 68, 184n85
Ramírez, Encarnación, 159
Ramírez, Guadalupe, 113, 126
Ramírez, Rosario, 112, 128
Ransom, Henry, 113, 126
Redondo, Margarita, 10–11
Republican Party, 111, 158
Rhode Island, miscegenation law, 25
Ronstadt, Federico José María "Fred," 10–11
Ronstadt, Friedrich August, 10–11
Ronstadt, Gilbert, 10–11
Ronstadt, José M., 11, **72**
Ronstadt, Linda, 10–12
Roosevelt, Franklin D., 31

Sage, Rufus B., 57
Salcido, Dolores, 125
Salcido, Ramón, 80
Santa Cruz, Atanacia, 8, **9**, 10, 124, 132, 158–59
Santa Cruz, Petra, **9**, 10, 132–33, 135, 156, 158, 205–6n1
Schiavone Camacho, Julia María, 20–21
Shaler, William, 47
Sheridan, Thomas E., 7–8, 188n21
Silver City, New Mexico, as location to circumvent Arizona's miscegenation law, 101–3, 116–19
Solomonville, Arizona, 42–43
Sosa, Dominga, 149–50
South Dakota, 161
spousal abuse, as cause of divorce, 142, 147–56
spousal sustenance, 139, 145, 148–49, 154–55
Stevens, Hiram, **9**, 10, 132–33, 135, 156, 158, 205–6n1
Stoler, Ann Laura, 14–15
Summerhayes, Martha, 58
swarthy, as racial epithet, 47, 50, 52, 63

Tennessee, 124, 128
Terrazas, Leonicia, 3, 21, 112–13, 126
Texas, 12, 45–45, 48, 59, 65, 68, 75, 96, 101, 112–13, 122, 152
Texas Rangers, 35, 158
Tombstone, 109, 195n24
Tombstone Prospector, 66
Torres, Isabel, 72
Treaty of Guadalupe Hidalgo, 5–6, 17, 23, 32–33
Tschudi, J. J. von, 49–50
Tucson Citizen, 68, 116, 140

Utah, 22, 171n33

Vallejo, Guadalupe, 60
Vásquez, Jesús, 10–11, **11**
Veracruz, Mexico, 56–58
Vermont, 132
Virginia, 3–4, 112, 158, 198n49
Virginia miscegenation law, 29–20, 32, 171n33

Walker, Chur-ga, 37, 43
Walker, John D., 37, 43
Walker, Juana, 37, 43
Washington, DC, 25, 29, 30, 126, 138, 140
Washington state, 103, 114–15
Weekly Arizonian, 67–68
Wisconsin, 80, 96
Wo, Hi, **119**, 128, 199n51
Woodley, Emmett, 3, 21, 112–13, 126
Woodley, Frank, 126
Woodley, Manuela, 136, 206–7n12
Wyoming, 171n33

Yet, Dong, 112, 128
Youstcy, Jacob, 149–51
Youstcy, Mariana, 151
Yuma, Arizona, 38, 63, 68

Zamorano, Guadalupe, 10–11
Zhu, Liping, 161

ABOUT THE AUTHOR

Sal Acosta holds PhDs in U.S. history (University of Arizona, 2010) and Latin American literature (UCLA, 1997) as well as an MA in Mexican American studies (University of Arizona, 2004). He is an assistant professor in the History Department at Fordham University. Acosta has published in the *New Mexico Historical Review* and *Latin American Popular Culture Since Independence: An Introduction*, 2nd edition, edited by William H. Beezley and Linda A. Curcio-Nagy (Rowman and Littlefield, 2011). His research interests include Mexican and Mexican American class and race and quantitative analyses of census data to answer questions about the nineteenth-century populations in the borderlands.